A Hundred Years
of
Railway Weighells

Sidney Weighell

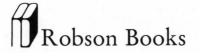 Robson Books

FIRST PUBLISHED IN GREAT BRITAIN IN 1984 BY
ROBSON BOOKS LTD., BOLSOVER HOUSE,
5-6 CLIPSTONE STREET, LONDON W1P 7EB.
COPYRIGHT © 1984 SIDNEY WEIGHELL

British Library Cataloguing in Publication Data
Weighell, Sidney
    A hundred years of railway Weighells.
    1. Railroads — Great Britain — History
    I. Title
    385'.092'4   HE3018

ISBN 0-86051-263-0

Printed in Hungary

Contents

Author's Note

For eight years I was engulfed in the work of the Trade Union and Labour Movement. Anyone with any knowledge of the job of a General Secretary of a major union knows that it leaves little time for reflection. I lived from day to day, drawing on the experience I had gained over my years of active service, at every level, in the Movement.

But since I resigned as General Secretary of the National Union of Railwaymen in January 1983 I have had time to look back over the three generations of railwaymen in my own family and see how the machines, the people and the way of life have changed. I've called the book *A Hundred Years of Railway Weighells* because it's almost that long since my grandfather joined the railways; if you add up the years of service we have all put in it comes to many more than that.

I am indebted to many people who contributed ideas, criticisms or comments. To each I express my thanks.

My special thanks go to Susan Rea of Robson Books, who first put the idea to me, and to Robert Waterhouse, who used his considerable skill as a journalist to list and to turn my scrawled notes into some semblance of order, to Dr Keith Bright and his colleagues at London Transport, to David Howard, Director General of Tyne and Wear Transport, to Denis Thorpe, John Armstrong and John Carr for their photographs, to Janice Potter who typed the manuscript, and finally to each of the family who dug into the past to find family records and pictures: my mother, brother Maurice, and sisters Elma and Brenda — not forgetting Auntie Nellie and Uncle Dick. And thanks, too, to my wife Joan who has had to bear the sight of manuscripts all over our new home twice in one year.

Beckwithshaw, 1984   S.W.

Foreword by the Rt Hon. James Callaghan, PC

The reader will put this book down saying to himself: 'Once a railwayman, always a railwayman.' For it certainly seems that enthusiasts, once they are bitten by the railways bug, are never able to escape. Sidney Weighell's book shows how true this is of the railwaymen of his own generation, and, although they may describe themselves as frustrated and disappointed, nothing ever totally destroys their loyalty and pride in the railways. One can only regret that such enthusiasm and devotion have not been better repaid in the past. As Sidney Weighell's book makes clear, a major fault has been that, following the modern development of the internal combustion engine and a massive road-improvement programme, successive governments lost their way, and could not make up their minds what the roles of road and rail should be.

Sidney Weighell is not quite accurate in saying that, when the Labour Government nationalized the railways in 1947, we believed that public ownership of them would be enough to solve the railways' problems. We did not limit ourselves to nationalizing the railways. The Attlee Government nationalized long-distance road traffic also. At the time, I was a youthful Parliamentary Secretary at the Ministry of Transport, and I recall the many speeches I made in the belief that we were to achieve our goals through the blessed buzzwords 'integration of road and rail'. I soon discovered that a powerful road haulage lobby, in addition to the Transport and General Workers' Union, had a very different idea of the meaning of the word 'integration' from the ideas of the railway unions at the time.

7

We never sorted the matter out. As the roads took more and more traffic, the railways became ever more defensive. Sidney Weighell remarks about the railway unions' attitudes: 'We were geared to opposing closures, but not to championing new developments.' In some ways, he is unfair to himself in saying this, for during his own period as General Secretary he always had his eye on the longer perspective, and this book shows that he is still looking ahead to the measures that are necessary to restore the railways to health and vigour.

He showed the same progressive outlook when he established a residential education centre for NUR members at Frant. Railwaymen have always been among the leaders in trade union and Labour Party education since the early days, and this showed itself in a heightened political and civic consciousness. The result was a profusion of Labour councillors, mayors, lord mayors and magistrates drawn from the railway unions, especially during the twenty-five years that followed the Second World War. Will there be as many in the 1980s?

Sidney Weighell is a remarkable man, and the fact that he became a victim of that miserable period in the history of the Labour Party and trade unions when intolerant left-wing extremists nearly hijacked the movement is no reason why the rest of us should forget his qualities. He is clear-headed, forceful and courageous. Not for him the role of time-server or messenger. He says in this book: 'I preferred to lead in the direction I believed was right for the lads on the job', and there is plenty of evidence that the rank and file of the NUR trusted his practical approach. I have known every post-war NUR leader, and they all possessed their own special qualities: Benstead's wisdom; Figgins's forcefulness; Campbell's shrewdness; Sid Greene's patience. But I have no hesitation in saying that Weighell's dynamism and far-sightedness exceeds them all.

It has been an honour to be asked to write this Foreword. I first came into close contact with the railways as a new Member of Parliament nearly forty years ago when I stayed for many years in the home of the Chairman of the Cardiff South Labour Party, Joe Drongeson, who was at the time the South Wales Organizer of the NUR. Like Sid Weighell, he was a former

North-Eastern man, and would have supported him in giving the palm to the old North Eastern Railway and its brilliant engineer, Nigel Gresley, whose Pacific Class locomotive was so outstanding that it set a target for the other companies to aim at. He is entitled to claim Gresley, but as Sidney's brother Maurice rightly reminds us of the dirt and disagreeable nature of the footplateman's duties, perhaps I may be allowed to put in a word for another brilliant railway engineer, Oliver Bulleid, who designed the famous Merchant Navy Class locomotive, one of whose purposes was to minimize the dirt and discomfort of the footplate. This successful class, designed in the twilight of the steam locomotive, surely entitles Bulleid to a footnote. His radical and exploring mind led to failures as well as success, one of which I was associated with. As well as being Parliamentary Secretary at the Ministry of Transport, I was also Chairman of the Treasury Allocation of Materials Committee during the days of rationing, and I especially found the materials necessary for him to build his experimental double-decker train. We hoped it would ease the sardine-tin journeys of the south-eastern commuters, but — alas — it was not popular with the powers-that-be after I left the Ministry, and I must admit they had a case.

Everyone who reads Sidney Weighell's book, railwayman or not, will be caught up in his infectious enthusiasm for the profession he was born into. This straightforward book will do more to establish the good sense of investing in a modern railway system than reams of propaganda, and the railway unions should buy up several thousands of copies and distribute them to anyone with influence.

And finally, when I finished reading this book, I could not resist a feeling of pride at one more demonstration of how ordinary people, born with no material advantages, could show such talent and character of the first order and, as Sidney Weighell did, place it at the service of his fellows.

House of Commons, 1984   J.C.

Introduction

The travelling public both loves and hates the railways. Ever since the first timetables were published and trains ran late passengers have had cause to curse their luck. At the same time the noise and excitement of railway journeys, the fleeting world as seen from the carriage window, the anticipation of power and speed which involuntarily grips people as they mount an express — all these have survived the great age of steam in today's High Speed Trains which travel almost twice as quickly as the steam-hauled services of only thirty years ago.

Railwaymen also have a love-hate relationship with their trade. They pride themselves on running the fastest, safest, least environmentally damaging method of moving between centres; they enjoy the knowledge that without trains London would jam up, mail would slow down, fewer newspapers would reach breakfast tables. They retain a sense of solidarity arising from the history of their unions, especially the National Union of Railwaymen which had a hand in establishing trade union rights and the Labour Party. But they hate the reality of the last thirty years: a workforce in continual decline; low investment by whatever government is in power; having to watch limb after limb chopped away from the network body. Railwaymen, not the Ministry of Transport or the British Railways Board, must face the traveller each working day and attempt to explain mishaps whose root cause is no responsibility of theirs.

This book is about railwaymen and railways seen through the eyes of Sid Weighell. Until his abrupt departure as General Secretary of the NUR in January 1983, when he was 60, Weighell had carved himself the most dynamic career of any railway trade-union leader. In the charged atmosphere of conflict during his final years with the union it was easy to forget his personal and family commitment to railways. As a third-generation railwayman his determination both to better the lot of fellow-workers and to ensure a future for railway operation was the driving force behind his often controversial actions.

In this book Weighell sets out the background to his rise from the unlikely powerbase of Northallerton, the wealthy North Yorkshire market town which, to the chagrin of local worthies, developed a tradition of God-fearing, co-operative-minded socialists among the railway community. These working people challenged the local shopkeepers by creating the Northallerton Co-operative Society, painstakingly educated themselves, and insisted on supplying Labour candidates for elections local and general. Of all these obstinate folk, who organized an entire work-ethic around Northallerton station, none was more energetic than the Weighell family.

Grandfather William Weighell joined the North Eastern Railway back in 1893 as a 25-year-old shunter in the Northallerton yard. He graduated to being a goods guard and then a passenger guard before retiring in 1934. An early member of the Amalgamated Society of Railway Servants, William Weighell was also a founder-member of the Northallerton Co-op. His son, Tom Weighell, qualified as a signalman but was soon NUR branch secretary at Northallerton. He had three years in his forties on the NUR Executive Committee before becoming Secretary of LNER Sectional Council No. 3, with responsibilities from King's Cross to Aberdeen, which he ran from an office-bedroom in his Northallerton terrace house. Tom Weighell narrowly missed being elected NUR President but became, respectable at last, chairman of the local magistrates and proud holder of the British Empire Medal and the MBE.

It was hardly surprising that the young, industrious Sid — bearing a striking resemblance, if the photographs didn't lie, to the equally pugnacious James Cagney — should choose to follow his father. Despite the family background of Baptist chapel, Labour Party and trade unionism, Weighell still had to educate himself. He left school at fifteen without any bits of

11

paper, having proved better at sport than sums (and good enough at soccer to sign on as a professional for Sunderland F.C.). The experience of the war years working on the footplate around the bombs and blackouts of Teesside in conditions of great risk and stress motivated him to get on, to 'equip' himself. A second, even more traumatic event, the death of his first wife and young daughter in a car accident at Christmas 1956, led indirectly to further years steeped in railway union matters so that when he eventually bid for high office he was the natural and overwhelming choice of the NUR rank and file.

Those who see Sid Weighell's career as pre-ordained might care to consider the case of Maurice, his brother. Maurice Weighell is just two years younger than Sid. He joined the NUR soon after his brother and he too became a fireman and driver. He too was Northallerton branch secretary, he also worked for the Labour cause at election times. But there the similarity ends. Maurice never wished to leave North Yorkshire. He moved, it's true, to Thornaby on Teesside in 1961 as an engine driver. He still drives locomotives out of the Tees Yard depot, often big company freight trains to Corby or Newcastle. Maurice stayed put. But he is every bit as capable, and argumentative, as his elder brother. Seeing them embroiled in discussion about railway life — the sort of thing Sid reproduces in Chapter Six — it would be hard to tell, if you didn't know, the plain engine driver from the former NUR General Secretary.

Circumstances and temperament made Sid rather than Maurice head for the top. As a Northerner brought up in a beautiful part of Yorkshire he hated London and the Southeast. Yet, forced to live there for twenty-five years he was rightly proud of securing a manor house in the cultured Sussex countryside for the NUR's educational training centre; and he left behind a gleaming new Unity House on Euston Road. One of the silliest consequences of Weighell's sudden departure from office was his not even being invited to the official opening of the building he made possible.

Sid Weighell may still be in disgrace with the NUR Executive; his standing with ordinary railwaymen has never altered. For the purposes of this book he sought out a wide range of railwaymen in and around North Yorkshire, where he has once more made his home. He wanted to know what they felt about lives spent in the service of the railways. He spoke to them not as the recent General Secretary but as a fellow-railwayman. Their response proved as friendly as it was frank.

It charted an almost unanimous feeling of despair about the way British Rail is today forced to operate. Weighell has high-lighted a skilled, loyal workforce which can see a way of life breaking down — and the service with it — as a direct consequence of government policies. The stories he has collected, often joyfully told, are tinged with sadness. This isn't the nostalgia of the steam freak. No sane railwayman mourns the passing of the dirty, unhealthy, uncomfortable steam footplate, or having to start work at five in the morning to polish smuts from the Harrogate Pullman. Sadness, rather, that the zestful days of steam could not have been translated into a brave, new, all-electric world with investment matching technology's potential, something as in France or Japan. After all, we invented the railways, didn't we? We could still be out there ahead of the rest.

This certitude of a railway system in decline became ever more concrete to Sid Weighell as he drove around the North-east searching out his rail roots. Everywhere he visited, the buildings in which he had once worked, or booked on for work, were no more. Thriving towns like Ripon, formally on the Leeds-Northallerton main line, are without a rail service. Northallerton station has been reduced to the same lowly profile it had when the York-Darlington line opened in 1841. And at Darlington there is little to suggest that it was ever a famous railway town. Gone are the loco sheds and the loco works. The original North Road Station survives, of course, as a museum. But it is surrounded by wire to discourage teenage vandals, whose artwork adorns, New York subway-style, the platform serving the Bishop Auckland branch line.

Trade union leaders have a reputation for fighting progress and its inevitable job implications. In retrospect, the NUR leadership can be accused of not fighting strongly enough the job-losses of the last thirty years. There has been a revolution on the railways, and the ordinary railwayman was principal victim. Nearly half a million fewer people work today on BR

13

than at nationalization in 1948. Japanese National Railways employ a payroll over twice that of BR to operate a service of similar dimensions.

That is not to say that productivity could or should not have improved. When Sid Weighell took over as NUR General Secretary in 1975 he was quite prepared to talk about new manning agreements — in return for new investment. He, together with Sir Peter Parker, the BR Chairman, set up a fresh impetus for railways which only broke down (as Parker spells out in an interview in Chapter Ten) when the engine drivers' union ASLEF failed to deliver their part of the bargain. Until then the railways had won friends in Mrs Thatcher's Government and were set on a significant, eleventh-hour recovery course.

Weighell argues in the concluding chapters of this book that railway investment must be taken once and for all outside the petty boundaries of party politics. By its very nature railway investment demands long lead times. You cannot plan, commission and build a railway in less than ten years. BR should therefore be able to commit investment at least ten years in advance, as does the SNCF across the Channel, instead of having to beg each year at the whim of a Cabinet almost certain to be forgotten in under five years. You cannot count on two hands the number of transport ministers Britain has suffered in the last decade. Weighell sets out the few sensible instances of post-war investment — the London Midland electrification, the Victoria Line Underground and the Tyne and Wear Metro. These, he suggests, are indispensable today. How many other 'indispensable' lines are we struggling on without?

The railways' case — as opposed to more motorways, for example — has been documented elsewhere. Sid Weighell, probably alone among the modern generation of trade-union leaders, had the intelligence to grasp the environmental benefits of reversing the railways' decline. Politically, the arguments have never been simple. There was, and remains, a huge pro-road lobby within the Transport and General Workers' Union and the Labour Party — a lobby based purely on self-interest. Weighell's support of the rail case was not entirely disinterested but he had the imagination to encourage and part-fund an independent lobby, Transport 2000, with

14

genuine regional strengths which, ten years on, continues to present factual, well-written information on better use of public transport and alternative transport — not just railways.

Those who have met Sid Weighell, or heard him discuss his life, will recognize the reassuring (or infuriating) consistency of his position. Whether drawn on industrial relations, political warfare, inter-union strife or the future of the railways, Weighell extends commonsense criteria based on a lifelong experience of decision-making and its consequences. If events forced him to become militant against Militant that was just too bad. He remained true to his concept of socialism, just as his quarrel with ASLEF was based on a well-defined sense of trade union justice. The background of chapel, the Labour Party and the NUR is always there, firmly established in generations of hard work, even though Weighell is his own man.

This is a book about railwaymen and railways written by a person unusual only in the discipline he has brought to control his own narrow interests in pursuit of what he believes to be the common good. Of course, Sid Weighell is not short on self-confidence. He has had little time for others in public life who were unable to demonstrate the same devotion to their tasks. He made enemies in trade union circles by his uncompromising style, his extreme hatred of extremism. But he kept his friends in the railway branches and depots around the country. They knew, instinctively, that he stood for them and their future.

Many battles are lost. One of the proudest and most distressing, because closest to home, was the case of BR's Shildon loco wagon works in County Durham. Sid Weighell fought successfully for a stay of execution at Shildon, where falling orders were threatening not just a famous (and modernized) works but a whole town, like Consett and Corby. Due largely to his intervention the evil day was postponed, but in the months since he left the NUR hope has vanished. Shildon was finally consigned to the scrapheap in June 1984.

During his last few weeks as NUR General Secretary, Weighell and his wife Joan were guests of honour at the Shildon Civic Dinner and Dance. There he was presented with the following verses, composed by the Personnel Officer of British Rail, Shildon, Jim Reid, which, suitably framed, hang on his study wall near other mementoes of a life on the railways. He's not quite sure why his colleagues called him 'Syd' unless it was an unconscious reference to his mother's wishes. The story goes that she intended to christen her son Sydney in celebration of the Sydney Harbour Bridge, commissioned from Teesside in the year of his birth, but the officious Registrar wouldn't allow her. The men of Shildon have had the final say.

Manchester, 1984   R.W.

A Tribute

By local members of the National Union of Railwaymen, Shildon Branch
Delivered on 19 November 1982 at the Shildon Civic Dinner Dance

Syd Weighell, you've been a stalwart over many many years,
You have battled for your members amidst their hopes and fears;
At heart you're a Railwayman, of that there is no doubt,
In the interests of your members you know what it's about.

Using strength, with care and thought, has always been your cry,
There's others, who are in our midst, who should but your way try;
Instead of confrontation, disturbance and the rest,
They should follow your example, and do the things that's best.

For all you've done for Shildon, we send to you our thanks,
When the chips were down, you led the way, in front of all the ranks;
We hope that things will brighten, and work will come our way,
When you shall be our honoured guest, on that auspicious day.

The railwaymen have lost a friend, to champion their cause,
Your efforts over all the years have earned you great applause;
On behalf of all your many friends, in Shildon and around,
We wish you health and happiness, wherever you are found.

Allan Walker (Chairman, Shildon Town Council)
Roy G. Jones (Chairman, Shildon Branch, NUR)

From a map showing the extent of the railway network in the North-East of England in 1900.

NORTH EASTERN ENGLAND

0   5   10   20   30 miles

1 *Birth of a Railway Nation*

~~~~~~

THE NORTH EASTERN Railway Company, formed on 31 July 1854 from an amalgamation of the York, Newcastle and Berwick Railway, the York and North Midland Railway and the Leeds Northern Railway, was the largest in the country at the time, boasting over 700 route miles. It was a grouping together of twenty small companies stretching from the North Midlands to the Scottish border — with important exceptions like the Stockton and Darlington Railway, generally regarded as the world's first fully commercial railway undertaking. The S and D, along with other essentially mineral lines, were to join the NER at a later date, just as the NER would merge into the LNER and finally become part of British Railways.

Take a look at the NER's famous route maps, set out in tiles at the bigger stations — a perfect example is still to be found on the Middlesbrough Down platform. The small town of Northallerton lies near the geographical centre of the map, its large lettering proclaiming an important station. Northallerton, on the dead-straight York-Darlington main line, a key link in the London-Edinburgh East Coast route, was also where the Leeds-Middlesbrough railway crossed at low level, and where the Wensleydale branch line terminated. I, like my father and grandfather, and my brother, grew up in a Northallerton railway environment.

Northallerton was, and remains, a rich, busy market town serving the big agricultural interests of North Yorkshire. But for a hundred years and more, from the 1840s until the 1950s, railway business and railway people were an integral part, perhaps even the most important single part, of Northallerton's prosperity. Markets, dairies, factories all depended on the north-south, east-west rail links for their custom. Northallerton station, today little more than a halt, was the town's biggest landmark: from its towering position on the banked main line it sported five platforms, a hotel, restaurant and waiting rooms, engine sheds and signal boxes. Almost 500 railwaymen saw Northallerton as their base, and when North Riding County Council built their new County Hall in 1906 they chose the site of the old race course, opposite the station.

Northallerton is just sixteen miles south of Darlington, the nerve-centre of the Stockton and Darlington Railway and the world's first true railway town. The prime reason for the S and D was, of course, to create a better, faster route for shipping coal from the mines of County Durham to the nearest port (Stockton) on the River Tees. The history of coal, steel and the Industrial Revolution in the North-east is inextricably bound up with the development of railways, just as the interlinked needs of Liverpool, Manchester and the other Industrial Revolution based on manufactured goods brought the Liverpool and Manchester Railway into existence shortly after the S and D. Railways provided the key to the revolution, a fantastic revolution which spread across and around the country within a decade. Almost overnight the map of Britain had been changed. Using railways, all parts of the country were within a day's journey of London and each other. Not only that, the urge to invest in these magic rail-roads, even to build and run them in direct competition, set fare scales which allowed ordinary people for the first time to travel real distances from home.

The reason why the North-east played such a major part in these pioneering days — witness the phenomenon of George Hudson, the York Railway King, of whom more later — was that it not only had the need for railways, it produced the raw materials for their construction. Just as important, it provided the engineers to make it all possible. George Stephenson, designer and builder of Locomotion No. 1, came from Tyneside, a self-educated son of a lowly pump-engineman who at thirty-one became engine-wright at the Killingworth High Pit in Northumberland. Stephenson developed steam locomotives for pit work, along with the all-important rails, for use within the collieries or on the existing wagon-ways. Building on other engineers' designs — notably John Blenkinsop's locomotive for the Middleton Colliery Railway at Leeds — Stephenson began the process of technical improvement from which emerged the sort of locomotive which served to pull trains in this country for 120 years, and is still working away around the world.

Stephenson was first in a long line of brilliant North-eastern engineers, civil and locomotive, who not only constructed lines over some of the country's most difficult terrain but provided the locos to run them profitably. Along with Stephenson must be remembered his son Robert, Wilson Worsdell, Sir Vincent Raven and my own particular hero, Sir Nigel Gresley. Because of their regional origins the country's leading railway companies (amalgamated under the terms of the Railways Act 1921 as the LNER, LMS, GWR and SR) each continued to design and build its own locomotives right up into the Second World War. Although Darlington and Gateshead do not compare with Derby, Crewe or Swindon as loco works — they have since disappeared — the LNER locomotives themselves stand up to any challenge. As I describe in Chapter Three, the Gresley A3 and A4 Pacifics, along with the V2 freight engines, proved themselves a match for all the Second World War could throw at them. Their versatility, and good footplate design, made them as pleasant as any steam locomotive could be to work. And the A4 Pacific, Mallard, of course established the world steam speed record of 126 mph in 1938 near Peterborough.

Darlington became such an important rail town because of its strategic position astride the East Coast route and between the coalfields on one side and the port and industrial complex of Teesside on the other. Middlesbrough, created as a railhead, quickly outstripped both Darlington and Stockton in size, especially after the discovery around 1850 of vast iron-ore deposits in the Cleveland Hills gave it the wherewithal to manufacture cheap iron and steel on the spot. In late-Victorian days Middlesbrough meant coal, iron and steel; it was a thrusting, bustling, heavily-polluted frontier town, and the two modes of transport that mattered were rail and ship. The huge Middlesbrough docks, familiar to my brother Maurice

21

All that remains today of the railway network between York and Newcastle.

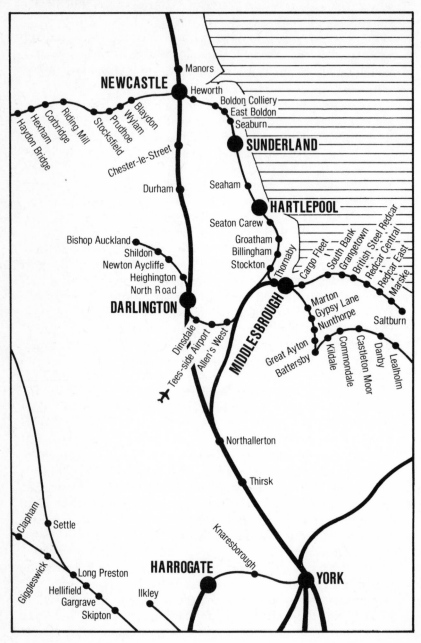

and me during the war years, were developed by the NER, which believed in owning everything contingent or abutting to the railways.

But Teesside is a relatively small area. You are soon out of it, whether into the Cleveland Hills, the North Yorkshire Coast, County Durham's uneasy mixture of industry and country-side, or the Pennines. The early railway builders thought nothing of taking on the Pennines. The Stockton and Darlington was itself extended to Barnard Castle and over a 1,400-foot summit to Tebay, the junction with the Preston-Carlisle line near Shap. Even earlier, as early as 1836, the Newcastle and Carlisle Railway linking the East and West Coasts opened. Despite their lack of experience — and the surprising fact that many trains up to 1850 on the Stockton and Darlington remained horse-drawn — steam was rampant.

What with the peaceful countryside in the south of the region, the market towns, the ports and docks, the primary industries and sophisticated engineering like shipbuilding, the moors and the mountains, towns as different as Harrogate and Bishop Auckland, great cities like Leeds and Newcastle, the North-east was a microcosm of Victorian England. Even in the railway age it remained, and felt, a long way from London. York, the headquarters of the NER, represented the centre of the world inhabited by most North-eastern railwaymen.

Indeed, for a short and crucial time the activities of George Hudson, three times Lord Mayor of York, dominated the national railway scene. Hudson, using his North-east power-base, became chairman of new railway companies around England and was even, it's said, on friendly terms with Prince Albert. Hudson fought many battles, both on his home patch and around the country, before accusations of irregularities began to stick. Ironically, his part in admitting the Great Northern Railway to York spurred investigations which eventually led to his demise. But the judgment of history is that Hudson was essentially creative, even if the volume of railways left behind by the mania he inspired proved an early embarrass-ment to railway travel in the days when it had a virtual monopoly.

With railways came railwaymen. The very early locomotive drivers operating on the Stockton and Darlington earned a handsome farthing for each ton-mile of coal they pulled, and this amounted to as much as twenty-five shillings a day. But by 1867, when the first NER strike is recorded, the wage claim was seven shillings a day for drivers, four shillings and sixpence for firemen, on the basis of a ten-hour day and sixty-hour week, with Sunday work as time-and-a-half. It was a time of high unemployment and the company had little problem in recruiting alternative enginemen from around the country. Some of the strikers were prosecuted but not imprisoned, others emigrated to America. Only twenty-five of the 1,050 strikers were reinstated. Although the men succeeded in their primary aim — to establish a ten-hour working day — the newly-born Engine Driver's and Firemen's United Society which had called the strike was smashed.

But, as has often proved the case throughout the history of trade unionism, adversity brought new strength. The railwaymen's cause was taken up by Derby's MP, Michael Thomas Bass, the brewer and a substantial shareholder and user of the Midland Railway Company. Bass spoke out for railwaymen in Parliament and encouraged them to organize. He it was who set up the *Railway Service Gazette*, forerunner of the NUR's *Railway Review*, to keep railwaymen abreast of the news and counter-management propaganda. After meetings in November 1871 held both in Leeds and London, a new union, the Amalgamated Society of Railway Servants, was formed.

Pay, working hours and safety were the new union's major concerns. The first thirty-five years of railway development had been so hectic that little thought had been given to the consequences of long working hours and primitive conditions in a competitive, time-cutting, cost-cutting environment. As timetabled trains got faster, the chances of bad accidents increased. Railway companies, especially the Great Western Railway, prided themselves on enlightened paternalism, going so far as building houses, schools, even chapels for their workforce. They argued: 'Why do you need to be in a union when we can give you all this?' But the union went ahead with setting up accident funds, orphan funds and sick funds. In mid-Victorian England there was no state machinery to support workers who fell sick or injured themselves; railwaymen wisely understood that they were, through the union, their own best benefactors.

On the NER the first semaphore signals came into use around 1850. Before that, drivers had to keep their own look-out. (In the early days of the Stockton and Darlington, faster trains would expect slower ones in front of them to pull over at the regular passing places. It wasn't unknown for some of the lighter horse-drawn vehicles to overtake heavy steam-powered freight trains, and the drivers of horse coaches hated giving way to steam.) Semaphore signalling, each signal box communicating along the line by telegraph and telephone, was to become the staple method of controlling trains. Not until the Second World War did the concept of central control take over the bulk of train operations. Signalmen assumed the major responsibility for safety, gaining the grade and status commensurate. They also, because of their practice at book-keeping — each train movement being logged meticulously — and their position at the nerve-centre of train operations, very often became the union branch secretaries. There used to be a long, unbroken tradition at Northallerton of signalmen branch secretaries, of which my father was part.

Despite all the concern, the fact remained that Victorian railways were very dangerous places to work, particularly for the permanent-way men. During 1873, for instance, a couple of years after the ASRS was formed, 782 men died on the railways nationally, or one in every 330. One accident well remembered in union circles happened in 1873 on the North Staffordshire Railway when an engine which had been used to push wagons up a bank was taken back down the line, leaving the wagons on the incline. The guard forgot to apply his brake and the wagons ran back down into the engine. Guard, engine driver and fireman all died. The guard, it was found out, had been on duty for nineteen hours, while the driver and fireman had both been on duty for thirty-two hours.

Over the years, the ASRS and the NUR which followed it have been instrumental in improving railway safety standards, as I describe more fully in Chapter Five, which deals with my time as relief Divisional Officer of the NUR attending inquiries and inquests. So much improvement has happened that the railway is today a much safer place to work, while the passenger is statistically safer on rail than he or she is at home.

The struggle to get railwaymen a living wage for a reasonable

25

working week has been just as long and wearisome. At the first Annual General Meeting of the ASRS in 1888, members decided on a national programme with such things as a guaranteed week, an agreed scale of wages and enhanced pay for overtime. Some concessions were made by the NER during 1890 in the form of a six-day guaranteed week, fewer working hours for goods guards and shunters and better pay for plate-layers. All the same, the railwaymen's average wage in 1895 — for a minimum sixty-hour week with just three days' annual holiday — was twenty-three shillings.

By that time my grandfather, William Weighell, had joined the NER in Northallerton and become a member of the ASRS. His wages, if anything, deteriorated over the next ten years — at a time when railway profits were on the increase. The problem was, and remained until 1911, that companies like the NER flatly refused to negotiate with the union. The union's only channel lay through petitioning Parliament — railway-men had at least been given the vote in the franchise of 1867 to better-paid working men. Even after a national Conciliation Scheme was set up in 1907 wages continued to stagnate. By 1911, only two years before the creation of the NUR (and, incidentally, the year my father Thomas Weighell, aged eighteen, started in a signal box at Northallerton), the railwaymen's average wage was still only twenty-five shillings and nine pence a week.

At a time of Edwardian affluence, with the companies well into profit and still untouched by the internal combustion engine, railwaymen were clearly being exploited. The national rail strike of that year led to the government of the day setting up a Royal Commission, which in turn led to a new conciliation process in which union officers were for the first time represented. The union had arrived, and within two years amalgamation with two smaller unions gave birth to the National Union of Railwaymen. But, for his part in supporting the national strike, my young father was briefly 'banished' to a signal box at Selby, the far side of York from Northallerton.

Meantime, two important judgments and one historic event established the union's unique ties with the Labour Party. The Independent Labour Party, founded in 1893, had soon enrolled members of the ASRS executive. At a London conference on

28 February 1900, as good as sponsored by ASRS, members of the TUC formed a Labour Representation Committee, the forerunner of today's Labour Party. The ASRS was one of the first unions to affiliate.

In that same year the union's experience on the Taff Vale Railway in South Wales showed the tasks ahead, while stimulating interest among ordinary workers in the union and the Labour Party. Taff Vale railwaymen were striking unofficially for an extra two shillings per week. The railway's general manager decided to bring in strike-breakers from London, and so the union gave financial backing to strikers. A judgment the following year in the House of Lords made the union pay damages and costs amounting to £42,000 to the railway company.

This test case appeared to show that a trade union (even one unrecognized by management) was responsible for the financial consequences of striking. What a setback to the young unions seeking to help their members! But affiliated membership to the Labour Representation Committee shot from 375,930 in 1900 to 969,800 in 1904. In the 1906 General Election twenty-nine of the Committee's fifty candidates were elected, shortly to form the Parliamentary Labour Party. In the House of Commons, joined by a further twelve left-wing Liberal MPs, the mood for better interpretation of the 1871 Trades Union Act grew. Finally, the government of the day accepted Keir Hardie's Bill, which became legislation as the Trade Disputes Act of 1906, legalizing peaceful picketing, awarding full protection to union funds and denying the right of employers to take civil action against the effects of a union dispute. This is the very legislation which is today under attack from Mrs Thatcher's hatchet-men.

The other judgment came from the actions of one William V. Osborne, ASRS branch secretary at Walthamstow, East London, who disliked having to pay his one shilling annual political levy to the Labour Party (a decision taken by a union Special General Meeting in 1903). Osborne opened legal proceedings in July 1908 to prevent the ASRS using its funds for political purposes. His campaign was taken up by the *Daily Express*, then as now the voice of reaction, and eventually the House of Lords ruled in his favour. This meant effectively that all trade unions had to cease paying their MPs (who were without a salary otherwise) and to withdraw from activities in local elections. While the three railway union MPs in the Commons had their salaries stopped, the twenty-one railway directors also in the House received their salaries as normal. The obvious unfairness of the Osborne judgment helped to convince the trade union members of the value of the Labour Party, and showed members of the Labour Party the value of trade union affiliation (still a major source of political argument). Four years after the Osborne judgment the anomaly was removed under the Trades Union Act of 1913, which gave unions specific powers to raise a political levy, but individual trade unionists the right to contract out.

This was the political climate in which my grandfather and father were brought up. It was a period of consolidation and profit-making for the railways, whose interests extended into docks, shipping, hotels, everything to do with transport and travel. The year my grandfather joined the NER it operated some 1,200 route miles of railway; by the time my father joined it had extended to 1,800 route miles. By the late nineteenth century the railway companies were beginning to apply modern marketing techniques to encourage travel: weekend tickets were first issued in 1880, day returns in 1895. In 1896 a 1,000-mile ticket was introduced offering a 20 per cent discount for first-class travel. To meet this new surge of travellers, coaches got bigger, trains longer. Ordinary people were again able to travel further than ever before. The NER employed a staff of 38,000 in the early 1890s which had swollen to 50,000 in 1913.

When it came to the unions' amalgamation that same year the ASRS linked up with the General Railwayworkers' Union and the United Pointsmen's and Signalmen's Society to form the National Union of Railwaymen, with almost 180,000 members. The other two unions, the train drivers and the railway clerks, remained aloof from this expression of working-class solidarity which equipped the union to face the challenge of the Great War and the totally changed society which followed. The railway companies, soon to be reorganized themselves into the big four, deliberately offered railway clerks and salaried staff better conditions to split their interests from those of other railway workers. The train drivers, ASLEF, regarded themselves as the elite, and still do, for that matter. Despite being footplatemen, my brother and I never considered joining ASLEF because its craft-union ethic stood for the opposite of the working-class solidarity we had been brought up to believe in.

The NUR clearly rejected sectional or parochial interests in favour of a united front, and a rationale of new structure was provided by Charlie Cramp, who was to become Industrial General Secretary of the union in 1920. He wrote, in 1913:

> The railway, providing transport as it does, must be regarding as an industry. All those whose labour in any way contributes to the carrying on of this industry are either railwaymen or railwaywomen, and thus part of the industry, their conditions are ultimately governed by the facts and prosperity of the carrying concern which does produce transport as its chief commodity for sale.

Note the reference to railwaywomen. At that time there was just one woman member of the NUR. But during the First World War some 55,000 women were recruited to help replace the 180,000 railwaymen who enlisted. Many of them joined the union, which itself swelled in numbers to 416,000 by December 1918. The war brought many other changes, such as the eight-hour day and, following the definitive general rail strike of 1919, a fifty-one shillings a week minimum wage much closer to the industrial average. But during the inter-war years, when railways were hit by the recession and the motor vehicle, NUR officials, my father among them, fought unsuccessfully to prevent wages being cut.

While all these momentous events were taking place within the union, the railway companies, the political system and the nation itself, the little world of Northallerton carried on peacefully enough. Northallerton has a long history: navvies constructing the York-Darlington main line in 1838 discovered Roman remains suggesting a Roman camp on the site of the town, which clearly owes its position to being on the main north-south communications route, equidistant from the North York Moors and the foothills of the Yorkshire Dales.

Northallerton's past, however, is as bloody as that of many crossroad towns. After the Roman invaders came the Norsemen, my ancestors probably numbered among them (see Chapter Two). The Normans also came that way, then the Scots fought at the Battle of the Standard at Brompton, just north of the town. The history books say that King David I of Scotland and 12,000 men were halted by an English force assembled by Archbishop Thurstan of York. Northallerton received its Royal Charter in 1200, and during the Civil War twice sheltered King Charles I, showing the conservative-royalist tendencies of the town which we railwaymen found mildly strange.

Northallerton was famous for its coaching inns, being on the turnpike from Boroughbridge to Durham. The 1785 mail-coach route from London to Edinburgh used the Black Bull Inn as its staging-post between Harrogate and Darlington. Northallerton's reputation for strong ale is put forward as one reason why the coach drivers liked to stop off.

After the coaches came the railway. Completed in 1841, the York, Newcastle and Berwick's main line together with the Leeds and Thirsk Railway low-level line in 1851, gave Northallerton a whole new dimension. To begin with, there were even two stations, and South Parade, a fine terrace of substantial houses, was started in 1860 to connect the town centre with the main station. With the completion in 1878 of the branch line to Hawes and Garsdale Junction, linking with the London Midland Carlisle-Settle line, Northallerton was at the agricultural and industrial crossroads of North Yorkshire.

Trains brought livestock to the market, built close to the station; milk from the Dales to the big dairy on the other side of the main line; and people to buy and sell their produce. Northallerton had been a renowned market town for centuries, with a charter going back to 1555 for a Wednesday market, but the railway put it in a new league. It also attracted a whole new breed of people, skilled working people alive to the opportunities and dangers of the Industrial Revolution. These railway people, my grandfather's, father's and my generation, were self-educated chapel-folk and progressive socialists. The merchants of our God-fearing town disliked and mistrusted us, outvoting us at elections. But they couldn't wish us away.

2 Socialism from the Market Cross

I WAS BORN in a small, rented, furnished terraced house in Gladstone Street, Northallerton, eldest child of Tom and Lena Weighell, on 31 March 1922. My father had joined the railway eleven years before as signalbox boy. By the time we came along — Maurice being born in 1924, Elma in 1927 and Brenda in 1928 — father was well established as a signalman, a socialist and a leading member of the NUR Northallerton branch.

Mother, who was five years younger than father, had known him most of her life from their mutual involvement in the Baptist chapel, where she played the organ and he preached — until the First World War that is, when his experiences in the trenches drove him away from preaching religion to preaching socialism.

Grandfather Weighell, a passenger guard based at Northallerton, was born at Osmotherley, on the fringe of the North York Moors, where his parents were farmers. He married an Osmotherley girl called Fanny Barker. He started work with the NER on 19 February 1893, progressing from a shunter to a goods guard and then a passenger guard. They lived in a railway house near the goods yard until grandfather retired in 1934. Grandfather died in 1949. My father was one of seven — three sons and four daughters.

Grandfather Hardisty on my mother's side was a successful Northallerton shopkeeper, born in 1877. His father had been a travelling man, a tinker who lived in a caravan and went from fair to fair until he was killed when he fell under the wheels of his vehicle as he tried to control runaway horses on a dangerous hill. Grandfather Hardisty was a natural salesman, building up his greengrocery business from next to nothing. He died of pneumonia in 1930. He had eight children, and all helped one way or another in his business, just as two of my father's sisters were employed at the Northallerton Co-op, which Grand-father Weighell had helped to found.

The meeting-point between my parents' families was the Baptist chapel, where Grandfather Hardisty was a Deacon. He was not, however, a socialist — he was more inclined to the Liberals — and mother had eventually to leave home before she could marry father.

Father died in 1977, aged eighty-four, just two years after I became General Secretary of the NUR. My mother is still alive and well, living just down the road from the house where she raised the family. She has been a chapel organist for almost seventy years, and is proud of still being 'relief' organist at a small country chapel. Between us, the Weighells — my grandfather, father, my brother Maurice and I — have put in 176 years of railway and NUR service. We were not unusual in that respect — many railway families count two, three, even four generations.

Grandfather was active in the railway union long before it was officially recognized, becoming branch treasurer. He also helped to establish the Northallerton Co-operative Society, which today has extensive high street premises. There are still old railwaymen in Northallerton who re-member him working trains up and down the Wensleydale branch, immaculate in his passenger guard uniform.

Grandfather, like most railwaymen, kept pigs in his garden. We knew when he'd slaughtered one because we first had black pudding, then a part of the pig would be shared out among all the relatives, to be hung up in the pantry.

Grandmother Weighell's sister, Martha, married a Mr Farnaby, landlord of the Chequers Inn on the moors beyond the village of Osmotherley; he also farmed a smallholding. He was a reluctant landlord, his sheep and farm being much more important to him than the pub. But the womenfolk helped business by providing afternoon teas and selling postcards of the inn. I used to visit the Chequers with its stone-flagged floors, plain deal table and a peat fire which — one of the

The Weighell family in 1918. Father is on the left and Grandfather is seated on the right.

Uncle George and Grandfather Hardisty outside the family greengrocery business at the turn of the century.

The Chequers Inn near Osmotherley where my great-uncle was landlord.

One of the elegant Officer Special coaches in which the railway management would inspect outside sites.

My grandfather, William Weighell, in the 1940s.

This photo was taken in 1932 when I was aged ten.

4-6-2 EXPRESS PASSENGER ENGINE

3 CYLINDERS

DONCASTER 1922.

HEATING SURFACE	
BES	2715 SQ. FT.
E BOX	215 ʼʼ
PERHEATER	525 ʼʼ
TAL	3455 ʼʼ
ATE AREA	4125 ʼʼ
ILER PRESSURE 180 LBS	

3 CYLINDERS 20" x 26"	
DIA. OF LEADING WHEELS	3 FT. 2
COUPLED	6 ʼʼ 8
TRAILING	3 ʼʼ 8
WEIGHT OF ENGINE	92 TONS 9 c
TENDER	56 ʼʼ 6
TOTAL	149 ʼʼ 15

The 4-6-2 express passenger 'Great Northern' engine. First of the Gresley Pacifics, it was built in 1922 in Yorkshire – the same year and the same county in which I was born. This photograph was personally signed by Sir Nigel Gresley.

One of Gresley's early LNER Pacifics.

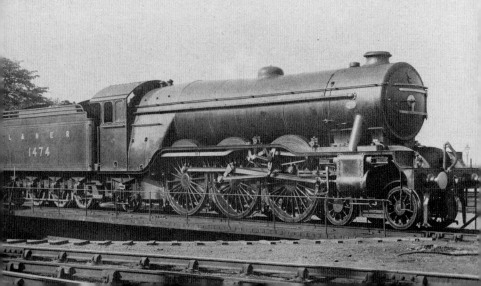

postcards claimed — had not gone out for 200 years. Hanging over the fire was a stewpot. Apart from an old wireless, the inn was quite cut off from the outside world.

Osmotherley is eight miles from Northallerton on the fringe of the North York Moors, and the Chequers Inn is a further three or four miles beyond the village, in a remote position. Yet it was a favourite picnic spot for townspeople on summer weekends. Underneath the chequerboard sign were the words: 'Be not in haste, step in and taste ale tomorrow for nothing.' Countless people would go in for their free pint only to be told, 'Go out, read the sign again. It's tomorrow you've got to come for the ale.' They were real Yorkshire folk, the Farnabys. Father used to complain that they wouldn't even serve him out of hours.

The story goes that the Weighell clan, who are only to be found in North Yorkshire, first came over with raiding Norsemen and settled along the coast around Whitby. Weighells are mostly farmers today. The name varies, being spelt -ell, -ill and -all, and we're not closely related. An experience which tended to confirm the raider theory happened on a tour to Scandinavia where people had no difficulty with my name, pronouncing it 'Vigell'. Sometimes in Britain strangers can't put their tongues round it at all.

My great-uncle on my mother's side was the manager of the two cinemas in town, one adjoining my grandfather's shop. This one, the Central, was prevented by grandfather (who had acquired certain rights of access when the cinema was built) from selling sweets or ices. Film-goers had to buy these at his shop before going in or when they came out — the shop stayed open.

All the family worked for Grandfather Hardisty's business, even Frank, one of his sons, who won a scholarship to the local grammar school and became secretary to the town clerk at Middlesborough before dying young. Frank was kept off school some Wednesdays to run errands. According to mother, her brothers and sisters were never paid a wage for helping with the family business, which went on as normal until the Second World War, though her father died in 1930. The sisters all had their jobs: Auntie Nellie and Auntie Mabel worked in the shop, Auntie Mary in the house. Uncles George,

Ernie and Bill all worked in the business. Their father never trained them. But then the three went off to the Second World War, and fresh produce became hard to find, although the girls kept things going during the war as best they could. The business was eventually sold for very little after the war.

Grandfather Hardisty, a deacon in the Baptist chapel, was also a special constable. He wore a dark suit, bowler hat and truncheon for these duties. The first time I, as a boy, saw him walking out of the shop dressed like that I was amazed. I don't know quite what he was doing.

Grandfather Hardisty was a businessman with a conscience. In those pre-war days fresh food wouldn't keep over weekends so on Saturday evenings he made sure that the poorer families in town who came to his market stall never went short. He would sell cheaply, and give generous portions.

On Grandfather Weighell's side, two of his four daughters — Auntie Nora and Auntie Annie — worked in the North-allerton Co-op store until they retired. Grandfather had of course helped set up the shop in the late nineteenth century, and most of the Co-op staff in the early days had connections with railwaymen. Railwaymen dominated its management committee around the turn of the century, a reflection of their concern for welfare and self-help. Today, revealingly, there are no railwaymen on the Northallerton Co-op committee.

My father, John Thomas Weighell, was born on 7 March 1893 and died 9 March 1977, aged eighty-four. Aged eighteen, he joined the NER at Northallerton in 1911 as a signalbox boy, but shortly after was moved to Selby for a time because he took part in the rail strike of that year, the successful strike for union recognition.

The story goes that when father and mother first married they had great difficulty finding somewhere to live as a result of father preaching socialism from the Market Cross. No landlord wanted a socialist among his tenants. And so at first they went to stay with my father's uncle, Robert Barker, who was a farm foreman at Kendrew's farm just outside Northallerton. They eventually found a furnished terraced house in Gladstone Street (which has now gone), but only because George Playforth, an active NUR man, persuaded his mother, who owned it, to give my parents the tenancy. It was

Mrs Playforth's own house, but because of her age she had gone to live with George. I was born at Gladstone Street. Later we moved to 15 Standard Terrace at the other end of town, then we moved to 7 Upwell Road, next to the infant school, where we first had a wireless. As we children began to grow, mother put pressure on father to buy 12 Arncliffe Terrace, in 1935.

Father, a forty-two, had just been elected to the NUR executive committee, which I suppose gave him that little bit extra for the new mortgage (he didn't believe in renting — it was dead money, he said). Arncliffe Terrace, which served until we had all left home, was a much bigger house, having four bedrooms, a bathroom, two rooms downstairs plus a kitchen, greenhouse and garden. Father took the small bedroom for his office. All the family were delighted at the move.

Grandfather Weighell always carried himself with pride and dignity. I remember him immaculate in his uniform. The guard, of course, is the man in charge of the train: nobody starts off a train without getting the OK from the guard. The name originates from the men who guarded stage coaches. The driver has never had quite the same contact with the public as the guard had. The guard would come up to see the driver about late running at stations, because he, not the driver, would have to make a report out. With all this responsibility came a pride in the job. Pride didn't always originate in a big pay-packet — job security was just as important.

The signalman, like my father, was also a man of authority. Other grades learnt to treat him with respect, and he was nicknamed 'Bobby' because originally signalmen were railway police. The signal box door had a big sign on it saying *Private*, you knocked and sometimes you were allowed in if you took care to stand on the mat with your dirty boots. The driver himself had status and authority, and in the yards the head shunter ruled his own world. You couldn't ignore this sort of authority. All those in authority were expected to exercise it — and they did. In the Thirties mass unemployment was a great force for discipline as people hung on to their jobs.

Then there was the inspectorate: the station inspector, the marshalling-yard inspector, the locomotive inspector, the permanent-way inspector and so on. Their uniform was a black suit and bowler hat. This didn't necessarily bring subservience, but their authority was respected. Men had a very clear idea of their job and the status it brought. If asked to do something outside their own grade duties they would say: 'That's not my job.' You would hear it frequently, and the inspector couldn't force him to do it. Most people had a pretty good idea of their responsibilities. Sometimes they might say to you 'Go and uncouple that wagon.' Well, if it was immediately attached to the locomotive, yes, that was a fireman's job. But ask me to uncouple between two wagons and I would reply: 'That's not my job' — that belonged to the guard or shunter.

Station-masters were quite something — they wore bowler hats, and, in certain mainline termini, top hats. I just remember top hats. After the Second World War with full employment the respect for the authority of supervisors was affected. Managements supply this authority if they wish to. Many a time supervisors have great difficulty in exercising authority over the workforce because management don't give them full backing. I've never believed in authoritarian discipline, but I think it sad that supervisors have often lost the support of their management.

One feature of management control was Officer Specials. The top permanent-way men or the operating superintendents would travel about the railway by a special coach pulled by its own locomotive. This coach had eating and observation facilities — quite elegant with armchairs and big tables. They would use the coach to inspect track, running over all sections of the railway to get a bird's-eye view of problems.

That was the world that my grandfather and father were brought up in. I only saw the end of it, because it changed very rapidly during and after the Second World War.

When father wasn't away on union business he still worked as a signalman around Northallerton. In his early years there were no fewer than fifteen signal boxes within a five-mile radius of Northallerton, which gives some indication of its importance as a railway junction. Father must have worked in most of them because he was for a time relief signalman (with a travel allowance...) bicycling around as needed. Later, when the modern power box opened at Northallerton in 1938 (see Chapter Five), he went there for a year or two. He was still relatively young in railway terms and could adapt himself to the new technology, a change the older ones who got first choice for the new boxes found painful.

My father and his brother Hammond (who became a policeman but died young) both went to the First World War, fighting in the trenches. When he returned father apparently spoke little about his experience but exchanged preaching in the local Baptist chapel for preaching socialism. He never talked about the war. I don't even know his regiment, but I remember he brought back some medals: playing with them one day, I put them on my chest out in a hay field, and they dropped off and got lost. I thought I was going to be given a good hiding, but my father took it philosophically.

The Baptist chapel, the NUR and the Labour Party ran through the kitchen, for my sisters as much as for Maurice and me. You didn't ask why. For a long time I believed everybody else's house was the same, until I eventually discovered we were unique in Northallerton. Socialism aside, our house, like others, rang with hymn-singing on Sundays, and we all attended chapel until our teens, when we were allowed to decide for ourselves.

Father was a good platform speaker. He had developed the art of talking sense without using notes, and he used his Biblical knowledge to argue the socialist, trades union cause. He was President of the Richmond Constituency Labour Party for many years. He didn't deviate all his life from his socialist beliefs, though he had to wait until 1945, when he was aged fifty-two, to see a majority Labour Government elected to power.

Father was on the NUR executive from 1935 to 1937, and a short time afterwards he became secretary and chief negotiator of the LNER Council, almost a full-time job. Most problems of the LNER involving the operating department grades would pass through the Council, which at its peak covered almost 70,000 employees.

The Council itself met for two weeks, four times a year, but there were also various sub-committees, involving numerous meetings. The railway headquarters was at York, but meetings could also be in Edinburgh or London. Any dispute about the facts of a case meant a joint inquiry, usually wherever the problem was. Father got to know the location of every station, crossing and signal box and marshalling-yard throughout the LNER.

Because of his job he was known throughout the company, and in the very early years of my union activities I traded on the name 'Weighell, Northallerton.' It gave me a chance to make up the gap between my small branch and the big, city branches. When I myself started to travel the country as a full-time NUR officer I was always asked: 'How's your Dad?' But I never felt under his shadow.

For some reason best known to himself, father never sought to become a full-time officer within the union; I think it was because he preferred to keep his home in Northallerton. He did run for President, however, and failed by an odd vote. Father was travelling to and from council meetings in London right through the war years, which was no fun with all the heavy bombing and crowded trains. There were still many staffing problems to be dealt with during those difficult years to keep the trains moving.

My sisters used to type for my father — sometimes he would ask them, much to their annoyance, to do typing when they were all dressed up to go out. It had to be done. I would have my football boots ready to go and play when he would ask me to collect trade union contributions. 'But I'm going to play football.' 'Play football when you've finished.'

When I first went to father complaining about my railway problems he would tell me the story of himself as the branch secretary going to see the Superintendent at Darlington, a man called T. B. Hare. The District Superintendent had considerable authority in those days. The NER was unusual in that the branch secretary had access when he felt he needed it to various levels of railway management. It helped to create a special authority for the branch secretary. My father had made an appointment to see Mr Hare to discuss a number of local issues. He was kept waiting half an hour in the corridor outside the Superintendent's office, then when eventually admitted he was given a chair in the middle of the big office some distance from the Superintendent's desk, having to struggle with his briefcase and papers on his knee.

He didn't complain, but when he returned to Northallerton he reported the circumstances to the NER's general-manager at York, Mr Jenkin-Jones. Mr Jenkin-Jones wrote back saying yes, he would make sure this sort of thing didn't occur again. So the next time father went to see T. B. Hare he was ushered into the office straightaway and placed in a chair immediately behind a desk face-to-face with the Superintendent.

Hare started off by saying: 'Let me congratulate you, Signalman Weighell, in having the courage to report your Superintendent to the general-manager.'

'That's where you made a mistake,' said father. 'It wasn't Signalman Weighell who reported you, it was the branch secretary of the National Union of Railwaymen and they are two different people. When I come here I'm a representative of the NUR, not Signalman Weighell. The only boss I know in this position is the General Secretary of the NUR, so if you now understand that we'll get on all right.'

This one small incident indicates how trades union representatives had to fight to establish their authority to speak on behalf of their members.

Before the First World War, my father had become a lay preacher, full of biblical eloquence. I suppose he had some sort of evangelistic style which suited the day, and later on when he left the chapel after his war experience, and became involved in the union, he used this eloquence to advocate the union cause. He believed that he wasn't going to change the world by preaching about it from the pulpit — he had to do something concrete to create and build trades unions and a powerful Labour Party.

He was one of the first readers of the *Daily Herald* in Northallerton and became active in the Richmond Constituency Labour Party and would address meetings all over the constituency, notably from the Market Cross in Northallerton. Northallerton was hardly a hot-bed of socialism. Father stood time and again as a Labour candidate for the local council without success, and so he finally abandoned that to concentrate on NUR work. Eventually he was, not without difficulty, appointed a JP. There were objections, and my father told the story that they were overruled after some influence exerted by the then NUR General Secretary in London. He ended up being the chairman of the magistrates in Northallerton where in his younger days nobody would take a blind bit of notice of him, and he was awarded first the BEM in 1955 and the MBE in 1966.

Shortly after I myself became General Secretary in 1975 we had a pay crisis on the railways and were within one week of a national strike. We'd been through the whole procedure and we'd turned down a 27.5 per cent (it seems a lot today!) tribunal award because we wanted parity with the miners and the power-workers, who had got more. I used to phone home almost every week to keep in touch, and told my father, long retired and in his eightieth year, the news. 'Turning down twenty-seven and a half per cent? You must be barmy.' I didn't try to explain. It just showed how the world had changed in one generation.

Father was a hard taskmaster. He wasn't going to carry me in the early years — he knew I had to learn for myself. I used to go back complaining to him about the way I was hammered into the ground at conferences. He replied: 'That's the sort of movement it is. It's about life and life is tough. The longer you stay in it the tougher it will get.' I didn't join the NUR or the Labour Party; I was born into it.

Sunday lunch was the main meal of the week, usually with all the family round the table. We fed well. We didn't take holidays in my childhood, except the occasional day out to Redcar, which was extended to a week in a cottage there just before the war. But food was a priority; father said: 'If there's anything goes short in this house it's not going to be food.' We had a garden beside the line, opposite a signal box where father spent some years, and later we had one at the back of 12 Arncliffe Terrace, and so there were plenty of fresh vegetables. Grandfather kept pigs and mother's family, of course, kept a greengrocer's shop. We often had a ham hanging up in the pantry together with half a side of bacon, and there were chickens and eggs in plenty.

Sunday lunch was traditional roast beef and Yorkshire pudding, but father sometimes couldn't be there — as a signal-man he had to work on Sundays occasionally. When this occurred Sunday lunch was taken to him at the signal box, often by one of the children.

Mother would give him the full treatment. We would set off across the fields from Arncliffe Terrace carrying a basket loaded with tureens and crockery, roast beef and Yorkshire pudding, all the vegetables and trimmings, carefully packed with tea-towels to keep it warm; father used to pull out his little table in the box, spread out his cloth, knife and fork, and sit down to his meal. I loved to work the signal box under his instructions as he ate. I was just about tall enough to reach the bells to signal trains. I answered the phone and pulled the levers to change the signals, not without difficulty. Years later, when told by obstreperous signalmen, 'But you've never worked in a box,' I would pull their legs by telling them how, as a boy, I had worked a signal box.

My brother Maurice, also remembers going to scrub father's signal box floor. Father would say, 'Don't be too particular, you might set a precedent.' Maurice sometimes stuck a green flag out of the cabin window to signal to passing drivers, on father's instruction. At the Northallerton Low Gates box he wouldn't let you close the level crossing, but he let you open it up after the train had gone through on the Leeds-Teesside line. Maurice remembers the smell of creosote sleepers drying in the hearth, a pungent, friendly smell of childhood.

It didn't dawn on us until some time after we moved to 12 Arncliffe Terrace, as we became increasingly active in the Labour Party and the house served for the local committee rooms, plastered with 'Vote Labour' posters, that it was called 'Blenheim'.

'You know where that name comes from,' we would remind father. Blenheim Palace was, of course, built for John Churchill, the first Duke of Marlborough, in recognition of his great victory over the French at the Battle of Blenheim, 1704. Winston Churchill himself was born there. '"Vote Labour" at Blenheim! — it's not right — get it altered to Keir Hardie House.'

'No,' father replied. 'It makes the point much more forcefully when we're operating from Blenheim.' So 'Blenheim' it remained, despite all sorts of quips. Father would add: 'And don't forget that Churchill was once a powerful advocate of public ownership for railways, when he stood as Liberal candidate at Dundee.' I call my present home at Beckwithshaw 'Blenheim' in memory of those times.

As a child, together with my brother and sisters. I helped

with union work — we didn't know at first what it was all about, but we learned. Of course, when I began to work on the railway I joined the union. But I didn't go to the branch meetings — I was never told I should go by father. It was about 1941 before I bothered about my first branch meeting — and that was in protest at rotten shifts.

I had complained to father about working so many Sundays. I remember him saying, 'Eh, don't you come to me [he was the branch secretary] if you want to get your working hours changed go to the local committee.' Shifts were decided by this elected committee along with the management. 'So how do I do that?' I asked my father. 'Well, you want to get to the branch, anyway,' he said. Having been pushed against the wall I wasn't going to leave it there. I asked where the branch met. 'Once every three weeks at the Durham Ox Hotel.' So I started to go.

Some months after, father told me that if I wanted to get on the committee there were elections coming up for four men. 'What have I got to do?' I asked. 'Get a nomination form,' he replied, 'get eight signatures and put your name in.' 'But how do I get the votes?' 'You get all the young firemen at the depot to vote for you.' 'All right,' I said, and I did it. To my surprise I was elected, at a very tender age, alongside two experienced engine drivers and a fellow representing the other grades in the depot.

Then my problems really started. They made me the secretary, and I had to equip myself to cope. It was shortly after that I was given the chance to qualify as an engine driver. I felt that this was important to me if I was going to represent drivers, firemen and other grades at the depot. I had to know as much as they did. Of course, when I became secretary of the local committee I used my position to get a number of firemen qualified as drivers, including myself.

I had to stand on my own two feet. The only thing father would do for me was give me advice about getting the information I sought and help me escape some of the obvious pitfalls during my twenties, when I established the beginnings of a reputation in the union.

Father may have been quietly ambitious for me — he occasionally said, 'Why don't you go in for that,' but I don't think he ever dreamt I would become General Secretary of the union. He taught me, however, that if I ever went in for an election I didn't do it frivolously.

I was elected as a delegate to the NUR AGM at Ayr in 1947 because branches thought they were voting for my father. The second time I stood for election, in 1948, he said, 'Go around and talk to people in the branches, so they know you.' I did, and the second time I got myself elected in my own right.

It was rough. I was expected to tackle things which at times were a bit beyond me. I had to do most of my learning at night after work literally by the guttering candle. I would apply for National Council of Labour Colleges postal courses on chairmanship, economics and so on. I used to go to NCLC and Labour Party summer schools. All this experience became the driving force that made me go out and buy a college for NUR educational activities soon after becoming General Secretary. At my insistence we bought this beautiful place located in forty-three acres of grounds at Frant just outside Tunbridge Wells because I believed that the union representatives have to be just as capable as management to enable them to cope with the complex problems of today.

I had to struggle to equip myself, as did my father and grandfather before me. So I was determined, when I at last had the opportunity, to provide proper educational facilities for the union's membership. I am proud to say that when I left office in January 1983 the NUR was second to none in this field.

Mother was always active and generous in helping others, and she took very easily to socialism. In the Thirties people really were on the poverty line. If you lost your job, or were injured at work, you could soon be desperate.

Once a year the whole house was taken over for the annual audit of the branch books. This entailed the visit of two auditors and a treasurer who would pore all afternoon over the ledgers. The NUR was and is a highly organized union, and the balance sheets — accounts of all monies passing through the branch — had to go through to head office for verification and inclusion in the union's financial statements.

I always rebelled against injustice to others. I used myself to object when asked to work ridiculous shifts in appalling conditions. I learnt to articulate the emotions and thoughts of the people I worked beside as one of them. No matter what level I reached in the movement there were always battles for power and policies, reflecting the realities of industrial working life. These struggles are inevitable when you get representatives from the heavy industries like coal and steel coming together to discuss their problems. Given my North-east background, and my temperament, I was bound to develop an abrasive attitude.

I was probably the most aggressive of the whole family at work — and the most passive at home (except that I would rebel if pushed). I was the quieter brother, too. I started out reluctant to get on my feet and express myself but ended up in a job which attracted more than its share of publicity.

I *was* intolerant of people fudging the issues as happens in the trade union and Labour movement — even though I understood why this has sometimes to be done. But, funnily enough, I didn't start to fight until I got into the industry. I was a passive schoolboy, interested mainly in sports. So much so that father would say: 'You know where you'll end up, as a navvy digging trenches.'

Exams and homework were less important than cricket and football. My teacher, Mr Taylor, used to tell father, 'There's nothing wrong with the lad; he's just lazy.' He was partly right, but once I had the challenge to equip myself I was happy to study through the night. Father would say, 'Why didn't you work like this when you were at school?' On reflection, I wish I had.

I found that I could concentrate much more effectively towards the end of the day. I don't know whether this was a question of adapting to the demands of railway-working, with shifts starting at all hours of day or night, or an in-built metabolism.

I had lots of friends when I was young, involved as I was in sport, but I soon discovered that I could survive on my own easily. I never acquired smoking or drinking habits, for which I was grateful later on seeing people under pressure reaching for their cigarettes or drinks in tough situations. I'm not oblivious to pressure, but I don't have to resort to such support-lines. If I hadn't been something of a natural teetotaller I could easily have become a heavy drinker given the number of functions I have attended where hospitality or friendliness usually meant a drink. I must have turned gallons of beer away, becoming a genius at excuses. To survive in jobs subject to great stress and strain you must be physically fit. I made sure of getting regular exercise, walking, gardening, swimming and — when I could — fishing.

Not that I was particularly ambitious at the start. Like everyone else in the war, I was living from day to day, and the only thing that drove me to higher levels in the union was the experience that whenever I tried to get things changed I always seemed to be at the wrong place! I slowly realized where the power was in the union — with the Annual General Meeting, the National Executive and the General Secretary. I learnt to take problems to the level where they were most likely to be resolved. I never set out with any desire to reach the top, and in my experience the rank and file are suspicious of position-seekers.

Power and authority have their own rewards, but they are also very demanding. Many people just wouldn't put up with it. You wouldn't do it, because of the aggravation on the way up, unless you were convinced and dedicated to the cause. You don't do it for the money — in the early years I didn't get anything at all. The fact that I remained single until I was twenty-seven enabled me to attend many meetings and conferences on behalf of the branch at my own expense, because it couldn't afford to pay. This enabled me to become known to representatives from all of the big centres in the North-east and eventually throughout the country. Northallerton branch had about 450 members at the time I was becoming active (it's now down to 90). Coming from a small North Yorkshire town you needed a lot of luck to make your way up to the National Executive Committee. You had to be in the right place at the right time and be equipped to take advantage of the chances.

Whole streams of people would come to our house, bringing their troubles — not just railwaymen. Father would give advice to anyone who chose to come with a problem. The poorer townspeople of Northallerton had nowhere else to turn in those days before the welfare services, and mother with her strong chapel background played her part. I remember in my younger days mother taking jugs of cocoa to the infant school nearby to help nourish hungry kids.

During the war mother would take in hospital visitors in need of accommodation. At Northallerton, in the town surrounded by airfields, there was an RAF hospital and planes would return from bombing missions with crews shot to pieces. Working at Darlington and coming home at weekends I found the house full of people visiting their war-wounded relations. Some of them were harrowing cases. Because mother was involved in the chapel we would have visiting Baptists from the Forces, many of them Canadians. They were just young lads of my age miles from home and very grateful to mother. She would give them a good tuck-in, since it was easier to get your hands on produce in a small town like Northallerton than in the cities. But what they enjoyed most of all, I think, was the home atmosphere compared with the harsh environment of the Forces. Mother still receives letters from some of these Canadian friends.

Years ago, when I was first involved in union affairs as a young fireman, trade union membership was not compulsory although most railway workers joined. My first responsibility was to collect union contributions from the men at the Northallerton motive power depot and pay them over to the branch secretary.

One day a fireman said, 'I'm not paying any more.' There was nothing much I could do about it. I remember saying rashly, to the offending fireman in a mess-room full of staff: 'If I was a driver I wouldn't take you as my fireman until you had paid your dues.'

Well, I soon became a qualified driver and the day arrived when I had to translate my threat into reality. I booked on one night at 6 pm and was waiting for my fireman when this fellow bowled in. He said he was booked with me and that he'd made a exchange of shifts with my fireman. The shed foreman had agreed it. I said, 'I'm not taking you.' Then the row started, with the shed foreman, who happened to be there, soon involved.

Fortunately for me, another young lad was booking on, an engine-cleaner, so I took him. But by the time I got back after working my shift the shed foreman had spoken to the shed master. There was a note from him wanting an explanation.

My reply was simply that I didn't think this fireman was fit to be on the footplate. Before I knew where I was I had been reported to the locomotive superintendent at Darlington, in deep trouble. Meantime this fellow had joined a union, chosing ASLEF rather than the NUR.

My father, when he heard about the incident, lectured me for sticking my neck out. 'What did you do that for?' he asked. 'At least he's paying his corner now,' I replied.

Father's advice was to retreat as swiftly as possible. 'You cannot win this one on your own.' So I went to Darlington and accepted that I made an error of judgement, repeating my belief that I didn't think the fireman was fit for the job. 'You're not the man who decides whether a fireman is fit or not — it's the inspector who decides that. When he's booked on you're supposed to take him,' the superintendent told me.

He read the riot act and I promised it wouldn't happen again. My view about trade union membership has never changed. One of my first acts as General Secretary in 1975 was to negotiate the toughest compulsory trade-union-membership agreement in Britain.

Three generations of Weighells, together with their families, have each tried to leave the world a better place then they found it. My grandfather was active in the early days of the union and of the cooperative movement; my father followed the chapel, the union and the Labour Party; I worked for the union and the Labour Party. It was my grandfather's and father's generations which created the union and the party. In their day, union contributions represented a much higher proportion of pay packets than today. My generation simply picked up the torch and proceeded to build on the sound foundations they laid.

I very rarely passed through Northallerton without looking up my mother. Now that I'm once again living in North Yorkshire I can see her more frequently, so I took the opportunity to draw her out on the early days. Why was it, I wondered, that my father Tom was so articulate when his own father had been a man of few words?

Mother: I don't really know. We both attended the Baptist chapel where I occasionally played the organ for Sunday

47

services. Tom would say, 'I'm preaching on Sunday, Lena. Pick me some good hymns.'

He joined the Army during the First World War and came home on leave at intervals. We went out together occasionally, but nothing serious. He came back from the war, but he was a different man. He'd seen the rough side of life, I should think, and his ideas were different. He would stand on the Market Cross on a Saturday night preaching socialism. When I was a lass I carried a banner for the Liberals — Labour wasn't thought of then in Northallerton.

When we married in April 1921 and were looking for a house I approached a local silversmith who had one to rent — he made all the cutlery for the Queen's doll's house. But when he found out that my husband was the one who spoke socialism from the Market Cross he wouldn't let me have the house.

Sid: Did you and your brothers and sisters receive any wages for working in your father's shop?

Mother: No, but mother would give us a few shillings out of the till, and see that we were fed and clothed. I was the eldest of twelve children, four of whom died in infancy.

Sid: How many shops did your father own?

Mother: Well, I remember living over one small shop. We had to move because we were overcrowded, so dad bought a house and shop further down the High Street. Later he bought the property which is now Wetherill's gown shop — a grand place with a bathroom, gardens and everything. Then he acquired three or four more properties for speculation, and a field for the horses up Stokesley Road.

My dad was the driving force in the house and the business. He'd buy and sell anything. He'd get hold of a load of herrings, maybe, and go round the town selling so many for a shilling. He'd do the same with rabbits, working all hours. That's how he made his extra cash.

But he had another side to him. I remember as a lass three or four posts in the middle of the road beside a street lamp. We used to play round them. One day a seat was erected round this lamp and folk from the lodging-house for down-and-outs would use the seat, just opposite dad's shop, to sit and talk. We never knew until dad died that he had paid for that seat.

During the last war the seat disappeared. We had no idea where it was until somebody discovered it at the back of Willoughby's, the builders. Brother Ernie collected it and offered it to the Council. It's now on the green in front of the Lyric cinema, placed round a tree. I've sat on it many a time thinking of dear old dad, who died of pneumonia after catching a chill in a hay field.

Your other grandad, Grandad Weighell, was of a quiet disposition and very friendly. Grandma Weighell was the driving force there. She had her good side, but she was very domineering.

Sid: You used to help all sorts of people during the war?

Mother: Yes, through the Red Cross. Miss Russell asked if I would take relatives visiting the wounded airmen at the RAF hospital in Northallerton. We were surrounded by airfields, and airmen often arrived back from their missions wounded or burnt. My own boys were in a reserved occupation so I thought it was my war effort to help these people. We had lots of visitors from all over Britain. Sometimes they stayed weeks on end, visiting their relatives at the hospitals.

If only we could recreate today the national unity, the comradeship and determination of those days, Britain would quickly find lasting solutions to her appalling economic and social problems.

3   *Working into the War Years*

I N 1938, AGED sixteen, I started as an apprentice on the LNER at the road motor engineer's department at Thirsk station. In those days the railways operated an extensive road motor fleet which both collected and delivered all sorts of goods. From this workshop at Thirsk we covered a wide area, including Northallerton and Ripon, servicing vans used by representatives canvassing for traffic, bigger lorries distributing railway goods around the countryside, and three-wheeled Scammell mechanical horses which delivered in towns.

I used to catch the 7.20 train each morning from Northallerton eight miles away, working a forty-eight-hour week for eight shillings. I soon learnt to drive, practising on the Scammells in the station yard. Probably my father helped me get the job — as the NUR branch secretary he would have known it was coming up and an engineering apprenticeship in the Thirties was regarded as fairly secure. He must have thought that this was best for me.

I wasn't very happy about starting work myself — and in fact I had begun a year earlier at fifteen. Being the eldest in the family I should have left school at fourteen, but for some reason I wasn't very attracted to work. I much preferred to stay at school and hung on as long as I could until the pressure from my mother made me go out and find something. My first job was also in the motor trade, but I wasn't there very long before the Thirsk apprenticeship cropped up. I was at Thirsk for just over a year, and I suppose it was a useful introduction to railway life.

I soon came face to face with the disciplines of working. I remember on one occasion the foreman asked me to do something about ten minutes before clocking-off time at 5 pm. It was a sizeable job and I wasn't very happy about it since I was ready to clean up before catching the train home. It took me nearly half an hour and I was watching out because my train went at 5.30 — if I had missed that I would have been very late home. But anyway the job had to be done, getting some bits and pieces ready for the next day's repairs.

When I came to make my timesheet out I put down half an hour's overtime. The foreman eventually passed this, so it went to the pay centre at York. As the overtime rate was time-and-a-quarter, my half an hour's overtime worked out at just one penny-farthing extra, and my claim caused quite a stir. The foreman would send for me and say, 'I've got another letter from York wanting an explanation why you are claiming half an hour's overtime.' So I said, 'You'd want to be paid, wouldn't you?' I got the money eventually, but he didn't ask me to do any more overtime!

I was allowed concessionary travel between Northallerton and Thirsk — one quarter fare — in the shape of a three-month season ticket. Once I left it in my overall pocket when mother put the overall in the wash. When I found it in the pocket the ink had run and you couldn't read it. Now, the railway authorities were much keener on small details in the Thirties than today. It was the time of the Square Deal for Railways, promoted by the private companies, who were worried as ever about cash. Travelling without a ticket was a real crime then. I was a bit apprehensive about this washed-out ticket when the ticket inspector came along the train. I showed him it, and he couldn't read it. He was speechless. I tried to explain how my mother had come to wash it. He was about to take my name when he said, 'Go on, but don't wash it any more.'

I wasn't particularly interested in mechanical things, but I began to understand the internal combustion engine. And I also realized that you had to take care of a job. The consequences of losing out and going on the dole, a very different kind of dole from today, gave everyone a more disciplined approach in the Thirties.

When the war started in 1939 there was no immediate change, but gradually railways began to assume a new importance. This gave me an opportunity to transfer to the locomotive department. At Thirsk there was a big marshalling-yard close to our motor repair depot and I became familiar with operational railwaymen. When I could I went into the marshalling-yard, talked to the shunting staff and began to see, for the first time, the great LNER locomotives like the Gresley Pacifics and to get an interest. (I had never been a train-spotter and, coming from a railway family, just accepted locomotives as an everyday matter.) So when an opportunity did occur at Northallerton I told my father I would like to move. They needed staff, I made an application, and in January 1940 I transferred to the locomotive department of the LNER, based back at Northallerton.

Now this proved a totally different environment. I was no longer working 8 am-5 pm — suddenly it was round the clock. I joined as an engine cleaner but in a matter of days, having acquired a smattering of knowledge about locomotives, I was put on to the footplate as a fireman. This was on shunting engines used at Northallerton both around the mainline station and at the goods yard. We called them 'pilot engines'.

I had never before that time been much fascinated by locomotives, and only when I got on the footplate did I begin to acquire a liking for the job. But it had many disadvantages and certainly there was no romance about being involved with locomotives as the war developed. You worked rotten shifts, often clocking on when other people were looking to enjoy themselves. I was eighteen, I liked to have a good time and go dancing, though I didn't practise pub crawling because I was a keen footballer and cricketer. I wasn't a masochist out training every day, but I used to keep pretty fit.

The Northallerton shed, opened way back in 1857, was built between the low-level line, which carried the Leeds-Teesside railway and the main north-south line, screened from it by the station. The lines had been built by two different companies, the Leeds Northern and the North Eastern. The shed was working trains on the Leeds Northern line and also the Wensleydale line from Northallerton to Hawes and Garsdale Junction, linking with the London Midland main line which ran from Skipton up to Appleby, Penrith and Carlisle. We operated both passenger and freight trains up the Hawes branch line, using G5 tank engines, plus J21 and J25 freight locomotives. We also worked from Northallerton the Harrogate-Teesside passenger trains pulled by D20 locomotives designed by Vincent Raven.

At Northallerton station we used pilot engines to sort out the considerable volumes of agricultural traffic — milk, cattle, sheep. The goods yard was at the other end of town, also with its own pilot engines. That accounted for Northallerton, but we also ran the marshalling-yard at Thirsk eight miles south, supplying it with men and locomotives, and we worked freight to the Thirsk town goods station, about two-and-a-half miles off the main line via a branch line.

As the war began to tell, the Northallerton depot expanded because it was used as a changeover place for some mainline crews. Trains were taking much longer to get from Newcastle to Leeds, and freight crews would change over in the hope of being able to return home within a twelve-hour shift — Northallerton crews worked them on to Leeds. During the war years the staffing at Northallerton increased to about 120 altogether.

Northallerton was a very important junction with the East Coast main line passing over the line to Leeds and the important Teesside industrial centres. During the war the authorities built a special line round Northallerton to duplicate the two overbridges in case they were bombed. In order to switch traffic they had a moveable section of railway on a pair of wheels. Thank God, the emergency never occurred. In fact, shortly after the outbreak of war, almost the whole track between Darlington and York was duplicated, with two Up and two Down lines.

The odd feature about Northallerton's shed, caught between the high-level and low-level lines, was that it had no turntable, or coaling facilities. These were to be found behind the signal box at the station, and they served not only Northallerton but the Leeds men who were working passenger trains to and from Northallerton. The shed closed in March 1963, and the buildings were demolished shortly after.

Altogether in the North-east, in the area bounded by Newcastle, York, Leeds and Hull, there were over sixty locomotive depots at the outbreak of war. Darlington Bank Top depot, where I transferred in December 1940, to fill a fireman's vacancy, was one of the most important. First opened about 1850, it had been rebuilt a number of times. A final phase of extensive alterations was completed in 1938/9, so that it then consisted of seven straight through-roads (or lines) with sheds and access both north and south. An old turntable shed stood nearby, as well as a modern coaling-plant where you just pressed the button for coal to come out. A second turntable at the south of the shed was big enough to turn Gresley Pacifics, seventy foot long.

We used to work trains north and south to Leeds, York and Newcastle from Darlington, also the very busy Saltburn line and up the coast to Newcastle via Sunderland. We serviced most of the Durham collieries and, via a branch line, took iron ore to the great Consett steelworks.

We also worked the Darlington, Barnard Castle, Kirkby Stephen and Penrith line both for passenger and freight. This had a branch to Tebay, linking with the London Midland Shap Fell main line. There was, too, a branch down to Richmond and, as the war developed, a line to Catterick Camp, the big military establishment. We took many a trainload of tanks, armaments and soldiers to Catterick. Darlington loco shed closed in 1966 after 116 years of operation.

In Northallerton drivers belonged predominantly to the NUR, like most of the North-east, because in the depressed areas — the North-east, Scotland and South Wales — railwaymen had a unity and comradeship which dismissed craft sectarianism. This comradeship began to break down in the Fifties as affluence spread. There has always been friction between NUR and ASLEF — I found it particularly when I moved to Darlington and began to get pressure put on me to join the train drivers' union.

A NEW BREED OF FIREMEN

Before the war you didn't become a driver until you were fifty or more; it was a very slow promotion process, and a fellow would spend years and years as a fireman. Then suddenly there was this great influx of youth on to the footplate, some as young as sixteen, most of them as green as grass. The old boys had to carry them to start with, and some didn't like that. Several of the older drivers were autocratic, many were characters — enginemen in the fullest sense. Their whole life was devoted to making steam engines go. Steam locomotives may have been less sophisticated than the modern diesel or electric machines but they required special understanding to get the best out of them. No one engine was quite the same as another and you got to know how each one would perform by its number and its class. The old-style driver was almost bred to handle steam; he wasn't a scholar, some had great difficulty in writing, so I often found myself writing reports for them and doing all sorts of paperwork.

In return, they could be loyal and helpful to us young firemen. One night I particularly remember we got back to Darlington with a passenger train from Tebay on our Class J25 small locomotive about 11 pm. The driver said, 'You'd better get some water, I don't know if we have enough to get us over to the shed' (this was only a mile and a half but the trip had exhausted our coal and water reserves). So I climbed over the tender to find the water column, which was attached to the station roof, and lowered it into the tank. Then I turned the wheel on at the side of the station wall, filled the tank and pulled the column out. Now you were expected to put the lid on the tank when you'd filled up, to stop dust getting into the water and blocking the injectors which fed water into the boiler. But I was so black, dirty and tired I didn't bother. I just climbed back on to the footplate and sat there.

A fellow walked over, knocked me on the shoulder — I'd seen him standing there in the shadows, I didn't know who he was — and said, 'What about that tank lid?' I was just about to give him a mouthful and tell him what to do with his tank lid, when the driver came over and said, 'Yes, Charles'.

I went to put on the lid, then I asked the driver who the hell he was. 'That's Charlie Foster, the locomotive inspector,' he said. He was the same inspector who passed me as a driver a couple of years later.

On another occasion we were instructed to relieve an express passenger train and take it on to Leeds. My driver was a big fellow called Alan Walker. He hardly spoke a word. The guard blew his whistle, the driver slammed open the regulator on the Gresley Pacific, the wheels spun, and half the fire went out of the firebox up the chimney as the fourteen coaches lurched forward. That's how he drove to Leeds. Talk about sweating. At the other end where we were relieved he took me to a pub just off the station and dumped a pint of shandy in front of me with a gruff 'There you are.'

At that time the LNER hadn't yet adjusted itself to the new intake of young people. The railway was and is a very disciplined industry. There is an extensive rule book; regulations about working trains and other railway operations have to be upheld in the interests of safety. You're dealing with the welfare of millions of people, passengers and staff, and you have to be careful . . . nobody would argue about that. Because of this, the industry has evolved a sophisticated disciplinary procedure, agreed with the unions, so that staff who commit offences and violate the rules can be dealt with fairly. To invoke this procedure you are issued with a Form No. 1, which sets out the offence and asks for a reply within forty-eight hours. Alternatively the offender can opt for a hearing accompanied by a union representative.

I noticed in my early days on the footplate, particularly when I moved on to Darlington, that these forms came up like confetti because of the younger people finding difficulty in adjusting to the disciplines of the railway. Men were doing jobs previously undertaken by those very much older, and management had to try to adopt different attitudes. Foremen and supervisors who once had great authority suddenly found themselves being challenged. This, together with the impact of the war, began to spread throughout the industry.

It was the start of a change of attitude which, of course, was carried much further after the war. People like me weren't looking over their shoulders. No longer were there all those millions of men out of work. I wasn't aware of it then, but these were the beginnings of the very-changed post-war society, and the experience on the railways was only one example. So, as you walked through the timekeeper's office to report for duty you'd see quite a lot of Form Ones posted in the window. I had them myself, and we youngsters didn't take them all that seriously.

You weren't sacked then, for obvious reasons. I was actually called up and redirected back to the railways as a reserved occupation. The only way you could join the Services was by volunteering for air crew. It was an exciting time for someone as young as me as the war began to develop. I was fascinated by Churchill's compelling rhetoric over the radio, especially the 'We shall fight on the beaches' speech. We soon began to see refugees passing through Northallerton after the retreat from Dunkirk.

By December 1940, when I moved to Darlington as a fireman, there was a constant stream of troop trains, tank trains and ammunition trains. Working in the blackout, in total darkness, was a frightening experience. This railway world, which I was only just getting used to, was swamped by great volumes of traffic, marshalling-yards full of trains. If you set off to work to York or Newcastle, you could take hours and hours to get through because of the sheer weight of traffic.

At Bank Top station, Darlington, where we relieved trains on the line behind the station, we had to change train crews going both north and south and we went there at all hours of the day and night. You just didn't know where you were being sent.

To meet the war need, the railways had been reorganized with a new control system. In the old days the signalmen regulated traffic, but by 1940 there was central control. Railways had been brought under government authority. These were the lifelines of the nation — everything was going by rail. Some traffic, especially coal for instance, which previously went by coaster was switched to rail. Steel from Consett, Hartlepool and Middlesborough suddenly had a great importance for the munitions of war; iron-ore and steel were in great demand.

When you worked a train to York or Newcastle you sometimes had to travel back as a passenger because of the long delays and it was difficult to get on trains because of all the troops crowding the corridors. When food rationing came, they established Forces' canteens at stations and depots which railwaymen could also use. That was all right, because it supplemented our normal rations.

Working twelve hours a day was common; sometimes I spent eighteen or nineteen hours on each shift. You often just couldn't get through; I've stood waiting at a signal for hours. It was tedious, tiring work. Even though I was still in my teens I would go back to my lodgings in Darlington dog-tired. Working in the dark, the pitch black, was the worst. You learnt quickly. If you didn't you stood a good chance of being killed or injured. The worst place to be in the dark was the shunting-yard, where shunting staff were in great danger from moving wagons.

One incident was particularly frightening. Going to relieve a train at Bank Top station to take it to Newcastle, we had to cross four sets of running lines — the Up and Down main lines plus two relief lines. We were crossing to the relief line to take over an express freight train going north; the three of us quite close together in the dark — the driver, myself and the guard. I remember being about to cross the main Up line when an express suddenly tore through in front of me. It had no lights on, and its steam was shut off because of the falling gradient. The only thing I heard was a hissing from the cylinder cocks which made me hesitate a moment before I crossed. Thank God — I would have been cut to pieces.

There were other, lesser, dangers like points sticking up in the loco and shunting yards. From time to time I walked into these with only minor injuries. I once split my eyebrow when I stepped off the footplate of a locomotive on to a curved firing iron, stood on the end of it and it knocked me over. Incidents like these happened time after time. I was one of the lucky ones — many railwaymen were killed or injured. The railways are a dangerous enough place to work in normal times.

The only consolation about war working, when you never quite knew when or even if you were going to finish your shift, was that at least you got paid for the extra hours. But that lost its attraction after a time, particularly if you were young. The national agreement had stipulated a minimum of twelve hours rest between one turn and another. That went by the wayside and later in the war, as people began to get worn out, they rebelled more and more at the hours.

Then there was the weather. The winter of 1940-1 when I moved to Darlington was terrible, we had trains buried in snow on the main line. On one of our routes, the line across the Pennines to Penrith and Tebay, we used snow-ploughs. There were great squads of soldiers keeping other lines open and telegraph poles had been knocked down by the weight of the snow.

Sometimes you'd be out for twenty hours.

Permanent-way men were especially vital to the service, particularly during the bombing raids of the Battle of Britain when miles of track could be destroyed overnight. It's a totally different occupation today, but in the war permanent-way repairs were still done by pick and shovel.

Even during the war years Sunday was the favourite day for permanent-way operations, especially relaying. So we were put on permanent-way trains at weekends. We were there just to move the wagons and then sat watching them work. When they had to manhandle freshly creosote-coated sleepers, lifting them off the wagons with no mechanical help, the creosote not only got on their hands but used to affect their eyes for days after.

Signalmen had the authority to call permanent-waymen out for snowstorm and 'fogging' duties. This meant that they were stationed at the distant signal with a coke brazier to keep warm and detonators to put on the track when the signal was at caution to warn approaching drivers. These men could be stood out there most of the night in the very worst weather conditions. Snow-clearing duties were again extremely dangerous. This involved clearing the points manually of snow and ice so that they would work properly. From time to time men working on this job in very poor conditions would be cut down by trains. Lack of sleep, caused by long working hours, was another very dangerous factor.

When I was lodging at Darlington war rationing got worse and my landlady, who was very good to me, had great trouble finding food for my bait tin. She used to pack sandwiches filled with brawn, which I couldn't eat. I would occasionally buy half a pound of carrots on my way to work at the greengrocer's; there was no fruit on sale at all. They must have been the best-fed seagulls in the war at Saltburn because I used to chuck the brawn out of the sandwiches as we were taking our food at Saltburn station and eat carrots with the bread. But you could sometimes get a good feed at the canteens they set up in the main stations and depots.

Going to the motive power depot just outside Gateshead at Borough Gardens was like being thrust back into the middle of the last century. I needed the toilets and was directed towards a low shed. There was nobody inside, but I found a long wooden seat with ten holes over a trough, everything open. Much later, as NUR General Secretary on a visit to China in 1976, I saw the same sort of thing but there had been some advance with little shoulder-high cubicles (you could see the head and shoulders of the occupants). The Borough Gardens arrangements must have been in operation since the 1850s. Archaic. Even today there are facilities around British Rail which disgrace a modern industrial society. Things have got much better, but there has always been a lack of resources to cope with the backstage demands of the railway industry, let alone the side the passenger sees.

Because of the primitive washing facilities at the depots it was often preferable to wash on the footplate before you booked off, using hot water from the engine boiler. The steam locomotive was a great producer of dirt — not only the coal on it but the ash out of the fire-box and a very fine black ash from the smoke-box. The men who had the worst job were the fire-droppers who worked permanently cleaning fires or chucking them out in the bigger depots, using long nine-foot shovels and crawling about in piles of smouldering ashes which played havoc with their clothes — not that they had much protective clothing. The ash was raked out of each engine in between shifts, the smoke-box door was opened and all the black ash cleaned out.

Some locomotives were easier in that they had a drop-bar in the fire-box which operated from the cab allowing ash and clinker to drop into the pit without using the shovel. Fire-droppers had a quota to do — about twenty each shift — so that by the time they finished those men had earned their money.

Just before I started working on the footplate the railways changed their practice of always allocating the same locomotive to the same driver or a group of drivers. There was still a semblance of group ownership shed to shed, but that all broke down as the volumes of traffic swelled with the war. Even then, locomotives still 'belonged' to a certain depot, and frantic efforts would be made periodically to return them to the depots for servicing and things like boiler-washing.

The pattern of a day's work allowed ten minutes for booking on — to look at notices, see whether there was anything in particular to look out for on the permanent-way or water troughs. You would then have forty-five or sixty minutes, depending on class, to prepare the locomotive — oil it and get the necessary tools together (it would already be coaled and watered). If after your shift, which was usually far more than the scheduled eight hours, you brought the engine back, sometimes you would be expected to 'dispose' of it. By that I mean you would clean the fire, smoke-box and so on to make it ready for the next crew to book on, finishing by coaling it and watering it.

Now there were other crews at the depots who did nothing else but preparation work — they never left the shed during their shifts. Sometimes I worked that shift, which nobody particularly liked; you had about an hour to complete each locomotive. The only bonus was that occasionally you could slip away early if you finished your quota of engines before the end of the shift.

When I started there was a profusion of locomotive depots. In 1940 in the Darlington area alone we had Darlington, Northallerton, Leyburn, Barnard Castle and Middleton-in-Teesdale, and West Auckland. Railways were a very labour-intensive industry, which had already peaked sometime after the First World War when not far short of a million people were employed, declined after 1919 and climbed again during the Second World War as NUR records show (1919: 481,081 members; 1947; 462,205).

Darlington was quite big by any standards, with 800 people; Northallerton much smaller, about 120; Leyburn had just six men, Barnard Castle about twenty and Middleton-in-Teesdale six again. The rural depots were small, self-contained units operating branchline services. When steam went after the war so did many of these jobs and of the sixty or so North-east depots only a handful are left today.

By any test, steam is hopelessly inefficient. The only

61

argument in its favour is that Britain is an island built on coal. Even as technology developed and engines had super-heating to use steam more potently, it could only have been cost-effective to run steam in an age when labour was cheap.

I got to know more about locomotives by studying at home. There was no time allocated during work hours. All they would allow you was time off to take the test. But we did have mutual improvement classes. I used to go in my own time on Sunday mornings to these Darlington classes. There I found models of the layout of steam engines to help me understand the principles and familiarize myself with the different working parts. Drivers and inspectors would give their own time to talk to anyone interested. There were never more than half a dozen of us, I'm afraid. But it depended on you — if you wanted to know, you got to know.

As I progressed, I saw the opportunities of qualifying to become a driver. My private reading was dominated by unions, railways, trade union agreements which I could learn from, old arbitration decisions. My father had an office with this sort of book. For some reason or another — and my son is the same — I can pick up and read anything. Anything that really interests me I find I can throw myself into. At school the environment did not stimulate interest, but when I have something to aim for there's no problem.

My father used to say, 'For God's sake put that book down and come and get something to eat.' I would be the same on the footplate. In shunting-yards I was always being chided by drivers, told to stop reading and put some coal on. The better-humoured ones would fire and drive, letting me read on. After a time, drivers would allow you to drive the locos in shunting-yards, then occasionally on main lines. You had to be careful and on the alert; the last thing that must happen was injuring or killing anyone in the shunting-yard or on the track through your negligence. The driver had to be sure you were competent before he allowed you to drive.

During my war years at Northallerton and Darlington I worked a huge variety of engines: the G5, a passenger tank engine, 0-4-4; the J21, 0-6-0, principally for freight; the J25 0-6-0 passenger and freight; the J39, also both freight and passenger; and an 0-4-0 Sentinel shunter with vertical boiler and cylinders, which was based in the small yard at Leyburn. (The Sentinel was like a small fish-and-chip shop. I had to qualify specially to drive it.) I also worked on the V1 passenger 2-6-2, and very regularly on the A5 tank engine between Saltburn and Bishop Auckland. Then we had the B16 4-6-0, a big freight engine allocated to Darlington, the D20 at Northallerton, a 4-4-0 passenger engine with huge driving wheels which used to roll so you had to have the agility of a ballet dancer on the footplate. The K3 Gresley freight, 2-6-0, would lurch along because of its wheel arrangement, but wasn't bad to work on.

And the best of the lot — the Gresley Pacifics, the A4 4-6-2. The Gresleys, because of their power and wheel arrangement, were good enough for every job. But others like the D20s and the D49s, named after the Hunts and the Shires, 4-4-0, were passenger locomotives whose wheels were too big for freight. We also worked the Gresley-designed V2 2-6-2 Green Arrow class out of Darlington — this engine was introduced in the mid-Thirties, and carried a lot of the burden during the war.

For a number of years we had as a special arrangement an A4 Pacific 4-6-2 of the type used to pull expresses non-stop between London and Edinburgh, standing at Darlington in case of engine failure. A set of men was detailed to this locomotive, just in case any mainline express locomotive broke down.

The heavy freight locomotives were the Q6, 0-8-0, very powerful; and, even more powerful, the Q7, which we used to work iron-ore trains to Consett.

Going back to the J25s, which we used to work over the Pennines to Tebay, the biggest tender engines possible over the old iron viaducts — they were shockers. I can still see myself, saddled with bad Durham coal, starting at Bank Top station, Darlington, first stop around the corner at North Road, and I was struggling for steam already. Firing one of those involved using a shovel and a long fire-iron, which you needed to break up the caking coal. By the time you got to the other end you had to take on more coal at Penrith and clean the fire just to get back. Because of this work you had no time to stop and eat, so there you were with the shovel in one hand and a sandwich in the other.

On the line from Darlington to Tebay and Penrith across the Pennines very old iron-built viaducts limited engine size for weight reasons. There was the part iron and wooden-trestled Deepdale viaduct, 161 feet high and 740 feet long, fitted, as I remember, with a wind-gauge which rang a warning bell in bad weather. Then the Belah viaduct was a massive structure, 196 feet high and 1,040 feet long. The line, as it crossed the Stainmore Summit, reached an altitude of 1,370 feet beside a signal box and a few cottages. The NUR had great difficulty in persuading signalmen to work in this bleak area at this box. Near the summit a small stream ran beside the line. We called it the 'Welcome Stream'.

Driving in the dark, you sometimes couldn't see for steam. You had to shut the regulator off to find the signals. During the blackout you had to keep the fire-box closed as much as possible. But when you opened it to put more coal on, even during air-raid warnings, a great shaft of light shot up and the driver would shout at you to get the coal in quick.

Especially down the Teesside coast, going to Saltburn, there would be anti-aircraft guns rattling and banging. Bombs dropped everywhere, though I luckily didn't have any direct hits. Newcastle, Sunderland, Hartlepool and Middlesborough stations were all bombed. You heard planes droning in the night, too, though I never knew whether they were ours or theirs. Of course, the East Coast route of the LNER was very vulnerable to attack from the Continent, homing in on the industrial centres of the North-east and our own massive air-fields. Later on in the war, I witnessed the 1,000 bomber raids head east from these airbases towards Germany.

In a sense the war was lucky for me. Because of the pressure on manpower, and because I equipped myself, I became a qualified engine driver at twenty-one. That wouldn't have happened before. I found I could work best at night; returning home from the backshift at 10 pm or later when the rest of the family had gone to bed, I would get down to learning the rules and regulations for my driver's test. What to do in case of accident or train failure, how you protect the train, even how to repair the locomotive and detailed knowledge of Westing-house and vacuum brakes.

When the test came the locomotive inspector took me down

Darlington North Road Station in 1933.

The last train over Bela Viaduct in 1962.

The unique semaphore signal at Alnmouth, 1952.

A cheerful snapshot of NUR delegates at the Annual General Meeting in Hastings in 1951. I am standing alongside the locomotive.

Tender locomotive on the turntable at Garsdale Junction. A palisade was constructed around the turntable to act as a windbrake.

Sheep are now all that run on the Redmire-Wensleydale line. The line was closed to passenger traffic in 1954.

to the loco shed, then took me over the locomotive, asking detailed questions about what made what work. I was required to drive a train over the Saltburn-Darlington route and complete a written test. Of course, because I was only twenty-one, he was that much more strict. But I found I had the ability to learn quickly and then articulate my knowlege.

Locomotives were run continuously. They came in to the shed to have the fire cleaned and be coaled and watered, and then they went straight out again. We ran the wheels off them. (Some were thirty years old.) It was remarkable how they kept going. We were required to work almost every class of LNER locomotive on any type of train. I worked the pride of the railway, Gresley Pacifics, on coal trains, for instance. The locomotive fleet ran and ran and ran, with the consequence that everything deteriorated. It did give you the experience on every class of locomotive — some good, some bad.

And, of course, the drivers varied — some didn't give their engines a chance; they just opened the regulators and expected you to shovel like hell. I used to shout to the drivers to let up a bit. Before the war, train weights were limited; when the war came locomotives were pushed beyond their capabilities. Often, on starting out, the wheels would spin when the driver opened the regulator, and half the fire would go up the chimney.

I remember often going up to Consett pulling loads of iron-ore. With the most powerful steam locomotive we had then you could only pull twelve wagons of iron-ore up the very steep gradient to the Consett steelworks. One winter it was so cold up there that when we came to turn the engine round at Consett my hands stuck to the turntable with the frost.

It was the same up at Tow Law. We used to go there with a Class A5 tank engine on local passenger trains, and at Tow Law we would fill the tank from water columns — part of these were made of leather, for flexibility. The leather could be frozen solid, so you had to hammer it to bend it to fit the tank. You earned your money all right.

I used to rebel occasionally at the long hours, and also against other working conditions. Sometimes I was wrong myself, and my father used to tell me off. I suppose, being young, I had an exaggerated sense of justice and fairness, which began to be aggravated by the conditions in which we worked. We never, in my part of the world, had any strikes or stoppages during the war in protest at the rotten conditions or the long hours. Everyone was conscious of the need to sustain the war effort. In many cases, railwaymen were working a damned sight harder, in more dangerous conditions, than some people in the Forces.

Railway shift-workers had callers-up if they lived within a mile of the locomotive depot. As a war-time arrangement you could make a special application for permits to purchase an alarm clock or even a thermos flask because of irregular hours (they proved unsuitable for the footplate).

At home in Northallerton my brother Maurice, who had also started work on the railway being only two years my junior, used to share a room with me. Sometimes the caller-up would come for Maurice. I would answer 'Yes' at three or four in the morning, turn over and go back to sleep. He would get up when the house woke up at about 8 am, go to work and swear the caller never came. Or it happened the other way round — there were always arguments.

You got to know each locomotive by its number. You could get a good and a bad one in every class. Particularly if it was stationed at your own depot you would know from the number when you climbed on at the beginning of the shift what you could expect. You learnt how to handle one differently from another. Some you had to coax along.

Being a fireman involves a great deal of skill, just as being a driver does. If you had an intelligent combination of the two you could probably work through. But if you found yourself with a rotten fireman, or a good fireman found himself with an inefficient driver, there were problems. The good driver, sensing difficulties, would ease back a little when he saw you were in difficulty.

You juggled with the level of water in the boiler and the steam pressure. Knowing every inch of the route was the key to good firing and driving. Established firemen were just as knowledgeable as their drivers on these matters.

Travelling on the footplate was a totally different world from being in a carriage. Some of the older locomotives, the ones with the bigger wheels, would kick and roll at speed. You had to learn to keep your balance so you could distribute the coal over a big fire-box in the places needed. It was a skilled job, putting the coal on so that the fire-box temperature was raised to give maximum steam.

The coal varied enormously in quality: Yorkshire coal was big and good, but it had to be smashed up with a hammer which meant additional hard work. We got a lot of Durham coal — dirty, dusty stuff which used to cake up the fire-box, so you needed nine-foot-long fire-irons for poking. At night, with blackout sheets to cut down the glare from the fire-box, the steam and the noise from all these moving parts together with straining your eyes, head out of the cab, to spot signals, life could be very tough.

In tunnels there were additional problems. One of the longest in the North-east, Bramhope Tunnel on the way to Leeds, was 2 miles, 241 yards long. The tunnel was on an incline and that meant when you worked a heavy freight train you might start slipping because of the all-pervading damp. We countered this by using the sanding equipment in the cab to put sand under the wheels. What with sparks flying and smoke everywhere, at times you had to get down with a wet handkerchief around your face just to breathe. If the train slipped almost to a standstill by the time you got to the other end you were really struggling to get your breath, coughing and spitting. Coming the other way from Leeds, of course, you could coast through on the falling gradient.

Bramhope Tunnel has a special, infamous place in railway history. It was completed in 1849, the key section of the Leeds-Thirsk Railway, linking Leeds direct to the North-east (the Railway only survives today as far as Harrogate). The number of navvies killed building this flood-ridden tunnel was so great that a special memorial to them, in the shape of a castellated tunnel, was constructed in the churchyard at Otley nearby.

James Bray, the Bradford stonemason who became the railways' principal contractor, is said to have used stone taken from the tunnel to build the mansion on his Moor Park Estate, Beckwithshaw, near Harrogate. By an interesting coincidence, I now live at Beckwithshaw myself, close to Moor Park, though I don't think the stone used to build the house I live in came from Bramhope...

Just before the war the York-Darlington main line had been modernized with electrical signals. Because the lights are placed at cab-level you can run a train at time-table speed in the worst of conditions and not need to see the signals until you are almost on them. You rely totally on the signals being correct with nothing untoward on the track. The running signals which control the driver are of the four-aspect type — green, double yellow, yellow and red.

A report in the *Darlington and Stockton Times*, when the new Northallerton signal box opened in 1939, was headlined 'Signalling Marvel at Northallerton.' The report noted the progress made in railway signalling from the original idea of a signal to stop a train to developments which would include the ability to keep maximum numbers of trains on the move, at the same time ensuring absolute safety at speed. All these developments were incorporated in the Northallerton main-line signal box.

The reporter, shown round the box by the station-master, found that it was equipped with the most modern electrical power signals. The box controlled sixty-two miles of track-circuited lines sectionalized into 146 separate track circuits. Some 58 signals and 33 pairs of points were operated, allowing 120 different routes to be set up.

All this, concluded the report, was a system which meant added speed and safety, and ensured that supplies got through 'both in the dark days of war and the grey days of peace'. The Northallerton box proved to be the prototype of modern power-signalling systems used throughout the country.

This was the ideal railway to work on. But off that modern track you were back on the old semaphore system. The signals were stuck up at different heights in different locations; you had to know the geography of each route, every bridge, to recognize the sound of the track which could tell you where you were in the fog. Sometimes during the war years it was almost impossible to see signals through all the steam coming from leaking piston valves. Drivers had to have good eyesight, and many were put back on to shunting tasks because they failed the stringent tests.

The job was exacting and unromantic. It wasn't the world imagined by the train-spotter or enthusiast. I often say I like steam locomotives on postcards. On the footplate what concerned me was — what sort of locomotive is this, is it a reasonable one to work, can it cope with the tasks being asked of it? It didn't matter if it was painted bright green or dashing blue or black. One of the best to work, because specially built for freight, was the Gresley V2. All Gresley locomotives had well-designed and equipped cabs, good visibility, comfortable seating. There was a water-pipe connected to the boiler for washing and for settling coal dust which made all the difference to footplate comfort. Gresleys were high-quality engineering. Nigel Gresley gained a knighthood in recognition of his outstanding contribution to locomotive engineering.

UNITY IS STRENGTH

During those years there was a comradeship among railwaymen. You worked in large groups in the locomotive sheds, which were thronging with people. This comradeship has been broken down today because many train crews sign on at booking points and rarely meet each other. In those days most people met in the mess-rooms between shifts; there was always chat and debate going on. I grew up in that atmosphere. We would discuss union matters, politics and working conditions.

It was the same at home, of course. My father wasn't a full-time union official: he continued to be employed by the railway as a signalman. The railway had, and still has, a sophisticated system of union representation, with very few full-time union officials. The negotiating machinery at local and regional level is manned by rank-and-file railwaymen who are given time off on full pay; this has two advantages — it saves union resources and provides representation by men who fully understand the working conditions of their members. At every station or every depot with more than thirty employees there's a committee of four (called the Local Departmental Committee — LDC) who meet the local management to discuss local problems; at places with fewer than thirty, two men suffice. In every region there is regional machinery, manned by rank-and-file railwaymen to deal with the problems of different groups and grades. Some of these are almost full-time. The regional and LDC representatives meet as and when required.

I naturally got involved in the union discussions at depots, especially after I started to take an interest in the branch. At Darlington there was a balance between the NUR and ASLEF drivers and firemen. I got pressure put on me by some drivers to join the train drivers' union. I remember one driver who gave me *The Lighted Flame*, the history of ASLEF, and said, 'You should be in our union.'

I was once on a running pilot with him, taking traffic from one marshalling-yard to another. We were standing opposite the modern signal box at the south end of the station. I was looking over the side at a plate-layer going about his work. The driver pointed down at him and said, 'What do you want to be with *him* for?' I said, 'Well, I'm with him for the same reason that I'm also with him up there' (pointing up at the signalman). 'Haven't you heard about unity being strength?'

And after all those years of aggravation since 1880 the train driver still doesn't get any special treatment; he is paid in accordance with his skill and responsibility like all other grades — he gets no better holidays, pensions or sick pay. Yet ASLEF have had this fallacious argument since 1880 — you'll be better off with us. It has never worked out. What it has done is create divisions between railway workers when we needed unity. Experiences like this made me go back and read up on the reasons why the NUR was created, what its original purpose was. I didn't just take it from my father, I had to stand my corner to argue with those other footplatemen. I wasn't satisfied with being silent. So I had to go back to equip myself.

And then my father would say that the ASLEF form of organization was contrary to working-class solidarity and principles. 'What do you want craft elitism for?' he asked.

All this was part of growing up on the railway which later stood me in good stead because if you want to represent people in industry you've got to be of them and from them; otherwise you can't hope to win their trust. You aren't able to articulate what they think if you don't know what makes them tick. A representative should be able to act in much the same way as the person he represents would act in the same situation.

So this hard grounding during the war years, learning my trade and about my colleagues, was an apprenticeship which served me well during the many pitched battles to come.

4   *Wensleydale: Memories of a Branch Line*

THE IDEA OF running a railway line up Wensleydale from the flat, fertile North Yorkshire plain at Northallerton to the inhospitable moorland of Garsdale became a reality in 1878, shortly after the Settle-Carlisle line opened. This mostly single-track railway, criss-crossing the Ure valley as it climbed gently to over 1,000 feet, was a much easier engineering task than the London Midland main line it met at Garsdale, the junction with the now-threatened route over the top of the Yorkshire Dales, which links Leeds with Cumbria.

Despite its usefulness as a through-route across the Pennines, the Wensleydale line, in its full thirty-nine-and-three-quarter miles, was closed to passenger traffic as long ago as 1954, well before the Beeching cuts. For many of its seventy-six passenger operating years my family and colleagues were involved in its well-being.

As a goods and passenger guard based at Northallerton, the Hawes branch line (known as such probably because Hawes marked the end of the LNER track; from Hawes to Garsdale trains ran by favour of the LMR) was a regular route in my grandfather's life. My father, a Northallerton signalman, controlled access to the Hawes branch, served by its own little terminus platform at Northallerton station. Both Maurice and I fired and drove trains up the line, which was not always the haven it now seems.

There were frequent goods services bringing limestone from Redmire quarry halfway up the dale to the steel furnaces of Teesside, a service which still keeps the bottom end of the line open, though the stone is now powdered and carried in fifty-tonne hopper wagons. At least until after the Second World

71

War the line also served the everyday needs of the small, mainly agricultural population.

This meant daily milk trains, trains full of sheep and cattle, and horse-box specials to the famous Middleham racing stables. It meant provisions for the village shops and wagons-ful of coal which we dropped off at each of the fifteen stations up the line. Every station-master acted as the agent for the sale of the coal, thereby sometimes doubling his wage if he was keen and efficient. Having obtained a station-master's position, together with a house on the pleasant branch line, a man never left beautiful Wensleydale.

Wensleydale has much the same number of inhabitants today but the transport environment is quite different. Everything comes by road. It's hard to evoke the days when rail was supreme, including special troop and munitions trains which brought soldiers to Leyburn, with its firing range (Catterick Camp is nearby) and supplies to link with the West Coast route.

Regular passenger services from Northallerton to Garsdale and back were worked by Northallerton crews and also a small 'link' of men based at Leyburn, where a certain amount of shunting was handled by a special lightweight Sentinel engine. These locomen enjoyed a pleasant, regular life compared with the shifts endured by most footplate staff. The first passenger train left Northallerton around 7 am, reaching Garsdale some two hours later after making sixteen stops. There was often over an hour to fuel and water the locomotive before the return journey to Northallerton. The last train at night terminated at Leyburn. By the early 1940s there were only four passenger trains each way per day, with none on Sundays.

Ernie Wade was the old boy who drove the Sentinel pilot engine at Leyburn. (The Sentinel was a tiny tank engine with a vertical boiler, adapted from steam road engines, which looked more like a fish-and-chip shop than a locomotive.) He kept pigs during the war and he had a pipe connected from the boiler gauge glasses into a milk churn. This milk churn was properly equipped for boiling his pig food. When you got into the cab there was a delicious aroma of all these mixtures cooking in the milk churn. They used to send us up there to relieve when he was on holiday. The motto of the Sentinel's makers was 'Ever watchful and on the alert' — you had to be so, because its tiny vertical boiler needed constant feeding.

There were plenty of freight trains, too. In those years the LNER tried out a freight bonus scheme; the quicker you completed the job the more you were paid. This move was resisted by the NUR because it eliminated jobs, but not successfully at the time.

When I first started, a fireman earned about two pounds seventeen shillings a week and a driver about four pounds ten shillings, worth more than that sounds today. So the bonus was worth while to many. But obviously the person who had to flog himself to speed the locomotive up was the fireman, and a year or two later when I began to form an interest in the union I opposed this kind of working. I argued with drivers — who perhaps had big families and needed the money — that I wasn't flogging myself to death to help lose jobs.

On single-track routes like the Hawes branch you had to slow down at each signal box to exchange tablets with the signalmen — tokens which ensure that you are the only train on that section of track. But drivers used to go like hell on bonus trains. Often, if I thought the speed too fast for the exchange (it should have been 5 mph), I would simply step back into the cab and refuse to attempt it. The drivers then had no option but to stop, which could take half a mile for a heavy freight train, to let me walk back with the tablet. If anything slowed down the rush, that did.

There were numerous crossing gates on this line. Time and again on the return journey off the branch at speed on the incline from Leyburn to Bedale we smashed through the gates. But management turned a blind eye because they wanted those bonus trains to continue.

Once I was approaching Leeming Bar Station at North-allerton end of the line, firing for a driver called Tot Ball. He slowed down correctly to the required 5 mph in preparation for the tablet exchange while I stepped over to the driver's side to get near to the signalman. Tot chewed tobacco and as I moved over and leaned out he just spat, hitting me right in the eye. He didn't do it deliberately, but I missed the changeover and he had to stop the train. I said 'You dirty...' and he just laughed his head off. I always watched him very carefully after that painful experience.

Freight trains stopped at nearly every station to detach wagons of livestock and coal. We also carried racehorses in special horse-boxes for the Middleham racing stables, but my best memory of the turf is stopping at a station, working a passenger train up the branch opposite the train coming down at a station passing place. We were chatting across the line with John Watson from Leyburn, the other engine driver and a keen racing enthusiast. Bob Hird, my driver, liked to back the horses so Watson shouted across, 'Bob, I've seen a miracle on the moor.'

'What are you talking about?' replied Bob.

'This horse, Dante. Small, but of good stock, just right for the Derby. Its speed is amazing.'

Dante was trained locally at Middleham and sure enough it won the Derby in 1945, backed by Bob.

The normal passenger train comprised just two coaches. On summer evenings, coasting down from Garsdale in the cool of the day, it could be really beautiful — Wensleydale looked good from the footplate, and the line was skilfully grafted into the gentler contours. But it was a different story in winter.

I remember one dark winter night coming down from Garsdale with a new driver called Mattie Bell from Tyne Dock near Newcastle. He had just 'signed' for the route, which meant that he had accepted full responsibility for working a train over it, but really I knew the way far better than he did. Being wartime, we were all in the pitch black — there were no station lights, of course. The only things to guide him were the signal lights. As we approached each station he started slapping the brakes on and off, then stopping short, frightened to over-shoot. Those vacuum brakes worked very fiercely with a small, light train. I told Mattie the passengers must be thinking they were on a switchback. 'Well,' he replied, 'I've got to get used to these difficult conditions.' And he did, eventually.

At Hawes station the fishmonger would be waiting for boxes of fish we carried in the guard's van, and he would start selling it direct from his van as soon as it was unloaded. So, some mornings, we would buy a couple of kippers from him, take them on to Garsdale Junction and cook them on the shovel there and then, while we waited to go back down. The shovels weren't dirty, of course, they were washed clean and bright before use.

You had to learn to adapt and live on the locomotive, especially when you were miles from anywhere. You couldn't make tea on the engine but we did boil up a kettle at Garsdale or any other station or signal box when the train stopped. You very soon earmarked the stops which provided a kettle on the boil: some signalmen were much more friendly than others.

This cooking breakfast on the shovel was standard practice with some crews, who brought their egg and bacon along with them. One day I was standing looking idly out of the cab, probably eating my sandwiches — I couldn't be bothered to bring food along for cooking — when, sniffing the fumes of smoke coming from the fire-box I automatically knocked the small lever which applied a special jet designed to prevent fumes from blowing back from the fire-box into the locomotive. Of course, this jet also sucked away my driver's bacon and eggs, which he had sizzling on a shovel inside the fire-box. I think I did this once or twice by mistake, not meaning to sacrifice his breakfast, but he learnt not to trust me and used a different method, getting the shovel red-hot then cooking his bacon outside the fire-box.

People who travelled the Wensleydale line felt that the railway was part of the community. My brother tells of an experience with some hikers.

'We used to have a few minutes at Hawes, with it being a change of railway company. This would allow a certain time for going through the train for tickets and things like that. I'm leaning out of the cab and these hikers come up. They had all the gear and an ordnance map; they point to a little, obscure footpath going across the railway and ask, "Could you put us off there, please?" It was the footpath down to the Moorcock Inn.

'I said to the driver, "There's a chap here wants putting off at the Moorcock Inn footpath."

'"It's not a bloody bus service," he replied.

'So the hiker passengers had to go through to Garsdale, and by the time we were coming back they had walked down on to the road below, back towards the Moorcock. They were shaking their fists and all sorts at us. But you couldn't stop because of the difficulty and danger of getting out of the coach without a platform. If they had been injured it would have been our responsibility.'

At Garsdale the station was a community in itself, and it was mainly railwaymen, London Midland men, who lived in the cottages nearby. The local lending library was to be found on the platform and a small village hall had been made under the water tank used to fill both LM and LNER locomotive tenders. The hall even boasted a piano and was used for dances and meetings.

The permanent-way men, signalmen and station staff who lived in the cottages had small-holdings and were part of the local community. You often found yourself chatting to an old shepherd, who seemed to call at the station for a bit of company. One day he told me how sheep went crazy after a sort of tapeworm attacked their brains. 'You know what you do? You catch the sheep, drill a hole in its skull, fish the worm out with a bit of wire and then everything's all right again.' I don't *think* he was pulling my leg.

When it snowed we used to drive snow-plough trains up the branch to keep it open. Many a time we succeeded when all the roads were blocked, and indeed the Wensleydale line was re-opened to passenger traffic during the arctic winter of 1962-63. The other very bad winter of 1947 was the only time I can remember the Wensleydale line, along with the Darlington-Tebay-Penrith line, closed because of snow. We ferried train-loads of troops up to the blocked parts to dig their way through, pursued by snow-plough trains.

My brother tells of one afternoon on the snow-plough when they were asked to take two butter baskets full of groceries from Hawes to Garsdale; they also gave a lift to a young man stranded at Hawes. Unfortunately, they stuck in a snowdrift about 400 yards from Garsdale station so the young man and my brother finished the journey on foot, carrying the baskets of groceries.

When they arrived at the station they found a steam locomotive almost covered by snow, drifts of snow all over the place and complete silence — not a sound. They took the groceries to the signal box and told the signalman about their problem.

They were in luck: snow-ploughs with a gang of men arrived from Settle. With their assistance they were dug out of the drift and made their way back down to Hawes.

As I was union representative at the Northallerton depot drivers would bring their problems to me. One driver reported how on a wintry night, working a Class G5 tank engine on the last passenger train from Garsdale to Northallerton, they were approaching Askrigg when there was a loud bang from under the loco. They coasted to a halt in Askrigg station and had a look around and found that an eccentric driving rod had broken.

They set to and removed the broken bits — no mean achievement with a coal hammer and a shifting key in the dark — centred the valve on the cylinder with the broken rod then attempted to move the train with a loco that had to work on one cylinder instead of two.

The driver opened the regulator and nothing happened. They were only hauling two coaches, as usual, so they asked some people on the platform, mostly uniformed soldiers, to give a push. Off they went and completed the thirty-mile journey on one cylinder and stopped at all twelve stations en route.

My brother also tells of a driver who had a friend who lived at Hawes and worked a quarry somewhere up in the hills. He liked to ride with Maurice and his driver from Garsdale to Hawes on the footplate. One night they were working a Class D20 with him on board. (Those D20s were terrible locos, really bad riders. They used to roll about.) At one point the engine gave a great kick and this man said to the driver, 'By golly, mate, she's an uneasy bugger this'n.' Very broad Yorkshire. And she was.

Garsdale station, high in the Pennines, sees gale-force winds; it was here that our passenger tender-engines had to be turned for the return journey. The turntable was hand-operated and, unfortunately, in a very exposed position. If the wind caught the locomotive you just couldn't stop it. The story goes that one spun around the turntable there for six hours, slowly rotating while all looked on helplessly. So the management decided to construct a sort of palisade around the turntable with sleepers stood end-up as a sort of windbrake. It was crude, as the photograph shows, but did its job. If you were forced to run tender-first that could be a very uncomfortable experience, with coal dust flying in all directions. The tank engine, obviously, was designed to work in both directions, and the G5 0-4-4 class locomotives did many years of good service on the branch.

Up on the line near the village of Newton-le-Willows there was a public school, whose young gentlemen would fill the train at Jervaulx Station each term-end. When they arrived at Garsdale or Northallerton to catch their connections they would swarm on to the footplate. I was amazed at their knowledge of locomotives, and I enjoyed showing them the fire-box, regulator and other parts of the cab. They understood me all right though their upper-class accents sounded out of place on the footplate.

I qualified very young to be a driver. One incident on the Hawes branch remains fixed in my mind, and it perhaps gives some clues about my approach to other problems in later years...

An even younger fireman — he was about sixteen, I in my early twenties — and I were working a passenger train on the branch. We started from Leyburn, bringing the train to Northallerton where I took on coal for the return journey, some eighteen miles. I remember telling the fireman to fill up the G5 class tank engine with water while I shot down to the shed to take care of some union branch work.

On returning I just had time to jump on the footplate before the signal was lowered to let us out and we coupled on to the coaches standing at the platform. Off we went up the branch line. We had reached the first station, Ainderby, before I checked with the fireman whether he had taken on any water. His face was a blank, so I stepped off the footplate, walked down the locomotive and lifted the tank lid. We were almost out of water, with nothing like enough to last us to Leyburn, with its ten-mile uphill climb from Bedale.

As I climbed back on the footplate I thought, 'Good God, what do I do now?' Then I remembered that a train would be coming off the branch; we were scheduled to pass it at Leeming Bar, the next station but one along the line. In the few miles between Ainderby and Leeming Bar I had to work out what kind of locomotive would be pulling this train, a tank engine or a tender engine, and if it was a tender engine whether it was likely to have plenty of water on board.

The fireman thought we stood a good chance — he said it was a big Class D20 passenger loco. As I ran into Leeming Bar I had to slow down to receive the tablet permit for single-track working. But instead of slowing down I stopped. I saw the other engine already waiting in the station and it was indeed just what I wanted.

My best chance was to get the other driver to swap locos with me. I called out to the signalman — 'I've a bit of a problem with this engine — it's creating difficulties. I want to talk to the other driver.' I walked straight over to the locomotive and spoke to its driver, George Raine.

'Eh, George,' I said, 'I've no water. You've got plenty, haven't you?'

'Aye,' replied George, 'I've a tankful here. I filled up at Leyburn and I've only been coasting.'

'Can I have your engine, and you have mine instead?'

'That's a funny one,' said George.

'I know it's funny,' said I (in fact it was totally unheard of), 'but I'm out of water — what else can I do?'

So we swapped engines via a simple points manoeuvre.

They never did know. The shed master came to see me some days later with a puzzled look on his face. He asked me what number of locomotive I had on such and such a day.

I said, 'Well, I don't know.'

'Well,' he said, 'we've got two engines at the wrong end — a tender engine at Leyburn when there should be a tank engine, and vice versa. How the hell did they get there?'

The incident reinforced the message which had been driven into my head the day I started on the footplate. Drivers told me that the most important statistic on the railway was the distance between each water column. They were as vital as petrol stations are to cars. If you didn't have water with a steam engine, you were finished.

Years after, old George Raine used to joke with me about the water, but nobody else ever knew — not even the signalman who helped me switch engines, or the guards. There proved to be just enough water left in my tank engine to get

George's train back to Northallerton.

By the time the Wensleydale branch line closed to passenger traffic on 26 June 1954, I had been a member of the NUR Executive Committee, seconded from footplate work, for a year or so. But my brother Maurice worked the line until then, and indeed continued long after with freight services. The enduring importance of limestone keeps the bottom half of the track in good condition, and there are occasionally other significant arrivals like the Royal Train, which has used Bedale as a quiet night stop during tours of Catterick Camp. When the Queen herself visited in May 1970, the Bedale platform was resurfaced.

Above Redmire the line soon peters out. The former track has given way to sheep runs. But road travellers, if they have eyes, can easily spot the route of the railway criss-crossing the Ure Valley. Given the obvious attractions of Wensleydale, could the whole line ever operate again? I believe it could, at an acceptable price, under the right conditions. I develop my arguments for reopening some branch lines in the final chapter of this book.

5 All Change, But Mainly for the Worse

WHEN THE WAR finally ended the railway system was exhausted. Railways and railwaymen had made a gigantic contribution to the war effort. Over half a million special trains, passenger and freight, had run during the war years, and we saw our share of them in the North-east.

The London and North Eastern Railway Company, LNER, was bankrupt in 1945, so there proved to be no resistance to the nationalization proposals of the incoming Attlee Labour Government. The problem was that after the 1947 Act which brought railways into public ownership, no government did anything of any consequence for another ten years to help railway investment. Railways, which had played a major part in winning the war, were definitely not seen as an economic priority. The system just had to struggle on, and it's not surprising that staff morale sunk as a result.

Change was in the air with people coming home from the war. Everyone was fed up to the teeth by the time war ended. I know we won, but most people were totally run-down, and needed something different. Despite Churchill's having inspired us to win the war, working people had no desire to see him carrying on during the peace. We felt that the Labour Party would bring the different times we so badly needed, and nationalization was one of the important parts of their programme. Railways were to follow coal into public owner-ship. I remember when the great day happened there were red flags hoisted at the pit-heads. Euphoria abounded — 'We're all right now — they're ours...'

When nationalization came to the railways in 1948 the same sort of feeling was common. Jokes were cracked like, 'Just be careful with our equipment.' There was a tangible feeling that the railways now belonged to us, not them. Nationalization was going to lead us to the promised land. The war had certainly precipitated change. There was the belief that, having sacrificed so much to protect British democracy against the Nazi tyranny, Britain itself ought to be a better place to live in. Returning soldiers made it quite clear that they were not going back to the old Depression days — they were going to change things.

I don't know what we expected in our industry — but it didn't come. The railways proved to be just the same as before. We were meeting the same management figures after the British Transport Commission was established and all the various parts of the system — such as the docks — had been taken into public ownership. The dream of the unions and the Labour Party had been translated into reality, but that was where the problems started.

Britain's devastation was deeper than anyone realized. We were flat on our backs and what it meant for the railways was that things were going to get worse. The resources just weren't there. I wasn't surprised, five or six years later, when the Labour Party barely scraped in at the 1951 General Election for a second term, which was not to last the course. I remember Aneurin Bevan explaining later how we just weren't able to persuade the British voter that further discipline was vital if we were going to bring about the changes we all desired.

What Labour achieved in their first post-war government was gigantic. Their problem was that the five years of austerity, following the five years of war, was too much for the British people to take. The Conservative opposition capitalized with slogans like 'Set the people free.' After these ten years it was almost impossible to persuade voters to make further sacrifices, and I for one wasn't surprised at the way things went. After barely eighteen months of Labour's second term the Tories took over and were there for thirteen years. The sort of changes that Labour was attempting required great self-discipline. They only succeeded because they still retained many of the powers — like rationing — given to government in wartime. Britain no longer had a great empire to sustain it — it was having to lift itself up by its bootstraps.

Strangely enough, the government had made a profit out of the railway operation during the war, working in parallel with the railway companies. But as I have said, the LNER itself was bankrupt.

Life for me carried on much the same at the end of the war, except that shift-working got easier (hours were at least shorter) and I began to become more active in union branch work. I was also involved at union district council level at York and Leeds. Also, I took more and more interest in the Labour Party and in 1948 became the Labour agent for the Richmond constituency, one of the biggest geographically in Britain and which included the towns of Northallerton and Richmond as well as Wensleydale and Swaledale. It was and is one place the Tories expect a huge majority — a terrible constituency from a Labour Party view, but what beautiful countryside! I was pushed into becoming agent because nobody else was very keen to do the job. I held the position until 1953 and was, of course, Labour Party agent during the 1951 and 1952 General Elections.

The constituency has about eighty or ninety polling stations scattered around North Yorkshire's countryside. We couldn't have someone at each of those — the only thing you could do was make sure that the main centres of Richmond, North-allerton, Catterick and Great Ayton were well covered. While I was agent we acquired a little Jowett van which could climb a mountainside, but went at its own speed.

This was just after the war, and petrol was still strictly rationed, but agents had petrol coupons issued to them based on the acreage of the constituency. You can imagine how many we received! They were as good as currency, and an amazing number of people would help the party in return for a few extra coupons. Many of them weren't Labour voters. The coupons also helped me to use my little second-hand MG sports car for party work.

Of course, we faced special problems in these rural constituencies. When it came to putting Labour stickers in their windows farm-workers had to be careful, especially those living in tied cottages. Preaching the Labour cause to the farming communities of Richmondshire was hardly easy. You'd only get a very few people to village meetings, and the best they would do was listen politely. So, most of the time, you were talking to dogs, stone walls, and black-faced sheep.

It was good practice all the same, and part of my apprenticeship for getting up in later years and speaking at Labour Party and NUR conferences. You need courage to stand up in the first place to address such conferences and a clear head to deliver what you have to say in a logical order with the minimum amount of referring to notes, especially when you're limited to ten minutes. It's a damned sight more effective to speak without notes.

At the same time I was also playing more and more football. I had started in amateur football locally, but I then went to West Auckland, who were a very hot amateur side. I signed for them as inside left early in 1945. When I was going to union meetings at York and Leeds on Saturday mornings I obviously had a problem in getting back to West Auckland in time for kick-off. I would take my boots with me to morning conferences ready for the afternoons and they would send a car for me.

While appearing for West Auckland I was approached by three First Division clubs, whose scouts must have seen me — Sheffield United, Newcastle United and Sunderland. The fellow from Sunderland came to watch me up at Tow Law and he persuaded me that Sunderland was the best bet. I didn't support any of those teams — in fact the team I watched occasionally during my schooldays was Middlesbrough because it was handy. One plus for Sunderland was that all their reserve-team matches were played in the North-east, so I signed for them in October 1945.

I was offered ten pounds to sign on with three pounds per match (equal to my railway wage) plus travelling expenses and a pound if we won. It was a very attractive pro-position — playing football on a Saturday was better in financial terms than going to work for a week. I didn't consider giving up my job, though. My father advised me firmly not to become reliant on such a precarious occupation. 'But don't forget to join the players' union!' Sunderland raised no objection to my continuing on the railway, so I carried both union cards. Since I couldn't get to training sessions at Sunderland during the week I made arrangements, two nights a week, to do physical training at evening classes held in Northallerton Grammar School. That, as well as physical work on the footplate, allowed me to run for ninety minutes on Saturday afternoons with no problem at all.

It was high-quality football I went into, all right. The reserve team was a blend of young lads like myself and old professionals who were there to bring them on. In fact, the half-back line was the one which had won the FA Cup for Sunderland in 1937 — Thompson, Johnston and Hastings. Those three taught me a great deal of football in two seasons, but I found it difficult to continue to compete because I was becoming more and more involved in the union and the Labour Party. I did travel once or twice with the first team — their normal inside left was Riach Carter — but it was quite something to survive in the reserve team. Those days we would get gates of up to 15,000 for reserve-team matches.

I don't know just how good I might have been; but even at the top of the profession you didn't go beyond thirty years of age and the pay then was nothing like as good as today's. It was a much more disciplined game in those days. Referees were in total control. There was none of this kissing and cuddling when someone scored. The scorer was just part of the team, not always seen as the most important part of the move which led to the goal. And you didn't have ten-foot-high barriers to keep the crowd out because the crowd was disciplined as well — they came to watch the football. North-east supporters were very knowledgeable about the game.

One problem was that as a local union representative I had to be very careful about setting an example. I couldn't be seen taking every Saturday off. I would purposefully swap shifts on to nights, trading away a good turn like early mornings, so that I could be free to play football. The money from the football allowed me to buy the second-hand MG sports car, so comparatively speaking I was well off.

After leaving Sunderland I continued to play for local clubs; I played for the village team at Brompton, near Northallerton, where we won all the cups going. I don't know why I chose Brompton, but I remember that teams for miles around feared meeting us.

In the ten years or so between 1942, when I first became

involved in the union (elected as a representative at the Northallerton motive power depot) and 1953, when I was elected to the NUR Executive Committee, I fitted in all manner of activities. I was a representative on Northallerton's trades council from the NUR branch; I was the representative to the constituency Labour Party; I went to two Labour Party conferences as constituency delegate in 1951 and 1952; I was one of the youngest delegates to attend the NUR annual delegates' conference in 1947 — I also went in 1948 and 1951 and 52. I was taking numerous written correspondence courses in chairmanship, economics and so on and, of course, I was Labour Party agent in two elections — 1950 and 1951. I took six weeks off work each time, unpaid and barely recompensed by the constituency Labour Party — which didn't have much money.

In the second campaign we'd been too ambitious and spent a lot more money than we should have done. I suddenly discovered that the agent was personally responsible for paying all the bills, and I was about £300 short. I remember calling an emergency meeting of the constituency party to find ways of raising the money. We put in desperate calls to Transport House but anyway we raised it somehow. Eventually I gave up the Labour Party (as well as professional football) to concentrate on the union.

Among Labour leaders at the time I had been inspired by Ernie Bevin — not by his oratory but more his presence. You could tell that he was determined, he had the look of a tank. Aneurin Bevan and Manny Shinwell were the brilliant speakers, Herbert Morrison quick and deft, Attlee a remarkable leader who kept the team together. That first Labour Cabinet after the war, including Cripps and Dalton as well, was a galaxy of talent which I doubt whether Labour has matched since.

The policies of that time were soundly based on bettering the lot of the working people — they weren't the sort of claptrap we see spewed out today by the extreme elements now in the party. The appeal went straight from the Cabinet through the parliamentary party right down to the traditional Labour supporters in the street. The only thing not going for the 1945 Labour Government was the depth of the problems it faced. I admit to being greatly influenced by the big figures who addressed the huge meetings arranged by the party in the North-east. Another man who impressed me was the Durham miners' leader, Sam Watson, who was on the Labour Party National Executive Committee and was always willing to visit the Richmond constituency. He would always speak at meetings and never charge expenses. In fact, he invariably put something in the collection box.

All this time I was meeting more and more railwaymen and listening to their problems — particularly getting to know the needs of other grades like signalmen, permanent-way men and so on. In those early post-war years there was far more interest in union matters, and in the Labour Movement, than there is today. It was a mass movement in every sense of the word, and if you wanted to get anywhere in the union you had to fight.

I found it a terrible battle coming from the small-town branch of Northallerton to compete with great centres like York, Newcastle and Leeds, each with thousands of members. My problem was to raise enough votes, coming from my relatively small base. Also, I was years younger than most of the competition. The war had accelerated my career, not only as an engine driver but as a branch official and area representative. Wherever I went on union business in those days, and for quite a long time after that, I seemed to be the youngest there.

I was, however, able to capitalize on the fact that father and grandfather had been ingrained in the movement; their experience overcame, to an extent, the difficulty of setting out from this small area of rural North Yorkshire. I was increasingly articulate, and was probably beginning to cause as much trouble to the establishment as other, younger men, caused me in later years. Years later I would say — 'Yes, I used to move resolutions like that once, I was going to put the world right in twenty minutes. Now I'm the General Secretary of the union it's a different world, and I'll tell you why it's different...'

There was a great tradition of debate in the NUR when I was making my way. The branch and district council meetings were brimful of men, good men, in far greater numbers than now. We had quality then, and there's a reason why. Between the wars the educational opportunities weren't what they are today. If you were born into a railway family the chances were you would become a railwayman too. They were good men, self-educated, articulate, intelligent and well-equipped. It all changed after the war. Railwaymen's sons no longer automatically followed their fathers. My son went to Keele University where he took an Honours Degree in Geology. Four years later he achieved a Ph.D at the University of Wales in Aberystwyth. My brother's son is a metallurgist with the British Steel Corporation. My sister's son also obtained a university degree and is an aeronautical engineer. With this sort of change, the traditional pool of working-class brains and talent has been siphoned off. Nowadays, the railway trade unions are drawing on people of a different kind. They're not inferior railwaymen, but there isn't the same background, experience and numbers to choose from when it comes to union representation.

You can't help but notice this in the sort of people coming through. There's no doubt that the quality of the NUR Executive Committee is different from twenty or thirty years ago. It represents a much smaller workforce, of course, about one quarter the size of what it once was.

In the 1940s and 1950s life could be tough for the aspiring union activist. Several times, in my early twenties I went back home from conferences where I had been cut to ribbons in debate and told my father I wasn't going to continue. They gave no quarter, but father taught me that if I got up without preparation, or frivolously, they would flatten me against the wall. Even so, you could talk quite constructively, but if they found something they didn't like they wouldn't hesitate to tell you. At other times, whatever your argument was, they would play the age card. But father would say, 'That's what it is all about — it is a tough movement, and the higher you go the tougher it will get.'

In that environment I developed a northern bluntness to survive which I have still today. I've mellowed over the years, but I still retain the northern characteristic which says in three words what some people need paragraphs for. I was to some extent influenced by grandfather at an early age. After he retired he often used to come round, and whenever you get a group of railwaymen together the talk goes to railways.

Anyway, father and grandfather were discussing in the greenhouse one day why the time set for moving resolutions at Labour movement conferences was exactly ten minutes — why wasn't it eight or twelve? They looked in Citrine's book on chairmanship and he didn't give any explanation. I remember grandfather saying 'There can only be one reason — if you can't say whatever it is you have to say in ten minutes you're telling lies.' He was a man of few words, and the longer you rambled on the less notice he took. You had to be able to encapsulate the most complicated issue in a few words for both my father and grandfather: if you didn't, they didn't listen.

Whenever I attended conferences in my early days, I made sure I knew what was on the agenda and then prepared myself if I was going to take an active part. To make any impression with North-eastern men you had to make your speech not short to the point of being unintelligent, but short enough to get straight to the heart of the matter and make sense. Father would say, 'If you get on your feet make sure you've got a point to make. Don't just get up for the sake of being seen.' So I started to get resolutions formulated through the branch to ensure that the right items were on the agenda at district council and later at national conferences. I found that once I'd written a speech out I could recall what I wanted to say without having to refer much to notes. I would just keep the notes in front of me as a reassurance, rather than get up empty-handed.

Shortly after the war I became involved in the North-east lodging dispute. Railways were trying to extend what we called double-home turns, lodging away overnight after a shift. There were very few of these in the North-east, but some bright spark on the Railway Executive wanted to extend them. I was involved in a whole series of unofficial strikes against the proposals. I was in favour of the protest, but at some stage it got out of hand.

It was then that I first met a man who was to become President when I was General Secretary, a fellow called David Bowman from Dundee, a Communist Party member. I had quite a few struggles with Bowman over the years, but when he became President I managed to reach an understanding with him. A strong President, as he was, and the General Secretary can together exert considerable influence over the National Executive. Similarly, if the General Secretary can reach an understanding through his ability with the annual conference he can fashion the union's policy to his liking; if he can't influence the annual conference he's in trouble.

After 1945 as a consequence of the war effort the whole railway system was in a state of decline. It had reached a point, probably unique in the history of the railways, where foot-platemen refused to take engines out of the shed because they were in such a poor state.

The quality of service deteriorated during the late 1940s and there was no longer war as an excuse. Already passengers were starting to complain and freight began to drift away on to lorries as roads and road transport started to improve. The motor vehicles which had been developed during the war were being adapted as goods vehicles and cars; the locomotives which had served so well were old and obsolescent. There was no specific move to modernize the railways until 1955, and that was both rushed and ill-judged.

For example, a good case had been established for electrification in the immediate post-war years but in 1955, when the decision to modernize was finally taken, British Railways opted for diesels as more immediate. The Continentals, by and large, decided to go straight from steam to electric motive power. One reason for British Railways' position is that our railway network wasn't so devastated during the war as those of Germany, France or Belgium, so we didn't have the same opportunity to build a complete new system.

Looking back with the benefit of experience, British Railways made the wrong decision. They indicated as much when they explained, many years later, the problems they faced. A British Rail Engineering paper presented to a Joint Consultative Council meeting for 17 January 1975 includes the following passage:

> Because a little prior development of diesel locomotives for British Railways had been carried out and because there was a need to compress the changeover into as short a period as possible to achieve financial advantages quickly, a large number of different designs and classes

were commissioned... There were originally thirty-two classes of main line locomotives.

A number of these classes soon proved either unreliable or expensive to maintain.

Between 1956 and 1968, when steam was transformed into diesel, some 3,098 diesel locomotives were built, with peak production of 450 in 1960.

In 1947 my brother Maurice and I crossed to the Continent on a railway study tour (my first trip abroad). We did this through the union newspaper. The editor of the *Railway Review*, Tom Ashcroft, made all the arrangements. Travelling through France to Switzerland was a hell of a job because French railways had been destroyed in the war. We had to follow a very circuitous route to get to Switzerland. But when we got to Switzerland, which hadn't been affected by the war, the whole electric railway system was a dream. And, coming from ration-book Britain, the food was a revelation.

In Switzerland railwaymen lived in a different world. They had no-strike agreements, but instead were guaranteed status, security of employment, good pay and good conditions.

They wore immaculate, military-type uniforms, the railway was clean and all-electric (using the country's abundant hydro-power). To us, coming from the dirt and grime of post-war British railways still powered by steam, Switzerland was a totally different world. We were there for a fortnight and returned the year after, attracted not only by our desire to see more but by the lure of as much good food as we could eat.

Swiss railways were really something, and still are today. That's also true, now, of most of Western Europe. Where we in Britain were once the world leaders we have now slipped back after years of neglect and political differences over the role of railways.

Despite the self-evident differences between countries, the mechanics of railways are similar worldwide and there is an international understanding between railwaymen. Because railwaymen have their own internal system of communications, they have proved themselves historically to be the best-organized workers in any industry. They have been among the leaders in most revolutionary movements in various parts of the world, including Russia and more recently Poland.

The very nature of their job makes railwaymen disciplined — in the early days railways had a hierarchy with a military flavour about it, even in Britain. You've got to have discipline, rules and regulations for railway operation when you are dealing with the safety of millions of travellers. The spin-off is that in organizing as a union, railwaymen are tremendous. In later years as General Secretary I would say to board chairmen: 'They may be your staff, but they will respond to a message from *this* general quicker than to one from you.'

Despite all the concessionary travel offered to railwaymen I found in my early days that I was something of an exception in my trips abroad. Many of the older men never went on holiday — some would rather have gone to work than take a holiday — principally because they knew no other life. They didn't know how to use leisure. Most of my generation were never like that. The only thing that deterred us was the cost. Some of the older generation just couldn't afford to go away. They only got a week's holiday in those days, but many wouldn't even take a day trip to the seaside.

COMMUNITY CONSCIOUSNESS, REGIONAL PRIDE

Railwaymen have always had a political and community consciousness about them. You'll find in the great railway towns like York, Hull, Derby, Doncaster, Newcastle, railwaymen became mayors and lord mayors, following a tradition of close involvement with local government.

Years ago when railways were at their peak many of these local authorities were dominated by railwaymen. I was often invited by railway mayors to visit their towns and cities. Soon after I became General Secretary the Mayor of Derby, an NUR man, invited me there. We agreed that he would send a car for me to the Station Hotel. I was waiting in hotel reception when a man arrived and told me my car was waiting outside. I followed him out, climbed into the back of the mayor's limousine and started to talk to this fellow.

'What does the mayor use this car for, then?' I asked.

'I use it for functions, and I find it valuable for trips to London,' he replied.

'Oh, so you're the mayor?'

He was. The fellow, quite unassumingly, had brought the mayor's car to collect me and he conducted himself with the same modesty throughout my visit. Yet he was at that period the Chief Citizen of Derby.

Starting soon after the war to travel in Britain on union business I came in touch with railwaymen from the other regions — the old Great Western and the London Midland and the Southern. They still had their former railway's loyalties about them. I found out that there were all sorts of different systems. On the Great Western, for example, you were compulsorily promoted to be a driver — wherever the vacancy was you went. We didn't have that on the LMS or the LNER — you went if you wanted to go.

Railway loyalites were still so strong that delegates would usually preface their statements by saying, 'I'm a London Midland man,' or whatever. When we moved into public ownership in 1948 the management obviously wished to standardize regulations, establish national promotional arrangements and do away with old railway practices and boundaries.

Railwaymen from the different regions fiercely defended their systems. There were all sorts of arguments between railwaymen you don't find today. The Great Western, for instance, had operated more paternalistically than other companies. They had developed a better pension scheme and the relationship between the company and its staff was different in some respects from others. At least the Great Western looked after its men in the very early days, pioneering pension schemes. Other companies wanted you to toe the line whether they looked after you or not. In the North-east, where the railwaymen's union had been the first to gain recognition in 1911, they were perhaps less subservient.

And then we argued about the different kinds of engines. Listening to Great Western men it seemed that their locomotives were second to none. One driver used to describe how a Castle class locomotive would start out of Paddington station. Because it had two cylinders, one on each side of the engine frame, when he opened the regulator he would see the engine rocking over, pushed by the steam going to one cylinder, then the other. He used to liken that to the Shire horse digging its feet into the ground pulling a heavy load. This was an absolute load of nonsense, of course.

They really guzzled coal, those proud Great Western engines. I used to say to them, 'You want a coal field of your own.' Being LNER myself, and maybe biased in my own turn, I thought that by far the finest locomotive engineer in Europe was Sir Nigel Gresley; all his locomotives were beautifully designed. Anyway, I was prepared to argue my part with foot-platemen from the other regions when I first met them at locomotive-grade national conferences in my early twenties.

Later on, in 1947, at the time of nationalization, I went to my first NUR Annual General Meeting where I again met the distinctions, only this time with different grades. I found that Great Western and LMS signalmen and guards had the same outlook as their drivers. Even on the union's National Executive Committee these old company loyalties survived in 1953, when I met with NUR members from the other regions.

I can't believe these loyalties were bred out of fear. I think the main reason, during the steam age, was that railway jobs were secure. They weren't very well paid and they were often hard work, but at least they had status in the community. All that changed too. People also gave their loyalty because they were proud of the railway they worked on. Engines were polished, the trains themselves were clean and tidy. By and large, the service provided for passengers was one to be proud of.

When you do give a good service it has the amazing effect of motivating staff. I couldn't help noticing in the 1960s when the London-Birmingham-Manchester-Liverpool-Glasgow main line was electrified, morale was raised magically by the introduction of new stations, new trains and new uniforms. Wherever there is new investment, even on a limited scale like the London suburban line from King's Cross to Hertford, the same happens. Passengers also complain less, both about the service and the level of fares. I find that people are prepared to pay reasonable prices if they think they are getting value for money. But if they are asked to pay through the nose for a bad service — as so often in Britain today — that's where they become unhappy. Poor quality at a high price: it's the road to disaster.

Before the war there was a much stricter attitude to providing a high quality of service. The consequences of poor performance by railwaymen were stark: they wouldn't be sacked, normally, but they might eventually be reduced in grade, which meant less money in the pay packet. As the service deteriorated after the war, work attitudes changed, too. Some railwaymen realized they could get away with sloppy practices, thinking, 'If he's not bothered, then neither am I.'

It is not generally known that very few, if any, of the old steam locos had speedometers, nor were drivers provided with watches (something not rectified until 1984). Yet they ran the trains to time. Drivers developed a feeling for the speed they were travelling. You could tell instinctively when you were running behind time, or ahead for that matter.

Guards, however, *were* issued with watches. Some developed the habit of walking to the front of the train at stations to remind the driver if he was running late. This was quite legitimate, of course; the guard, after all, was in charge of the train. But the practice generated some banter between drivers and guards. The most common crack when the guard reminded the driver that he had lost a few minutes since leaving the last station was the reply, 'I'll see if I can find them on the way back.'

RAILWAY DISCIPLINE

The history of railway discipline was a subject I found increasingly interesting. Because of their nature, railways have always needed very strict application of safety procedures. But at times this strictness has verged on the militaristic and right from the early days until after the First World War officers came straight from the Railway Engineering Corps of the Army into the railway hierarchy, with a set chain of command and uniforms to boot.

Before the Railways Act of 1921, which created the four main companies, there were about 120 big and small railways up and down the country. Some of these railways had developed without any rhyme or reason. To control this great force, the biggest labour force in Britain at the time with towards a million employees, discipline was fierce. If a man disobeyed orders he could be out on his neck, and unions were barely tolerated when they started in the 1870s.

This is the atmosphere my grandfather lived with and my father too in his early days. But the unions began to exert themselves even though the companies at first wouldn't recognize them or tolerate them, and by the First World War proper procedures for union negotiations were forced on the companies by government involvement and union demands. A large number of unnecessary accidents and deaths at the end of the nineteenth century brought about pressure in Parliament by sympathetic MPs and made governments look more seriously at railway working practices. One of the things established was a correlation between long hours and accidents.

The disciplinary procedures negotiated in the early 1920s have been refined and improved, but still stand today. Any man committing an offence is charged under a Form One. This form states the alleged irregularity, asks for a reply within forty-eight hours or gives the option of a verbal hearing accompanied by a union representative or fellow employee. This 'advocate' will state your case, the management will listen, and then decide if there should be punishment. Form Ones can be for small offences like absence or being late on duty, or for more serious ones like passing signals at danger, or damaging locomotives — any infringement of the rule book is subject to disciplinary action. Form Ones can also be issued for poor personal conduct such as being insulting to a supervisor.

Every railman has a service record — a record both of merit and disciplinary action. It is there when the man goes for the hearing, and the person conducting the hearing will make his decision taking the record into consideration. It is a fair arrangement, and the union is involved at every stage. The minimum 'sentence' would be a recorded caution; the second level of punishment is a reprimand, then suspension for a day, two days or a week. More seriously, you could be reduced in grade for a period or permanently, which could have catastrophic implications for the pay packet. The final sanction is the sack. All these punishments can be appealed against at another level in the managerial structure. On the LNER you had a chance of a second appeal if you lost your first one, but today British Rail operate one standard agreement.

Northallerton Station in Victorian times. It was to become the biggest landmark in this thriving market town.

Northallerton Station today, now used as little more than a halt.

My early footballing days.

Aged twenty – and already active in the Union.

Father (in the middle of the photograph) showing the top brass the Northallerton signal box shortly after it was opened in 1939.

A train pulling out of Consett Station in 1950.

With my brother Maurice at the vandalised signal box at Consett. Steelworks once dominated the surrounding area – now they have all been cleared away.

These disciplinary proceedings are regarded as very important for the union, which issues advice to members that they should consult a branch official before filling in a form in reply to any disciplinary charge. I myself regularly went as an advocate to the locomotive superintendent's office at Darlington, representing my members at disciplinary hearings.

There was a strong tradition in the North-east that the branch did its own work as far as possible. If there was some exceptional case you would probably call in the Divisional Officer from Newcastle. The Northallerton branch used to insist that we provided our own advocates — very rarely did we use the services of the Divisional Officer. This provided valuable experience for me because I dealt with all the cases involving the locomotive depot. I was still in my early twenties when I first acted as advocate, and I became a regular visitor to Darlington. I always conducted myself properly because I was representing the NUR. All the same, the motive power superintendent wasn't very pleased about my regular visits: my age appeared to rub him up the wrong way. I think he was glad when I departed in 1953.

I've had Form Ones myself for being late on duty and other minor offences. Working shifts you were almost bound to be late sometimes, and if you could give reasonable explanations you were usually all right. The more serious charges like passing signals at danger had to be fully investigated. They were usually oversights, human errors, by the people concerned — often in the sort of difficult conditions I've described elsewhere. One explanation may have been that the driver may have 'signed' a route without properly knowing it.

Every driver who works a train from, say, Newcastle to York, must sign to say that he knows that route. He is given time to learn it, go over the route and familiarize himself with all the details like signals and the geography of the track — the bridges, tunnels, gradients, and so on. Only if he signs a route can he work a train, and having signed it he agrees that he knows the route. If he then does anything wrong he can't plead ignorance.

There are so many things that can go wrong. For instance, if a part of the train becomes derailed, the train crew must immediately proceed to protect it, and everything else on the line.

Every accident at work which causes a staff absence of more than two days is reported and a decision taken by a Ministry of Transport inspectorate about whether there should be an inquiry. If there is any doubt an inquiry will take place on the spot to see whether a rule has not been enforced or was inadequate.

The bigger accidents, of course, merit inquiries held in public, to establish the cause and make recommendations to prevent a repetition. Later on, when I became relief Divisional Officer, I used to attend these MOT inquiries. I also attended inquests into railway staff deaths, where the union representative acts rather as a solicitor might in asking questions to establish what happened.

All these inquiries and inquests are conducted with the union involved at every stage in order to protect its members' interests and they are obviously vital to the proper running of the railways.

One time I received a Form One which I particularly resented and took all the way through the system acting as my own advocate. It came about during the war when, booking on at 4 am, I had a sixteen-year-old engine cleaner with me as fireman. He didn't turn up. So I took an engine from Northallerton on the low-level line round to the goods depot, about two and a half miles, by myself. That was contrary to the rules — you were supposed to have two men on the footplate whenever you moved over running lines. I didn't tell anyone. I wanted to keep the job going at the shunting-yard at the other end so I drove the engine round on my own.

I thought the fireman would arrive eventually, and he did at about 7 am. I didn't say much to him, but what he forgot to tell me was that he had had a row with the foreman and the foreman reported that he had been late on duty. I had booked him as if he had come, as he should, at 4 am. I was charged under the disciplinary procedure as falsifying the timesheet.

I went to Darlington and explained the circumstances but the superintendent brushed me aside. He decided to record a severe reprimand. I decided to appeal and the hearing was held at York. The fellow who heard my case is still alive, the Industrial Relations Officer for the Eastern Region a man called Sidney Judson. I acted as my own advocate and again explained the circumstances.

He said, 'I agree your motives were right, but we can't have locomotives on running lines with one on the footplate. You know that perfectly well.' I agreed.

So he said, 'All right, we will not let the reprimand stand on your record card, but I'm severely reprimanding you verbally. Don't do it again.'

We used to laugh about it in later years when we met at headquarters meetings in London or York. But being an advocate was tremendous experience and taught me to marshal facts and arguments.

FULL-TIME FOR THE UNION

In those ten years or so I encompassed so many activities that people say to me. 'Did you have any kind of social life?' The answer is that I did; and I loved Saturday night dances and the pictures which were the main form of entertainment in the 1950s. I also liked to play and watch both cricket and football.

I met my first wife Margaret at a dance. She was a children's nurse and her people, Jim and Marjory Hunter, had a poultry farm outside Northallerton. When I married, aged twenty-seven, we soon had two children, Jennifer and Anthony, and I began to understand the demands of a family. I was away a lot on union business as well as still playing football, and I don't quite know how Margaret coped with it. We lived in a rented house in Northallerton, and three years after getting married I was elected to the NUR Executive, which meant that I was away Monday to Friday.

My wife was very understanding. I don't think the fact that I was away quite a lot created any problems, even though I was then raising my sights to become a full-time officer of the union. Unlike many other unions, you have to pass a test in the NUR before you can be considered for a full-time post as Divisional Officer. This is to make sure you're capable of attending Ministry of Transport inquiries, inquests, and dealing with the financial affairs of each branch. The test takes two days, and is both written and oral. I had passed it when I was only twenty-six and had it under my belt when, in 1953, a vacancy arose for a Divisional Officer. I was nominated by the Northallerton branch. After a national ballot I succeeded in gaining election by a very good majority. In June 1954 I left the NUR Executive Committee and resigned from the railway. My life as a working railwayman was at an end, and I became an employee of the NUR.

I took up my appointment as a Divisional Officer at the union's head office in London: my responsibilities were to relieve other Divisional Officers as necessary in various parts of the country, located around the main railway centres. I had my eyes on the Leeds Division if and when it became vacant. My wife Margaret and I planned to settle down in that area; we both preferred to live in Yorkshire.

For the next one and a half years I travelled the country as a relief Divisional Officer attending inquiries and inquests, addressing branch and district council meetings and dealing with many other problems. My wife and I had moved and settled in St Albans in January 1956, fully believing that in a year or two I would be back north in Yorkshire in a division of my own so that we could live more normally.

All these hopes were shattered by a car accident at Christmas 1956 in which Margaret and our little girl Jennifer both died. The accident, which happened at Newark on the bridge where the old A1 crossed the East Coast mainline, altered the whole course of my life. My broken jaw — I woke up in a Sheffield hospital — was the least worry. Luckily my son Anthony emerged almost unscathed, but I was so badly shaken that I was out of commission for a year. I went back to Northallerton to stay with my father and mother, and eventually moved to my parents-in-law's farm, to help my recovery, and for a long time I had no wish at all to resume work. I worked around the farm, learnt to fly-fish and eventually realized that I couldn't hide away for ever. Slowly, I started to work again, first by helping out the Newcastle Divisional Officer; then I resumed travelling in my old job. As Anthony was living with his grandparents in Northallerton there didn't seem much point in settling down anywhere — the simplest thing was to carry on as union relief officer to return home at weekends to be with my son.

The following years were the most difficult of my life. I don't know if you can ever get over such a tragedy.

What is certain is that those years spent travelling the length and breadth of Britain got me so well known, and gave me such an experience of the NUR, that when I came to stand in the election for Assistant General Secretary in 1965 — having passed the examination set by the union to qualify for this post — I was far ahead of any of my rivals.

As relief officer I covered all the important centres of Britain, filling in for officers on leave or holiday. While in Edinburgh or Glasgow, Newcastle, Leeds, Manchester, Liverpool, Cardiff or wherever, I was responsible for the NUR branches within each division. I dealt with local disputes on railways and other transport undertakings we organized. Sometimes I was in a place for several months if the man was off sick.

Travelling around Britain, talking to different railwaymen from different regions, with different backgrounds, I realized that problems in different regions had to be tackled in different ways. As a northerner I found I had to tone down my bluntness in the West Country, for instance. This proved to be valuable experience for me, giving me the ability to tune my approach to the circumstances. In local disputes, you usually have to play it by ear. Sometimes you have to be adamant, sometimes pliant.

SAFER THAN SITTING AT HOME

My other responsibility was to attend Ministry of Transport railway accident inquiries. These inquiries cover both accidents to staff and accidents to the travelling public. The purpose is to try to ensure that whatever caused the accident doesn't recur, and that the information gleaned from each inquiry is put to use. There are repeated checks to test whether the equipment, the men and the rules drawn up for running railways are adequate.

Because of this process railways in Britain are the safest in the world, and railways in general are the safest form of transport in the world. Statistics show that you are safer travelling by rail than you are sitting in your own home.

Safety was of overriding importance throughout these years. At the end of the day railway safety depends on the skill and vigilance of staff. It has to be a highly-disciplined labour force, one that understands railway operation, the type of people who are able to operate efficiently with the minimum of supervision. Signalmen, drivers and guards must often act immediately on their own initiative. Circumstances arise daily in which they have to apply their special knowledge and experience. Without such a disciplined labour force the railways would be in chaos.

Now you can't help noticing that the treatment by the Press of railway accidents is totally different from the way they treat road accidents. Thousands die, and hundreds of thousands are injured each year on British roads, with hardly a mention in the newspapers. I know railway accidents look more dramatic, with carriages maybe scattered across the track, but even then only two or three passengers might be killed and it's front page news.

All this may itself be a backhanded compliment to the railways, since the scarcity of accidents provides their news value. Such treatment, however, does draw unfair and unnecessary attention to railway safety. I wish that more attention were given to the annual road accident figures, which are horrific whichever way you look at them. Why no headlines like '8,000 killed!' or 'Population size of Derby's injured!' The value of railways as a safe form of transport — let alone all the other environmental arguments — is not high in the national perception.

As relief officer, I never had to attend a major railway accident inquiry. Thank God, these accidents are few and far between. My work was normally individual accidents, often involving only railway staff.

It's interesting to note that the inspectorate which conducts inquiries into railway safety is totally independent of railway management. The inspectorate was established within the Ministry as a result of Acts of Parliament passed in 1840 and 1842 empowering the Board of Trade to appoint railway inspecting officers recruited then, as they are now, from the Royal Engineers.

They are ordered to inspect and report on newly-constructed lines, they investigate the cause of all accidents, and over the years the inspectorate have established an excellent working relationship with both management and unions. Their joint operation is to discover the facts and put the thing right. It's not their wish to hound individuals or put too much blame on them for dereliction of duty. The purpose is to try to ensure that the same accident doesn't happen again.

George Stephenson was himself a great influence in the wording of the Safety Acts. He wrote in the early 1840s that it was vitally important that these rapidly-developing railways were given criteria by which their safety could be judged. The union, too, first made its mark with the railway companies by campaigning against the long hours which it rightly believed were an important factor in the unacceptably high accident rate. The first breakthrough followed a petition to the House of Commons from Derby's MP, Michael Bass the brewer, which led to regulations on the length of the working day.

The NUR's legal department, a very expensive department to run, deals not only with helping railwaymen but also the families of those unfortunate enough to be injured or killed. No matter how much litigation might cost, the NUR picks up the tab to ensure that railwaymen are protected. Railways are dangerous places for railwaymen, especially in winter, and every winter there are unfortunate accidents in the snow or fog. The object is to try to keep them to the absolute minimum, and figures have been coming down year after year.

The NUR has frequently told the government that the safety standards required of the railways, combined with the speed wanted to compete with other transport on commercial terms, put unfair burdens on the industry which aren't shared, for instance, by motorists or road hauliers. Building roads, maintaining them and policing them is all financed by the community; on railways we have to stand these costs ourselves.

On relief, because I went to all these big centres, I found that the volume of work varied. There were easy periods, and I got to know all the cricket grounds like Old Trafford and Trent Bridge. Living out of a suitcase on my own in hotels I did have a lot of spare time in the evenings. In the winter I went to football matches, particularly midweek ones, to make things a bit more enjoyable.

'NO PRIZES FOR BEING SECOND'

During my period as relief officer, I met my second wife, Joan, in Manchester, where she was working for a short period as a market researcher. We married in November 1959, but I carried on as relief Divisional Officer until 1962. I spent seven years trailing round the country, and if anyone in the NUR didn't know me after that it was because I wasn't trying. They got to understand me and recognize my values.

I can't say that I passed the time formulating ideas for my later life. Even after the accident I was still hoping to return to Yorkshire, but a number of things happened. The man at Leeds, a Mancunian, decided to stay on in Yorkshire. So I finally opted to take a union headquarters officer's job, and plumping for that in 1962 really decided me to go for national office. Not the General Secretary's job at first. At HQ I was virtually doing an Assistant General Secretary's job, so I thought I might as well be paid properly.

During the long years of the relief work I found I had time to study the union's history in greater depth. I was also learning all the time about the union as I travelled around. I was happy to sit up into the night trying to work out solutions to problems I faced and didn't at first understand. For instance, to be competent to help sort out industrial disputes in the big workshops at Doncaster or Derby I had first to find out the make-up of British Rail Engineering.

Because of all this experience and the amount of time I spent travelling, together with my ten years at HQ as Assistant General Secretary, I was probably the best-equipped person ever elected General Secretary. There was no section of the membership — docks, hotels, London Transport, railways, the lot — which I didn't know. I had dealt with all their problems at some time. As a result, I made many valuable contacts.

Years later when I met both management and union representatives again, sometimes to do battle with them as Assistant General Secretary or General Secretary, I knew a great deal about them. I didn't keep notes on my experience, I just absorbed it. I never liked to know less about the job than the people I was dealing with.

So far as my own personal ambition is concerned I had no intention of becoming General Secretary of the NUR. Circumstances gave me the chance for what I had always believed was completely beyond my reach. However, after a few years as Assistant General Secretary, meeting all sorts of people — politicians, management and trade unionists — at every level I began to realize that I could compete on equal terms. I could more than live with them. Later, meeting government ministers to deal with railway problems, I found I knew at least as much as, if not more, than they did about the industry; half the time you would be telling them what the world was really like outside.

In my early days I was very self-conscious. It was always a struggle to get on my feet at the branch meetings. I'm not naturally extrovert. After years in the job I could happily chat and mix with the lads and I liked to attend social functions with members, their wives and families. But deep down I prefer peace and quiet — preferably on my own.

There are two obvious sides to me: one enjoys the challenge and battle of the trade union and Labour movements; the other craves for the countryside and the fishing-rod. I have always been torn between the two. I detested London, but lived there for twenty-five years because the union headquarters and power were there. I took part in the life that went with the job, the social side of it, simply because it was part of the job.

The challenge, and a belief in what I was doing, were the things which sustained me during my rough eight years as General Secretary. And then, of course, I never liked to lose. Whenever I played football or cricket I wanted to win. When I first became involved in union activities my father would say: 'There's no prizes for being second. If you want to win all the stops have to be out. You'll have to get off your backside.'

Many a time I've been defeated, and accepted it as gracefully as I could, but I certainly set out to win. My God, the things I did to survive! While I was fighting the adrenalin flowed, but after some of the prolonged battles I felt drained and turned to trout-fishing to recharge my batteries.

6 Conversations with Maurice

M Y BROTHER MAURICE, just two years younger than me, grew up with me in Northallerton. We are different people, but we have always enjoyed being brothers. As children we were very close; schoolfriends wanting us to come and play used to ask for Bogie and Gear, both good railway words.

Maurice himself started work with the LNER in the North-allerton locomotive department in August 1940 when he was sixteen. A year later he qualified to become a locomotive fireman. After the war he passed as an engine driver at North-allerton, where he was also branch secretary of the NUR for many years before he moved to Teesside, based at the Tees Yard (Thornaby) shed.

Maurice still drives locomotives from Teesside. His experience and opinions reflect something of the strength of the NUR grass-roots membership around the country, traditions and skills which are disappearing along with railwaymen.

NOT JUST SHOVELLING COAL

Maurice: When I started, aged sixteen, we were thought very young to be on the railway in wartime, so to begin with we were given lots of odd jobs.

I used to help Bill Gordon, the boilersmith at Northallerton, with work like patching the tanks of side-tank engines. Somebody had to go inside while he tightened the nut on the outside, and that somebody was me. There wasn't very much room in those side tanks, and I was a bit frightened that in going into such a confined space I might not get out.

If spare parts were needed for locomotives under repair, I would be told to catch the train to Darlington to obtain the right part at the Bank Top Locomotive Depot. If, when I arrived there, they hadn't the part in stock I would go on to North Road works, which was a massive place. It was amazing to see all those locos in different stages of manufacture as I found my way to the brass-shop or the coppersmith.

Work at Northallerton proved hard. I was already used to a full-time job in a radio and cycle shop, where I had been kept busy serving in the shop, charging accumulators and repairing bicycles. But hard manual work was new to me. After my first day or two my hands were red-raw. I spent most of the time shovelling ash and clinker from the locos into wagons and sweeping up in the shed.

Sometimes if a locomotive smoke-box door was faulty they would even get us to take it to Darlington. That really was heavy work. We had to push it on a four-wheeled barrow about half a mile to the station platform at Northallerton. These doors, which weighed three or four hundredweight and were five or six feet in diameter, were from the front of the engine. When they buckled with the heat they would allow air into the smoke-box which reduced the vacuum needed to create the draw on the fire to generate intense heat in the fire-box. So they were important as well as heavy.

Another job we got was preparing sand for the locos. It had to be dried or it wouldn't run through the sand pipes on to the rails. You had to unload the wagon first. You first dried the sand in an archaic stove. Then you threw it into the container through a sieve to get all the stones out.

From very early on we understood the principle of steam locomotion. Cleaner lads like us used to discuss it eagerly as part of our apprenticeship. We knew what these spare parts were, and what function they had on the loco.

When I was just seventeen I passed the test which allowed me to work on the footplate. The day after my seventeenth birthday the Northallerton station-master, who was also shed-master, sent for me. There happened to be a tremendous staff shortage because of the war and footplatemen were at a premium. But in order to become a fireman I had to know the procedure on how to help protect the train in the case of a breakdown, with detonators and so on, how to implement Rule Fifty-Five to inform signalmen when you are stopped at a signal (most important because under the old semaphore signalling a signalman could forget about a train being on the section), and so on. It wouldn't have been fair on the driver to allow me on an engine otherwise, even if I understood how to shovel coal.

Mind you, putting the coal on requires a certain amount of skill — you don't just chuck it through the hole. Each shovelful is placed in position and you get better through experience. I wouldn't say that at that age I was skilful — but I was capable of doing it.

When you were firing on some of the bigger wheeled locos, especially Class D20s, rocking and rolling, you had to be careful not to hit the fire-box door, because if you gave it a full-blooded swipe it would jar your right arm straight to the socket. And then there was coal all over.

Eventually, after a grounding on 'pilots' (shunting engines), I was allowed to fire on local passenger and goods services. But until I was eighteen I wasn't permitted to work nights or to start before 6 am. That was the only time in my career I haven't been on rotten shifts. As soon as I reached eighteen these became part of my life. Footplate working involves starting at 2 am or 10 pm, or any minute throughout the day and night; they are terrible hours — unbelievable, really.

After a year at Northallerton I followed Sid to Darlington, where we shared the same digs. He was already in the passenger 'link'; I started in the shed link as a junior fireman. (At large depots work is allocated into these 'links', with a man working only the turns in the link which he is allocated by his seniority. As senior men in the links retire, then others move up to fill their places. When I went to Darlington in 1942 there were fifty-two turns in the shed link. That meant that you did each turn once a year, and nearly all started at a different time.)

In the shed link we were mostly concerned with getting engines ready for the mainline men coming on duty. Our workload was governed by agreements on what constituted a shift. Sixty or seventy minutes were allowed for preparing a big loco, whereas the smaller ones were allocated forty-five minutes.

We were given a list of seven locos to prepare each shift. The list stated where they were going and what time they were due off from the shed, the last usually being about an hour before the shift finished. It was hard, dirty work requiring a good relationship between the driver and fireman to complete matters satisfactorily.

Some, though, were much quicker than others. There was a tale about one driver who was on a 2 am shed turn. His wife woke up and, finding him asleep beside her, nudged him saying 'Come on, you're late for work.' 'It's all right, pet,' he replied, 'I've been and come back again.'

During the war Darlington used the system of fire-dropping. At some other depots footplate staff used to clean the fire, ash-pans and smoke-boxes and also coal, water and sand up the engine — stabling work they called it — but at Darlington men were employed specifically as fire-droppers.

Huge wet pits were dug with big gratings over them, the locos were brought into position beside the pits and the fire-droppers cleaned out the fires with long shovels, throwing the ash into the pit. Then the smoke-box at the front of the loco was cleaned in a similar way, after which the ash-pan under the loco had to be raked out.

You can't imagine what life was like for fire-droppers. It was a version of hell. There was always a lot of activity at the wet pits, especially at night when the engines were returning to the depot.

The most difficult job was finding all the items of equipment needed to comply with the rules. You had to search for a box of detonators, two red flags, a gauge lamp, a coal hammer, a brush and shovel, a pricker and a slag shovel, two gauge glasses, shifting keys to change gauge glasses, and all that sort of thing. It proved virtually impossible during the war crisis years. You would wait for engines coming in and then you would pounce to get the gear off them. Passenger engines had their own gear locked away. When they came in the fireman would hand everything together into the stores against the engine number. But the other engines had to fight for it, and you could wait all day to put together a complete set of equipment.

Sid: One reason men were allowed to go as soon as they completed their work was that they wanted locos through as quickly as possible. Locos couldn't be kept standing.

Maurice: In ordinary times the railways were delighted to get sixteen hours out of twenty-four for a steam locomotive. In wartime conditions they had to try to get the maximum out of locomotive and men. So they introduced a system where once you had clocked on, you went to Bank Top station and waited for trains coming in from all over the place. The foreman would shout your name and the engine number. Then he would tell you where you were going to go. That was interesting because you got all the different classes of locomotive, even some off other regions. Mind, they weren't all good ones. Some of them were very poor. They used anything with wheels on for freight in those days.

We were once even given a Gresley Pacific to take a train up the Hawes branch line. I don't think there was ever one up there before or since. There was supposed to be a weight limit on the Hawes branch, but that day they didn't bother. There were a few raised eyebrows from station staff when we passed that day!

You must remember that those lads who joined in 1939 and 1940 were put on the footplate because they needed engine crews desperately. When we started there were men old enough to be our fathers who were still firemen. Some did have sons who started when their dads were still firing.

The old drivers weren't hard to work with. I was quite surprised. Some of them were advanced in years but they were always willing to show you. Of course, there were one or two awkward ones, but taking them generally I thought they were very fair. They relied on you to do your job. They didn't want to be telling you everything. They were prepared to help you, but they didn't want to be always saying, 'Do this, do that.' When you're on a steam locomotive there's always something to do, and it's 'Put some coal on, put this on, shut that, do this, do that.' They wanted people who were taking notice, interested in their job, so that the next time you worked together they could see you had improved and were a bit better than last time.

If you were showing an interest and improving — as you did improve — they were quite happy to keep on helping you. But if you weren't getting any better I suppose they soon got fed up — I think I would too. After you've been on the footplate a bit you're either improving or you're as good as you're going to get.

Often we would go fifty-fifty with the driving. When you showed that you knew what you were doing, that you had a bit of commonsense and that you could be trusted, they were quite happy to let you have a drive. That's how I learnt to drive. They would usually pick the easiest parts to fire, the downhill runs, but that didn't matter to us — we were glad to get a drive. A lot of old drivers, even though they were getting on, liked to fire a bit. They liked to think they could still do it. There is sense of achievement in good firing. It's not just a matter of throwing coal into the firebox.

FOOTPLATE CHARACTERS

Sid: What about the characters you worked with?

Maurice: Well, there was one driver with a reputation for being a bit erratic. He'd had one or two incidents during his career which had restricted him to the shed. He was the self-appointed shed barber, he wore a dickie-bow and a little 'tache with a doggie cap, and he smoked cigars. He was able to dress like that because the very dirty shed work had been taken off us by the fire-droppers.

The story goes that when he was driving passenger trains he kept running to the end of the platform with the train at one particular station. Some passengers asked him why he couldn't stop a bit nearer to the exit because they had a long walk. It was one of those single-line platforms on the Penrith line where you had to go through a shunt to join the platform, and the next day, going a bit fast, the driver went up the ramp at this end of the platform, causing a serious derailment. Anyway, he put his head out of the cab and asked, 'How's that?' That's what he was like. He had a little bag with shears for cutting hair and he wasn't bad, but I would never let him touch mine because I didn't trust him.

I also remember working at Northallerton with old Bill Howe, who came from Ferry Hill, County Durham. Five feet five and a half inches, something like that, a rounded fellow, used to dress in black trousers and black waistcoat with a great big watch chain across the front, an overall issue jacket and driver's hat — his only concessions to uniform. Bill literally waddled to work, smoked a corn-cob pipe and assessed you with sharp little eyes. He was a man of very few words and when he laughed he used to shake. He fascinated me, although he wouldn't bend to help me shovel coal, probably couldn't anyway — he had a struggle to get into the cab. He just used to sit and smoke his corn-cob pipe, stick his head out of the window and go. He didn't seem to bother whether he had steam or not. He would reminisce meaningfully about the old days when he was made to polish everything.

Every steam locomotive was individual. You could get two of the same class built at the same works and they would be completely different. So you had to recognize and understand quite quickly the peculiarities of a strange engine. If you were messing about and took a long time to recognize the symptoms you were in trouble. Once the steam gets low you can be struggling all the shift.

You don't need a specially high IQ to be a fireman but you want someone with his buttons on a bit. It was quite something at seventeen or eighteen, just an infant railway-wise, to step on the footplate of a big locomotive as a fireman.

You're always in danger on the railway, that's the nature of the job, so you have always to be careful. In the war blackout it was worse. I once fell into a pit outside the straight shed at Darlington; I climbed out of it, staggered about, and fell straight into the next pit. When I say 'blackout' I mean completely black. And if you've ever been in a motive power depot, especially on a Monday morning, when all the engines are cold and they're lighting them up with fire-lighters — you'll know you get fumes, smoke and dark, and it's a dangerous place.

It takes about four hours to get steam up, and this can be longer if an engine is cold. If it's cold and you try to rush it, the boiler will start to sweat and then it will take as long as it likes. Being a lighter-up is a rough job, as well. I occasionally did that at Darlington. When we were travelling from home at North-allerton we would have to leave home at 10 pm on a Sunday night to start work at 6 am on Monday morning, because of the

112

train service. So at midnight I would go to the shed foreman to ask if he had a job for me instead of waiting six hours for my own turn of duty as fireman. He invariably gave me lighting-up or throwing fires out of the pit.

'Yes,' he would say, 'you're just the lad we're looking for. Go over there...' and he would give you a long list of engines' numbers for lighting-up. A fire grate can be as big as forty square feet — some are nine feet long — and the first thing you have to do is cover the whole grate with coal, leaving a hole in the middle. You then light your fire-lighters and put them in the middle, placing a bit of coal on top of them. The fire-lighters were fixed to four pieces of kindling wood. The theory was that the draught coming up through the ash-pan would be concentrated through the centre of the grate, and the fire would catch and spread.

The thing about lighting-up was not to be in too much of a hurry because the quicker you went round them the quicker you had to attend to the first one again. You soon learnt that. It was a rough, rotten job. When a fire's first lit the smoke doesn't go up the chimney, it comes out of the fire-hole into the cab. You get hellish black with smoke and soot.

I passed the driver's exam in 1951, aged twenty-seven, back in Northallerton — it involved questions and a practical. Having passed I was eligible to drive any type of train, even though I remained a fireman. I was designated 'passed fireman', and drove on a day-to-day basis covering sickness, holidays and special trains. It was to be some years before I was appointed a full-time driver. Before the war you were likely to be nearly fifty before you obtained promotion to driver, and the same applies again today. We have lads in the shed at Thornaby who have years and years of experience and still aren't appointed drivers.

During the period I was at Northallerton, I did leave the footplate for a time. The station-master at Northallerton recommended me to go into control at Darlington. This meant helping control all trains in the Darlington area, including Teesside, and link with York and Newcastle. You started off by 'wiring' trains, notifying each area about the movements of trains and what the loads comprised. I was there about eight to ten months, but being inside didn't suit me. I was assistant loco controller, and they used to ask me to apply formally for the job. But I was reluctant to burn my bridges, so I kept my options open to return to the footplate.

I also became Northallerton branch secretary of the NUR. They were looking around for someone: Sid had moved on, my dad had finished, so it landed on my table. I also got involved in politics as Labour agent in local elections. I could identify with Northallerton people and their problems. When I left in 1961 I kept up my union work for a year or so on Teesside, and had some success too. But then I just dropped it.

As a 'passed fireman' I mostly worked the Hawes branch up to Garsdale Junction, the Wensleydale line. It was LNER up to Hawes, then we had running rights to Garsdale. We would see these funny fellows on the LMS at Garsdale with their shiny-top caps and their clogs. They all wore clogs on the LMS, the footplate staff, I don't know why.

We also used to run to Harrogate through Ripon. That was in the days when you weren't allowed to make smoke at Harrogate. They were very, very particular about smoke. So we took special care if we stopped at the station there.

Sid: I don't remember any other station in the North-east as particular as Harrogate, even though you weren't supposed to make smoke in any station.

Maurice: Ah, well, they thought they were different. Working up Hawes branch with a full load on firing a P3 freight loco throwing out coal lumps as big as your fist, it's not a question of making smoke but getting the coal in as quick as you can.

Sid: Did you find it a hard life on the steam engines?

Maurice: That was the first thing that struck me when I joined the railway, the sheer physical effort that was required.

Sid: Did you have problems keeping the steam going, waiting long hours at signals?

Maurice: Not really. But in winter the engines would cool down and you got cold. Often steam would envelop the cab. If you stood a long time when the fire was dirty you could have problems, or you might run short of water.

One of the things that used to puzzle me before I became a

114

fireman was — where does all the coal go to? I'd seen them get rid of five tons of coal, yet you could put a shovel-full on your fire at home and it would last all night. That problem was soon solved when I got on the footplate — it's such an intense heat. If you weren't quick firing it could burn the back of your hand, depending on the type of fire-box.

Sid: You got to know each engine by its number, and you had a good idea what it would be like before you stepped on the footplate.

Maurice: We also worked a lot of engines that had been in stock during the inter-war years which came from the old Great Central and Great Northern.

Sid: Did you ever work one of those American locos that came over on lease-lend? I got one. It was shaped like the old American high-footplate machines, but not as big as them and without cow-catchers. There was only one gauge glass, with taps alongside the boiler which you could open to check the level of the water. It was all right. We also had austerity War Department (WD) locos, built to the same austerity principle as clothes.

Maurice: I remember the tail-end of those at Thornaby. Nearly all of our loose-coupled mainline freight trains were hauled by austerity locos.

Sid: If you drive about the North-east looking at railways and heavy industry the changes are dramatic. If you live in the South you don't see these dramatic changes. Remember, for instance, when we took holidays as a family every now and then in Redcar, going by train past Middlesbrough. The ships that were in that dock. It was a thrilling journey. Now they've all gone.

Maurice: Well, they built Teesdock nearer the river mouth to fit larger ships. Of course, there are sidings but they use their own men and locos now to serve these docks. Everything's moved towards the sea. In fact, they started at one end of the Tees and desecrated it right down to the other. The local authorities have been left with the problem of tidying up, and they've done some remarkable work. The Ironmasters district beside the river near Middlesbrough, where some of the first ironworks were, has been transformed with grass and trees, and ponies grazing.

In the old days people had to live where the industry was, there being no public transport. In some cases they lived inside the ironworks. All those tiny terraced houses have gone now. Our stations are mainly unstaffed, too. The small stations have been levelled off, with just a shelter, because they're vandalized. Middlesbrough station was like a cathedral, but a bomb fell on it — that knocked half of it down. Then after the war they took the other half down.

GETTING USED TO DIESELS

Maurice: In 1961, ten years after I qualified as a driver, I was finally promoted to fill a full-time driving vacancy at Thornaby, where I still work. After ten years of having to fire and driving occasionally as a relief man, I thought I'd cracked it. What happened? Not so easy. I went back to the bottom link. I was back to preparing seven engines every day, but as a driver now not a fireman. When I moved from Northallerton to Teesside with the job I found life very difficult, moving from a small rural town to a big industrial area. I knew everybody in Northallerton. Suddenly I was in a place where I didn't know anybody. It wasn't very nice. It took me a long time before I got settled.

I wouldn't think of moving back now, though. It's too big a time gap. There must be someone I know back there, but I never see them. It's strange how often you go back without meeting anyone you know. Working on Teesside was no problem, though I didn't want my children to follow me on the railway. Nevertheless, there are some good jobs in the administration for lads with qualifications.

All this nostalgia about steam amuses me. In the York Railway Musuem you hear the old railwaymen recalling their days on the railway. I can understand — there is a certain aura about a steam loco. I wouldn't like to work on them again, but I can understand why people are taken up with them.

The modern motive power depot at Thornaby was built to replace the old Newport shed at Tees Yard, and also the sheds at Middlesbrough, Haverton Hill and Stockton. It had a big coal cracker plant. They brought the engines in and, just as we did at Darlington during the war years, they put them on the pit and the fire-dropper cleaned the fire. Then they were brought round for oiling — and that's where I started again, for the first year that I was there.

By that time the diesels had arrived. We actually started with them at the back-end of 1961. When I first went to Thornaby we had about fifty 'turns' in the shed link — that was a set of men signing on every half hour to stable and prepare the engines which came into the shed. A steam locomotive requires an army of men to prepare it and look after it. But when the new era came with the diesels, the first thing that happened was that these men were no longer required.

So we had a mixed view of this change. I looked forward to it myself. I welcomed the diesels. I'd had enough of the other game, and might have left the railways if diesels hadn't come. These steam locos they run about with today in pristine condition, just during daylight hours and only in summer — they are not railways. Everybody says how grand they are, but that's not the real railway.

With the arrival of the diesel we spent quite a long time doing very little. We just had to sit it out until such times as the job picked up. Then we gradually got reinstated, and by that time the diesels had completely taken over.

Sid: Yes, 1958 saw the launch of the diesels. Up to that time British Railways had about 16,000 steam locomotives but by 1964 the diesel had replaced them. You had to change from driving steam to diesel — how long did you get to learn?

Maurice: The initial training period was three weeks. We had to start again right from scratch and learn what was what. Then, as the different types of diesels came along — they came thick and fast at the start — they would give us only about a week on each new loco. By then we knew what a compressor, an exhauster and a generator were. At first we didn't know, or they had to assume we didn't know, because men had spent a lifetime on steam engines. Suddenly they were in the midst of all this electrical gadgetry.

British Railways appointed instructors. We were fortunate because, being a large depot, they usually brought the instructors to us, but in some instances you had to go to them. It varied from engine to engine — maybe you would have to go to Gateshead to learn a particular type, or maybe to York.

We had to learn to work ten or twelve different classes of loco. We started with a BR Sulser 2, the Birminghams, the English Electric Type One, Type Three and Type Four, the Hawker-Siddeley, then the DMU (diesel multiple unit), and the shunters. By the time we were reinstated, however, only a dozen shed turns remained. Now there are about eight. At the time there was some unrest because we felt they didn't use the men who were surplus to the best advantage. But on the whole we adjusted fairly easily to job losses; we knew they were going to happen and at that time there was plenty of work about. We were fairly confident that after a while we would be reabsorbed into the system and that it would be all right. There were no compulsory redundancies.

Sid: People perhaps began to be happy about the different working environment — the depot itself had to be much cleaner, dealing with diesels.

Maurice: It was all change. The first thing that happened was we lost half the shed because we didn't require the space. We retracted into a smaller, more compact unit. The work was much better; it was a lot cleaner, life was transformed. They scrapped the old overalls and started dishing us out with the new blue uniform. We wore a collar and tie, and mostly came home clean.

In the old steam days we had no baths or showers at the shed, even though we got filthy. At the Northallerton depot when I started, there wasn't even a wash-basin — just a dirty old bucket near the fitters' bench. It was ludicrous. Men worked as a matter of course in Victorian conditions. They (the LNER) didn't believe in making people too comfortable — they wanted them to work.

When we came to this new shed it had showers and toilets and everything. I don't believe the shed was planned with diesels in mind, maybe it was. However, interestingly, there are bits over the shed doors, not brick or concrete, which can be easily taken out; I understand that they are like that so that when the electric locomotives come the pantographs will go through. It certainly looks like it. If so, we're still waiting for them twenty years later. Anyway, a shed that will deal with steam will do perfectly well for diesel, apart from maintenance requirements. You just don't need so many units to do the same work.

I can see why they first introduced diesels because they could run them on the same track as steam without any permanent-way engineering. They should have done this for an interim period while they built the electric railway. But they haven't. They needed urgent action to get rid of steam. Where they've failed is in not fulfilling the programme to electrify. Of course, if Sir Vincent Raven had had his way we would have been electrified on the North Eastern donkey's years ago.

Sid: What it needed was a planned programme, with the East Coast electrification following on the London Midland, and the diesels could then have been moved onto subsidiary lines, but they didn't do that.

Maurice: So now the diesels are being run into the ground. One day they'll go and there will be nothing left.

Sid: 1984 is the year for deciding. If we don't take the decision to electrify we'll have to take the decision to rebuild another generation of diesels.

Maurice: They should have doubled the number of HSTs by now to run and maintain the schedules set in the new timetable. They're running them into the ground because they can't take them out of service long enough to do the necessary work on them.

MODERN WORK PRACTICES

Maurice: A diesel locomotive is available twenty-four hours a day. Quite often they come in, fuel them up, have a quick look at them and go straight out again without the engine stopping.

In my experience diesels are very reliable. The ones that were no good were soon got rid of. One I can remember with the cabin in the centre of the locomotive and a diesel engine at both ends was poor. The design was fine from a driver's point of view, but they weren't reliable. The Birminghams didn't last, either. They build locos bigger now, because the type of work has changed. What they want is a bigger unit to pull freight-liners, company trains, oil and steel trains. They're bigger and better. I haven't yet been on the latest ones, the 56s and 58s.

It's funny how the whole industrial pattern is interwoven. The oil-refinery was built beside the River Tees when they reclaimed Seal Sands — so we got the oil trains. Then they built the ore terminal at the Redcar steel works, so the ore, instead of going from Tyne Dock to Consett, started to go from Redcar and we got the ore trains. We had eight trains a day going up there, each with eight 100-tonne wagons, pulled by two Type 37s. The wagons were fitted with special couplings so that they could drop the ore by revolving without being uncoupled. The full trains were moved by British Steel Corporation staff using an electric device alongside to put them on to the unloader a wagon at a time without uncoupling. By the time this train was empty another loaded one would arrive.

Sid: What a difference! When I went up to Consett in the steam days we were pulling twenty-tonne wagons. We used to divide the train at Lanchester and take ten twenty-tonners up. You say you used to pull eight wagons, each weighing one hundred tonnes.

Maurice: That's right, but we were using two Type 37s, 1750 hp each. It's expensive for the management having two big locos tied up, with eight of those trains a day (one would maybe work two or three trips in the day). However, you can drive two or even three of these locos in multiple with just the one driver.

We have very few loose-coupled trains now — they're nearly all fitted couplings with permissible speeds of forty-five miles per hour, sixty miles per hour or even seventy-five miles per hour. We get the steel coil trains, going to Corby and elsewhere, which can be taken at sixty miles per hour. Also trains with steel slabs and ingots to Scunthorpe. Petrol and oil trains from the refineries are also permitted to travel at sixty miles per hour.

I used to work the DMUs up the coast to Newcastle and down to Saltburn and Whitby. There is a programme for re-furbishing some of these units but they are sorely in need of replacement. Most of the lines I drive now have modern colour-link signals — there are not many semaphores left.

Sid: So driving a diesel — good visibility, not stretching your neck to look high or low for semaphore signals . . . and protected by automatic warnings signs?

Maurice: Oh, yes, that's extensive. Every time you run past a green light it rings a bell in the cab. If it's other than green it blows a horn. You've then got a few seconds to cancel the horn with a button, and if you don't the brakes are applied automatically.

In all locos there is a safety device called a 'dead man'. This is either a foot pedal which is depressed or, in the case of the DMUs, is incorporated in the engine throttle which has to be depressed by hand. In either case, when the dead man is released the throttle closes and the brakes are applied.

Sid: Well, all that makes the job different and easier . . .

Maurice: Yes, it's easier in *that* respect, but it's a different machine you're driving with new pressures all of its own. A steam locomotive is the most basic of instruments: its principle didn't change over 130 years. But these diesels are highly-sophisticated things, and it doesn't take much to stop them. To start a diesel loco you have to have certain requirements — oil pressure, water pressure, fuel, and so on all of which must combine to make a starting circuit. If any electrical contact doesn't 'make', the engine won't start.

Because you've got this huge diesel-electric plant behind you it's mentally more taxing than steam. And you're mainly by yourself. You're not conscious of being on your own, after a while. But with two people you can say, 'Well, what do you think we ought to do?' or 'You do this and I'll do that.' By yourself you can only do one thing at once and you think, 'Which should I do first?' It's always easy for inspectors who have had three or four days fathoming an incident out to ask, 'Why didn't you do this?' but I have to make the decision on the spot.

Say you're going along and suddenly everything goes quiet. The thing stops. Believe me, there is no silence so profound as a diesel that dies on you. If you know there is no danger to an adjoining line or your own, you don't have to protect your train. It's a question of where's the nearest phone, can I get to it quickly, and can I find out what's wrong with the diesel? You have to use your judgment about the indications, and sometimes you can put your finger on it straightaway. If a phone is near, you generally have a word with the signalman and say, 'I'm having a bit of difficulty, I'll go to have a look and come back in a few minutes.' In the meantime, I may need some assistance, so I warn the signalman to tell control about my problems.

For times when other lines are affected by an obstruction the only difference now is that we have track circuiting clips. Most of the railway is track-circuited: anything that happens on the line is shown in the signal box nearby. These clips are specially designed — a pair of them is joined by a wire. If there's an obstruction on the opposite line the first thing you do is employ these clips, putting one on one line and one on the other. This shows in the signalbox that that track is occupied, and also sets the signal controlling that section at danger.

We still have detonators as an added safeguard — we put them down when we go forward to the signal box. The guard at the back does the same at the rear of the train. Most guards are now to be found in the back cab of the diesel as most trains are fitted with continuous braking systems. Except in the case of HSTs drivers have no communication with the guard.

There *is* a pressure in going faster and taking heavier loads, I suppose, but I'm not really conscious of it. It doesn't bother me. But it does affect a few drivers. They have to be found a job in the shed or on the yard pilots. It's a hell of a funny job being alone on a footplate. On single-manned turns there must be facilities off the loco where, between the third and fifth hour, you can go and wash your hands, go to the toilet and get something to eat (the PNB or physical needs break). If you're double-manned it doesn't matter — 'as and when the opportunity arises' still exists as it did years ago. But sometimes the PNB facilities just aren't available.

The younger men coming through today are completely different from me because they're classroom-trained. One of the greatest problems with the single manning of locos is — where do drivers learn their trade? They are very difficult people to produce, engine drivers. On the Continent they've tried all sorts of methods. We used to serve twenty years apprenticeship on steam locos and we were still learning. It must be difficult for the young lads of today. They have just six months in the classroom to learn about diesels and railway operations. Then they go outside for practical experience. It's a long process and there's lots to learn. We have several now at our shed who qualified as drivers this way. They're all right, too, even though they have no railway background at all.

Sid: Working on steam engines you could tell by the sound of the track just where you were. Do you still judge route knowledge by the same old yardstick?

Maurice: You still use bridges and other landmarks, but you can't hear a lot of the sounds you used to hear before. The diesel engine itself is noisy, and whereas you sat with your head out of a steam locomotive to hear things, this is all happening outside on a diesel.

But you don't need these aids so much because of better visibility and signalling. Colour light signals are set at regular intervals; so long as you get the sequence right you are fine.

From Northallerton to York on the main line you get a light every three quarters of a mile for thirty miles. With semaphore signals you have to know exactly where you are because the distant signal is predominant. This distant signal is to give the driver advance information about the other stop signals. If it is clear you can expect to find the rest of the signals off. So it is important that you know exactly where you are all the time.

Now at York, for instance, you get a light with a number, telling you what platform you're going on to, whereas in semaphore days you had virtually a signal for every platform. It must have been very difficult for people running into York or Leeds or Newcastle.

That's why the record of the railway is so good — because signalling has kept abreast of modern requirements. And track. The mainline track, as a result of efforts put in for the HST, is marvellous now. The old-stagers wouldn't know what had happened. No clickety-click now — it's just silent. You can look back along a freight train and at sixty miles per hour it's as steady as a rock. But when you get off the main line you notice it.

Sid: The East Coast route we worked had a long reputation for fast trains — the Aberdonian and the Flying Scot and all that. The first diesels produced to take over from steam weren't fast enough, so they designed the Deltic, a great powerful thing. A fleet of about twenty-five of them successfully operated the East Coast main line.

Maurice: I only worked one once. We were at Newcastle waiting to work a train to Tees Yard during the night sometime. The phone rang and it was for me. The controller said: 'Will you conduct this express from Ferry Hill to Northallerton? Something has happened on the mainline track, and the express driver doesn't know the alternative road.' So I said 'Aye, right-oh.' He gave me the platform number and I walked down. There was this Deltic. I'd never been on one in my life but I climbed aboard.

I sat in the seat and the driver said, 'Are you going to drive it?'

'Yes,' I replied.

He asked, 'Have you ever driven one of these before?'

'I've walked past a few of them.'

So off we went. This matter of conducting another driver is necessary because everyone who is passed for driving duties has a 'route card', which shows each route he is authorized to drive. It is necessary for drivers to learn the details of different routes and having done so to 'sign' for each one. When he is required to work on a route he does not sign he must be provided with a conductor, someone who does sign the route and will take responsibility for the train. They're usually good these chaps, they'll let you drive if you want to because it's sometimes easier to drive the thing yourself than to tell someone else where the signals are.

Deltics are 3,300 hp, and that's about the only difference between them and some of the locos I regularly work. The cab layout is exactly the same. So there was no problem in not having driven them before.

Of course, we get the same rate of pay whether we're working in the shed or driving on the main line. Mostly I think

124

drivers accept that, they don't like classification.

Sid: But you may get some drivers working quiet country lines in remote areas like the West of Scotland or East Anglia, who get exactly the same rate as men working on high-speed trains in congested metropolitan areas. I've always argued that you *ought* to classify them. Every other grade of railwayman is classified — signalmen for instance are paid for their skill and responsibility. The reason I argue this is that today the train driver happens to be about £15 per week lower-paid than the highest class of signalman. The signalmen have slowly over-taken drivers' wages.

Maurice: Drivers accept the equality. They play hell about having less money than the signalman, but they don't seem to appreciate that a signalman has got classification. I think drivers have an inbred hatred of classification.

Sid: What experience have you had working with coloured railwaymen?

Maurice: There was a period in the Sixties when we had at Thornaby quite a number of Pakistani and West Indian rail-waymen. They were all right. Good blokes. They had a bit of difficulty with the language sometimes, which used to worry me. In an emergency if you got an excited fellow on the phone not speaking his first language — it was a genuine fear. Some went to London, and we do see one or two of them nowadays on the long-distance trains as passenger guards, but a lot of others left.

Sid: There is no discrimination in the union or the industry. When anyone joins the railways they get a seniority date, and this alone determines seniority for promotion. Every railway worker gets the same protection agreements designed to provide fair treatment to all.

How about shift-work? We were both brought up with it, weren't we? It affects the home, but we learnt to live with it. Today, many consider it to be anti-social. Is it a deterrent to people joining the railways?

Maurice: There were several trainee-guards at Tees Yard who when they got to know the times they had to start work just left. Until you have to get up to start work at 2 am you don't realize just how bad it is. Some lads have to leave when they marry because their wives are afraid of being on their own at night.

Nobody has worse shifts than we do in our department. We start every five minutes of the day. There's no six-to-two and two-to-ten. As a rule you get the same job or 'turn' for a week. If you start at 2 am you go to bed when you finish and then you get up about 7 pm but you can't sit about to 2 am, you have to go back to bed again. By the end of the week you don't know where the hell you are.

They're terrible shifts and you never get used to them. Particularly when it's fine weather and neighbours are out in the garden — you get woken up and you can't get back to sleep. It most certainly affects your social life and the whole household, who try to be quiet. But you can't control neighbours. Starting at 9 am is almost unheard of. If I ever start at a time like that I wonder who the hell all these people are going to work.

Sid: There is more flexibility now to arrange the shifts. Despite the trouble about flexible rostering, these rosters do give railmen the chance to arrange shift-working to their own advantage, with rest days strung together.

Maurice: The diesel's available for twenty-four hours so the men have to have an availability to match it. A lot of the work that used to provide good day turns has gone. Mineral trade, the coal traffic, used to work between 7 am and 7 pm. If you worked a mineral link you were all right, but most of the North-eastern collieries have closed now. All the dock pilots, again daylight shifts, have gone too. We're left with company trains; companies want the wagons loading during the day then moving overnight. So a lot of the work tends to be at night, it's just one of those things. They definitely put people off from working on the railways.

Sid: What about actually working the trains?

Maurice: I find the brakes are much better on today's trains. When diesels were introduced air brakes came too, and they're far superior to the vacuum brakes we had previously. You've

126

got much more control. The permanent-way men nowadays get an audible warning of approaching trains in areas of restricted visibility from hooters placed at the trackside. We sometimes see a man with a chequered flag who warns the look-out man when a train is approaching, on lines used by the high-speed trains. They're also tightening up on us footplate staff wearing high-visibility jackets and making sure we take author-ized routes (wherever you are required to walk on or near the track there's an authorized route).

Sid: But the old pick-and-shovel permanent-way man has gone now, hasn't he?

Maurice: Oh, he would have been dead, killed off because he didn't move fast enough; he'd see this yellow dot coming around the corner then it would take the shovel out of his hand. They don't stand on their shovel now — they get as far away as they can. When you go out on these track-laying or maintenance jobs it's all planned like a military operation. There's a machine to do everything.

When we're laying the welded rails we just inch forward, sliding the rails off the end and taking up short lengths of old track. We have a slow-speed loco for that job. This is an electronic device fitted to the loco first developed for power station merry-go-round trains, keeping the loco at a constant five miles per hour, one mile per hour, and so on even though the engine is producing up to full power. Using these sorts of machines the permanent-way men can do in four hours what might have taken a gang of one hundred men a week.

But there are problems with today's track. Signalmen can stop you to let you know, through automatic sensors they have, that one of your wagon axles is running hot. So you go back to take a look — and you try to walk along this marvellous track. There are no footpaths now. You're walking over broken cable-ducting, pushing past bushes and all sorts. The stone ballast is very high. In some places where you stop to use the phone you can't reach the handle to get back on the loco! The long-welded track, with concrete sleepers, requires much more ballasting. Because of the depth of ballast it spreads across a wider area, and the old path has been gobbled up.

Sid: Yes, trains running at a hundred and twenty miles per hour give the track a terrible pounding, and all that ballast is needed to support it. High-speed railway is expensive railway. To concentrate on the high-speed mainline track they've had to neglect other areas. I suppose if you go somewhere like the Whitby branch very little has been spent?

Maurice: Yes. With the old permanent-way system, where each length had its gang, the gangs knew the bad places which they used to keep right. Now you never see a plate-layer unless it's an emergency job, part of a mobile gang which goes from one emergency to another. There's no method now of a gang building a length up to a standard and then maintaining it. Also, we're losing track in our area. They're taking goods lines out all the time.

Sid: They're robbing Peter to pay Paul. Where they've had two tracks of running line they're taking one of them up to use it to replace track somewhere else. That's the sort of desperate state they're in.

Maurice: Also, the marshalling-yards are slowly disappearing. At Tees Yard we had a huge yard, an Up-side and a Down-side each with twelve reception roads, both with humps, control towers, retarders, etc., and with forty-two roads in each yard capable of holding eighty wagons each. Well, the up-side hump has closed, and the down-side receptions have been reduced from twelve to six.

Sid: Anyway in three or four years from now it won't matter to you, will it?

Maurice: It doesn't matter much now . . . I reached that happy stage a year or so ago. I simply get through the day, or night. I think Thornaby will just about last me out. My record is pretty good. There's one caution on my record in forty-odd years' service, that's all. That's it, that's my record.

The Gresley V 2 Class LNER 'Green Arrow' locomotive.

Low Gates signal box at Northallerton. Father worked this signal box for a number of years in the 1950s.

The south end of Darlington Bank Top showing the locomotive depot in 1938 at the time of its reconstruction.

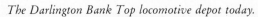

The Darlington Bank Top locomotive depot today.

Outside Buckingham Palace in 1966 after Father had been awarded the MBE. From left to right: sister Brenda, Father, Mother, sister Elma and brother Maurice.

With Bob Bonner, NUR executive member, in the cab of a Japanese 'Bullet' train. In 1972, as Assistant General Secretary, I led an NUR delegation to Japan.

With members of the construction team on a tour of Merseyside's new loop and link lines in 1976.

7   *Running Down the Railways*

I T WASN'T UNTIL 1955 that the post-war modernization plan for the railways was conceived. I had been appointed a full-time officer of the NUR in 1954, so I saw at first hand this plan being launched. Everybody now realizes that the 1955 plan lacked vision. After Labour lost the 1952 election there was inevitably a different approach to running the nationalized railways. Although the legislation came later, in the 1960s, the new Conservative mood was to begin to remove the railways from an umbrella of social obligation to a purely commercial remit.

Road transport was already beginning to offer an attractive alternative for British industry. The main fault of the plan was that the people who drafted it seemed to believe that railways could carry on for the next twenty years in the same way as they had since the mid-thirties. The best part of the £1.5 billion plan was a commitment to electrification, which eventually led to the modernization of the Euston-Glasgow main line; but most of the immediate cash, apart from dieselization, went into modernizing and expanding great marshalling-yards like Carlisle Kingmoor, Sheffield Tinsley and the Tyne yards. Those yards never in fact carried anything like the quantities of freight planned for them; they were never more than half busy. The reason for this, which the planners quite failed to see, was that wagons were to be bigger, moving much faster from A to B, and they would not need marshalling in the same way — indeed industry, putting more premium on time, would not want it.

It wasn't just the planners. The NUR also failed to understand the signs. British unions have a weakness in that they concentrate their efforts on raising living standards through the pay packet. I have long believed that, having advocated the public ownership of railways, trade unions should accept a responsibility to make a success of the industry. It's a difficult role, for unions have always been wary of change, especially technological change, which usually means fewer jobs. Sad to say, unions prefer to bury their heads in the sand, with the main object (if they can't resist change) of getting a bigger pay packet for those still in work. The British trade union movement has limited its horizons, concentrating mostly on the pay packet; our European colleagues have long sinced raised their sights to provide a whole range of other benefits like longer holidays or earlier and better retirement provisions, and shorter working hours. They have also been more prepared to take a positive role in the future planning of their industries.

Dieselization was in the air about the time I became a full-time union officer, when BR wanted to introduce the first diesel railcars for suburban and secondary services. I remember going to Northern Ireland in 1953 as part of a joint NUR/BR delegation looking at this type of diesel operation, particularly the manning implications. I could see then that these diesel mutliple unit sets could be the salvation of some rural lines. The union offered no resistance to this new technology; the only point at issue was manning. After numerous difficulties over the years, the matter has been resolved; today the vast majority of Britain's trains are operated with one man in the cab.

In 1956 there were about 16,000 steam locos. By 1964 diesels had completely taken over after eight years of tremendous change. I was involved in some of the manning and pay discussions this entailed. By any test the steam locomotive was far less efficient than diesel, itself easily bettered by electric. I never quite understood why British Rail didn't decide to go straight for electrification or even half-diesel, half-electric. By and large, the changeover period was successful, although the diesel locos had all the usual teething problems.

Many railwaymen needed to be completely retrained, not least the maintenance engineers, who had to learn a new set of skills in a completely different environment. Diesel workshops, dealing with delicate electrics, had to be kept far cleaner than the old steam sheds, which were sometimes simply converted as at Thornaby on Teesside. Stations, too, became a lot less dirty. Over a century of soot and muck was eventually cleaned away. Some of the older men found it difficult to adapt to the changes, and of course a lot of jobs went. The ones who stayed had to make do with just a few weeks of retraining, having to cope with technical problems they often didn't readily understand.

One of the consequences of the diesel was that it broke the natural flow which had existed throughout the steam age from cleaner to fireman to engine driver. With no natural apprenticeship and (today) very few second men in driving cabs, a new driver's experience of locomotives is bound to be limited. You have almost to bring him out of the classroom and put him into the cab. You can train anyone in the abstract, but steam drivers (except in unusual circumstances like the war) had a whole backlog of experience on the footplate before they took over.

The electrification of the London Midland route from Euston to Birmingham, Liverpool and Manchester was conceived in 1955 together with the East Coast main line from King's Cross to Leeds and York. But after the powers that be had shown their usual second thoughts and hesitations, they decided to limit the electrification programme to the London Midland region. It was extended to Glasgow only after another prolonged delay.

The Southern had been electrified by third rail for years, of course, but it's hard to compare the Southern with the LM or LNER, limited as it is to the suburban South Coast. Overhead electrification, of the sort standard in Europe, was obviously the way ahead. About half the £1.5 billion for modernization was allocated to electrification. The East Coast route was abandoned through fears of increased costs and that the two main lines together were just too big to handle. Did we have the resources, and could we stand major disruption of the country's two most important main lines? This sort of electrification does mean building a whole new railway on the old, and you must keep the train services operating whilst constructing the new railway — a very difficult task.

The Euston-Manchester-Glasgow line has proved itself

cost-effective beyond doubt, and the benefits could have been foreseen by the government of the day by taking European examples. But it was impossible to persuade politicians of the need for a commitment to more mainline electrification, even though the Suez crisis of 1956 had showed dramatically how vulnerable diesel oil supplies were.

At the first suspicion that it might be difficult, the government abandoned the East Coast plans. But I can't remember any outcry from my union at the time, because not one of us had the foresight to see the implications. We were geared to opposing closures, not to championing new developments. In 1984 we're still waiting for the East Coast route to be electrified, yet its case remains just as sound as the West Coast route.

Of course, electrification means remodelling on a huge scale, not just putting a few wires up. Euston station, for instance, was totally rebuilt along with Birmingham New Street and Manchester Piccadilly. The track and the signalling, to cope with a new railway moving at 100 mph, was all new. In fact, the prototypes of the new power signals were first built on the York-Darlington main line through Northallerton in the late 1930s. The new electric locomotives weighed only eighty tons, much lighter than the steam and diesel-electrics, but more powerful too. Whereas before to get over Shap you had to be assisted by a powerful loco in the rear, these new electrics built at Crewe would zip over Shap with an equivalent load.

Modern signalling was also a vital element in the success of this route, though, because a handful of centres could now control the whole system, it gave great power to signalmen as a grade, who demanded and got special treatment — and bore out my prediction as a young man that they would easily overtake the train drivers in wages and importance. The NUR policy is to negotiate wage levels based on skill and responsibility and grade people accordingly; ASLEF sticks at one fixed rate for all drivers irrespective of skill and responsibility.

After the London Midland route became operative in 1966, the number of passengers travelling by the new electric railway rose dramatically. But instead of continuing the impetus we muddled on with diesel locomotives and diesel multiple units. We lost time, and a great deal of the railways' natural advantage over other means of transport was never picked up

again. If we had started earlier, and continued with a programme of electrification, we would be in far better shape
today.

There was an element of surprise about the 1955 plan. Not
for the first time, the authorities suddenly found themselves
with money which they felt they had better spend quickly — so
that many details of the plan lacked vision. The railway board
spent money like local authorities using up their allocation at
the year end. The electrification of the Euston main line was a
glaring example of what should have happened all over Britain,
and stands today as a monument to the blunders made around
it. This bit of railway, opened almost twenty years ago now, is
still successful today, still competing with all forms of
transport including aircraft between London, Manchester and
Glasgow. Apart from a couple of London suburban schemes
(King's Cross-Hertford, Bedford-St Pancras) nothing has
happened since then.

A league table recently compiled confirms that Britain is
bottom for electrified route miles among comparable developed nations. Top comes Sweden with 63 per cent of total
track, the Netherlands 61 per cent, Italy 52 per cent, Japan 38
per cent, West Germany 37 per cent, Spain 36 per cent, France
28 per cent, and Britain 21 per cent. It shows when you go to
Europe.

The most notable thing from my point of view about electrification schemes was their effect on staff morale. This relates
back to the question I posed about much earlier times: Why
was there such loyalty to the railways? It's to do with morale.
The new clean, efficient London Midland railway, which staff
could boast about, returned railway workers' pride along with
their new uniforms. I was constantly moving between the
regions as NUR Assistant General Secretary when the railway
opened in 1966, and I couldn't help noticing the difference in
attitude. The moral is — give people the right tools and they
will do the job properly. It's not surprising that after so much
neglect morale is today at rock-bottom among railway staff.

Railwaymen did not object to Euston Station being
rebuilt — the protest came from Sir John Betjeman and his
like. I'm not arguing about the merits of conservation.
Victorian termini like St Pancras and Paddington are great

architectural monuments; but I object to the railway having to maintain and pay for these monuments, starving it of resources for modernization or better staff working conditions. There are something like 450 listed buildings owned by BR, and they look beautiful when restored like Manchester Victoria or St Pancras. My only argument is — who pays? If there's a preservation order it's a national monument, and the nation should find the money. What BR gets to help preserve historic buildings is chicken-feed. The railway police force is another archaic burden which the Board shouldn't have to carry.

When the London Midland line was finally electrified in 1966 they had virtually rebuilt the whole railway — track, overhead lines, rolling-stock and stations. On the East Coast route, still waiting for the go-ahead, all that now needs to be done is to put up the gantries and re-equip with electric locos and new carriages. Bridge, tunnel and station work has already taken place in preparation.

The Eastern Region was, however, determined to maintain its fast-route status (traditionally the two lines to Scotland were highly competitive, the Royal Scot fighting to get to Glasgow before the Flying Scotsman reached Edinburgh), and so it specified a new, big, fast diesel-electric to pull the Scottish expresses and found it in the Deltic class. About twenty-five Deltics were built, 100-mph engines which were claimed to pull the fastest timetabled diesel services in the world. They have only in recent years been superseded by the diesel High Speed Train (HST).

Even after the decision to electrify the LM, a lot of hiccups and governmental about-turns ensued. Each stage of electrification had to be authorized separately as the government, increasingly worried in the 1960s about mounting railway deficits, all but changed its mind. It ought simply to have taken the decision and got on with it ... There's no doubt that the economics of an electric railway get better the greater the area the network serves.

An electric railway, together with multi-aspect signalling, allows you to run trains at maximum speeds close behind one another. This sort of operation (all too rare in Britain) is the classic case for railways — fast, easily regulated, safe, low on energy consumption and environmentally contained. It is the best way yet developed to move people and freight between cities. Yet, despite the fact that all the routes intended to be in BR's ten-year electrification programme passed the tests set by the Thatcher Government, a decision on them is still awaited.

Euston station, now almost twenty years old, still represents the almost ideal solution for a big mainline terminal. The concourse separates train operation from other passenger needs. Tubes, buses, taxis and cars are all fed into the station. It's clean (except where litter takes over, dropped by the least considerate travelling public in Western Europe), and it's simple to find your way around in. The London Midland remains a benchmark for the rest of BR.

MACMILLAN ENDS THE SOCIAL ROLE

In 1960, Prime Minister Harold Macmillan, speaking in Parliament, said: 'The railway system must be remodelled to meet current needs and the modernization plan must be adapted to the new shape.' This initiative led to the Transport Act of 1962. Now, the 1962 Act dismantled the British Transport Commission which had been set up under the Transport Act of 1947 to co-ordinate the various sectors, including docks and hotels as well as railways.

The 1962 Act divided the Transport Commission into separate boards — railways, docks, waterways and London Transport. The British Railways Board was given a commercial remit and the social role of railways, implicit in Labour's Act of 1947, and the coordinating role which is the essence of good transport policy, was swept aside. Each authority had to attempt to operate commercially.

This freed, even encouraged, BR to look for closure of uneconomic lines, something identified with the figure of Dr Beeching. There were transport users' consultative committees which made out cases for certain lines to stay open, but the Minister took the decision in finality.

The railways had until then been a common carrier — anything you took to a station had by law to be carried. But it was relieved of this burden. Railwaymen's morale sank even lower as competition from the car and the lorry grew and grew. This factor was far more consistent than government transport

135

policy — except that both major political parties gave transport a low priority in government.

Sometimes being Transport Minister didn't even guarantee you a place in the Cabinet; and there proved to be a huge changeover of these ministers. Indeed, between 1975 and 1983, during my period as General Secretary, there were no fewer than eight transport ministers. Even this rate of change was overtaken between June and October 1983 when David Howell was replaced by Tom King, who was followed by Nicholas Ridley. A massive turnover of ministers is bound to have had effects on a department of such national importance.

British Railways Board chairmen also came and went; we had Sir Stanley Raymond, Sir Richard Marsh and Sir Peter Parker, followed last year by Bob Reid, and there were others who only stayed for about five years each.

Acts of Parliament concerning railways also came and went with about the same speed. One Board chairman, Sir Stanley Raymond, a railwayman himself, said he spent more time moving filing cabinets than considering the movement of freight and passengers. The only constant features were railway management, staff and trade unions.

Not only that but the labour force has been greatly affected by continual re-organization forced on them by this volume of legislation — legislation which often changed the nature of their employers. Now privatization threatens their future. This has produced a demoralized management and a demoralized workforce and the whole thing was made worse at the General Election of 1983 which returned to power a government which doesn't care a damn whether railways operate or not, and is bitterly opposed to public ownership.

After the Macmillan Act, Beeching was brought in to analyse the railways in the light of the new circumstances. I believe that he was short-sighted. He forgot that local and rural services were tributaries to the main routes. There's no doubt that the system was ready for rationalizing: some lines were senselessly duplicated; there were some elements of Beeching which made sense. I think it was because of that that the NUR didn't oppose him more strongly. The union did fight workshop closures, but when you looked closely a lot of them had been built to suit a particular railway company's needs and you had to admit that some would have to go after standardization of locomotives and rolling-stock came in.

Beeching's analysis had to be made, but management and unions simultaneously failed to create a future policy for railways based on those aspects of Beeching's proposals which made sense. We could have started many of the changes to branch lines to make them more efficient much earlier. Yes, there would have been union resistance, of course. But the lines in East Anglia or North Wales, for example, could have been made a lot more cost-effective with a new signalling system, new rolling-stock and new manning levels. Eventually, when the only option was total closure in East Anglia, the NUR agreed to pay-trains — guards collecting tickets, leaving stations unstaffed. That saved the lines. Really, we were reacting too late. Unions should have been more positive. We ought to have realized that for the public service to survive and prosper there would have to be changes in work practices. Unions could have raised their sights by making the industry more efficient and competitive — after all, we had been advocating public ownership since 1894 on the grounds that it would provide an efficient transport system. But we were only one symptom of muddled thinking from government-level down. Looking back, long before I was General Secretary, the union did present a lot of advice about running the railways, but it ducked many important issues on the more effective use of manpower and resources.

It had already come to terms with the end of steam and all that that meant on the job front. Steam was very labour-intensive, as were the old systems of signalling. The union recognized perfectly well that steam was totally inefficient, that the old manual signal boxes, controlling about five miles of railway each, were obviously on their way out, and that the old pick-and-shovel permanent-way men would be overtaken by machines.

We accepted these major changes and in many cases raised the pay and working conditions of railwaymen. Unfortunately, we had so much to react to that we ignored the longer perspective. Even today we are failing to plan how to live with new technologies, how to exploit them to our advantage, making life easier and working fewer hours without losing jobs.

In other words, to change the emphasis of our negotiations to a shorter working week, year and life. In the Sixties we accepted job cuts for the promise of higher pay! 'Tomorrow you'll be smaller but a well-paid labour force', was management's cry. That didn't happen to the extent we had hoped. The NUR membership, at its peak about half a million, is now down to 141,000; it never got the rewards offered for job sacrifices. Of course, there was a lot of natural wastage, because railwaymen were an ageing labour force. And in the Sixties there were plenty of jobs going elsewhere, which made the union less concerned than it would be today. We were the first union to negotiate lump-sum payments on voluntary redundancies. I remember negotiations for redundancy payments to workers on the old former Great Northern line, which closed completely. But, having cut back the obvious limbs, British Rail was then quite unable to put the right investment into the lines that remained.

Barbara Castle's Transport Act of 1968 only continued the divisive process begun in 1962. She also wanted separate accountability, but to her credit she sought to identify the social role for railways. We used to ask her, 'Who's going to co-ordinate all these separate undertakings?' 'I'll be the co-ordinator,' she replied. She couldn't co-ordinate, she hadn't the time, and anyway it was too difficult a job. There were constant arguments with the British Transport Docks Board after they were separated from railways about ripping up rail tracks because they ceased to be interested in how traffic came to or left the ports. That would never have happened if the co-ordinating role had been preserved within one overall transport authority. We could have adapted to the changing methods of trade, such as containerization, as indeed we have at Parkeston Quay today, a railway-owned port where NUR men work the cranes which unload the containers from the ships and on to the railway wagons.

1983 TRANSPORT POLICY

Unfortunately it was not until 1983 that the Labour Party presented to the British people a new transport policy which had not only been approved by the whole of the Movement but was created as a result of a series of conferences attended by representatives of the transport unions, the TUC and the Labour Party.

I made available all the facilities for these conferences at the NUR Educational Centre at Frant, Sussex, because it was vital that we should produce a policy statement acceptable to every trade union involved with transport. So many times in the past, divisions between road and rail unions had presented problems to Labour administrations.

The policy statement spelt out in clear terms how the problem should be tackled:

> It has become increasingly apparent over recent years that a sensible transport system cannot be achieved by relying on market forces. On the contrary, such reliance must lead to an unco-ordinated system which does not represent the best use of resources: the essential needs of many people are not met, and there is a damaging effect on the environment and quality of life. Intervention by both central and local government is essential in order to ensure that we achieve a coherently planned system which serves the community as a whole.

Planning, Co-ordination and Integration

Our objectives are to create a safe, efficient and comprehensive transport system to move both people and goods; to make the best use of resources; to provide a network of public transport services throughout the country which ensures that social needs are met at fares people can afford; and to safeguard the environment and the quality of life in the towns and countryside.

These objectives can only be met if we cease to look at each transport mode in isolation and consider transport as a whole. Our aim is to ensure that each mode performs the functions for which it is best suited, thus using resources to maximum advantage. However, this can only be done with planning and co-ordination between the various modes. This means, for instance, better public transport interchange facilities, complementary time-tabling and well advertised connections, through-ticketing wherever possible, and, in the field of freight,

139

the development of trans-shipment facilities. Both central government and local authorities have an important role in co-ordinating arrangements.

At national level, we believe that the development of a sensibly planned and co-ordinated approach by a Labour Transport Secretary would be enhanced by the creation of a National Transport Authority. Although day-to-day responsibility for transport operations would remain in the hands of the relevant operators, the Authority would have a major influence over broad policy.

Within the framework of the government's policy objectives, its main functions would be:

> To consider and advise the Secretary of State for Transport on investment needs and proposals and on the use of taxes and subsidies;
> to monitor and report on the provision of local transport services and to promote co-ordination between transport modes;
> to make recommendations on the provision of road haulage operator licences and the development of long term agreements on freight movements.

This National Transport Authority, which would be chaired by the Secretary of State, would aim to bring together all interested groups and including representatives of the trade unions, management, local government and transport users. Additionally, effective bodies representing users' interests are needed in all transport sectors to monitor performance, investigate complaints and advise on present and future policy options.

Unfortunately, in the years leading up to the 1983 General Election all the energies of the Labour Party were sucked into internal feuds and Labour came to be seen as less relevant to the solution of the country's problems. Those elements in the party who caused the trouble were responsible for Labour's electoral disaster and must carry the blame for the grim future which now faces thousands of railway workers.

The London Transport Underground is a railway system like any other which operates about 450 trains underneath London every week-day, handling more than 1,750,000 passenger journeys. As the major rail union, the NUR has been involved in organizing LT's staff for many years and between 1961 and 1965 it was my lot to take part in NUR negotiations with LT.

LT was brought into public ownership by the creation of the London Passenger Transport Board in 1933 when Herbert Morrison was head of the London County Council. Labour dominated the LCC at the time, and this was one expression of Morrison's commitment to public ownership. The NUR by far is the dominant union on the railways side of LT, claiming about 75 per cent membership.

For me it was a natural progression, from one set of railway negotiations to another, with a few differences. Obviously LT carries passengers only — though some cross-London lines permitted freight. The nearest thing to freight is at night, when the current is switched off and permanent-way trains move about the system. But the main difference was the contrast between the London Transport Executive and the British Railways Board as employers. LTE were far more generous because they were more commercially viable. The first thing I did was to raise my sights in negotiations. Put simply, if I asked for one shilling on main lines I would ask for two bob on LT. At that time there was parity of rates between some key grades of BR and LT, but outside that LT workers were at an advantage. For many other reasons, too, LT were better employers than BR, easier to deal with. They hadn't (and haven't) the crippling burdens that the main lines must carry.

My appointment as NUR headquarters officer with responsibility for LT brought me permanently to London in 1961 after my long period as relief Divisional Officer. I moved with my wife Joan and son Anthony to Bishop's Stortford. Later, as Senior Assistant General Secretary, I had another spell from 1970 to 1975 dealing with major LT problems at top level. The most interesting event during my association with LT proved to be the building and commissioning of the Victoria Line.

This line, linking north-east London with south London via King's Cross, Euston and Victoria stations was authorized in August 1962. The idea of the line had been floated as early as February 1949: one more example of the length of time which even good, sensible transport plans take to materialize in Britain. The Victoria Line was the first major addition to the underground system since the war.

It was always accepted that this fourteen-mile railway across London, serving sixteen stations, would never pay for itself in strict financial terms, but that it was vital to the transport needs of the capital. In its first year of operation it carried over seventy million passengers, and it is carrying even more today. It has been highly successful by any test; anyone who has travelled on the Victoria Line during peak periods must wonder how London ever managed without it. It was, and remains, different from other underground lines — with the capability of being totally automatic so far as trains and signalling are concerned. When the line was authorized in 1962 the development work on this automation was still incomplete, and I was quickly involved in the negotiations around this new concept.

The other main dilemma was how to construct the line without interfering with other services. There were all sorts of staffing problems relating to access to railways at night — existing railways — to help the Victoria Line.

It was, to me, an exciting concept — and I enjoyed seeing station and train designs on the drawing boards. The contracts for construction benefited British industry all round the country. I couldn't help noticing a £2,000,000 contract for Head Wrightson, the Stockton iron foundry, to provide the cast-iron tunnel-lining segments.

It was the sort of development that we as a union had been advocating for public transport. No new section of tube railway had been built across Central London since 1907 (fifty years earlier), and we were therefore very enthusiastic.

I went to see the trains under construction, and then again when the trial runs were in progress.

We had, of course, to agree the operation first of the experimental Victoria Line train on the Woodford-Hainault shuttle-line at the end of the Central Line system in Essex. A prototype train was installed there to simulate the exact circumstances. George Brassington, NUR Assistant General Secretary, was leading the negotiations from our side — I was the headquarters officer. We had to consider the implications of this revolutionary system — since employed elsewhere in the world — which operates through impulses in the track.

The system was designed by LT's chief electrical engineer, Robert Dell. He, with A. W. Manser, the chief mechanical engineer, and the Westinghouse Brake and Signal Company, developed the automatic concept. It's beautifully simple, really. Once the train operator closes the doors and presses the twin 'start' buttons, coded impulses from the track cause the train to accelerate, coast and brake to a halt at the next station, obeying any other instructions on the way. All the driver does is watch the operation. He can use his manual override in the event of failure or emergency. He's there for that reason — and also to reassure the travelling public, since it's a bit disconcerting to see a driverless train roaring into the station.

I think LT always accepted that it would not be feasible to run fast, crowded trains through miles of tunnel without some responsible person on board. There was never any conflict about having a driver; the conflict came over pay. Since there's no guard on the Victoria Line trains, what was to be the rate for the man operating the train?

The problem from our point of view was that his skill and responsibility was not greater than the driver operating non-automatic trains. In those days of fairly full employment we were more concerned about money than jobs. And so the negotiations revolved round the saving of the guard's pay and how much the driver should take. Fare collection was another part of the negotiations, since the Victoria Line was being planned to incorporate the new automatic barriers which are now common on LT. This involved an open attitude on our part not least because of its implications for the rest of the underground system. These automatic barriers help passenger flow, act as a deterrent to fraudulent travel, and reduce operating costs. If extended to cover the whole network the savings would be enormous. In fact, the managing director of the underground recently estimated that about £15,000,000 annually is lost on the underground through fraud, plus a similar amount on the buses.

We eventually negotiated a rate for the new grade of automatic train operator after failing to argue skill and responsibility. What we arrived at was in fact based on the crude consideration: what wage did you save at the back end? The operator should have a proportion of it.

Some years later, as Senior Assistant General Secretary, I had to deal with a most interesting claim for automatic train operators who wanted more money because they argued that their skill and responsibility had been increased. They advanced very complex reasons. I was sceptical about this new claim, but the executive committee insisted we pursue the case. So we eventually ended up before the LT Wages Board, the arbitration level equivalent to the Railway Staff National Tribunal. The trade union nominee on the board was George Lothian of the building workers, a TUC General Council member.

I made the case as eloquently as I could. It sounded all right. So the chairman said we should go to have a look at its operation. He picked the day and the time, and we set out from LT headquarters at 55 Broadway, without being given any other details. We just took the first train that arrived at our station, showed our credentials to the train operator and joined him in the cab. It was pretty crowded — there were four of us — but the driver pressed the start buttons and then turned his back on the direction the train was going so that he could tell us how difficult his job was. He was going on about the stress and the strain of the job while the train rocketed forward automatically. I couldn't get near enough to kick him. He should have had his eyes glued to the track in front and told us that he had no time to talk. Then the train stopped itself, he glanced at the TV screen, pushed the buttons and turned his back again. That was his routine for six or seven stations.

When we got off the chairman thanked the operator. As we walked away, George Lothian contrived to get beside me and said: 'What do you want me to do with that lot now?' I said, 'Forget about it, George.' Needless to say, the wages board decision went against the claim.

Victoria Line trains were the first to be silver in colour rather than the traditional red. That was because they are of

144

lightweight aluminium alloys, unpainted and much more economical to maintain. We were aware that this would involve some job losses. But the Victoria Line meant LT expansion and in the workshops we could see the advantage of this kind of change in terms of business. The carriages were built to high comfort levels, quiet, well-planned for the standing passenger. When the Queen opened the line in March 1969 it was something for everyone to be proud of.

The line is capable of being extended, and its principle could be applied to the whole underground network. It was, for instance, designed to handle great masses of rush-hour traffic with maximum stops of seventeen seconds. To do that, doors, exits and moving staircase flows have all to be right. Platforms are put side-by-side with other LT lines where possible, and there are also direct links with BR suburban lines. I myself used the changeover at Tottenham Hale with the mainline Liverpool Street-Cambridge route. But as the BR line service to Bishop's Stortford deteriorated, I sometimes chose to use the M11 motorway to Blackhorse Road on the Victoria Line, park my car there, and travel on to Euston. It proved quicker than going by BR train. I first started to use the route because of a mainline railway strike and found out myself how passengers change long-established transport habits during strikes, to the consequent loss to railways.

The sad thing is that the example set by the Victoria Line has never been followed up. The conflict between the GLC and the government over fare structure has not helped. Fares aren't the only factor in successful railway running; the quality of the service is equally important. We argued with the GLC, 'For heaven's sake don't overplay the fares debate. If there's a certain amount of money to put into London Transport use it to improve the quality of the service, the stations and the stock, or at least create a balance between investment and fares.' If Ken Livingstone, the leader of the GLC, had done that he wouldn't have faced the fares backlash he received from the Tory Government. But the GLC under his leadership has been more interested in playing politics than providing a good transport system for London. All the same, LT, like the rest of the rail system, is desperate for investment. Just compare the London underground with the Paris Metro!

The man at the top level of LT when I was responsible for LTE negotiations was Anthony Bull. His attitude was first-class. I always preferred to talk with someone who understood the job and spoke straight and to the point. In short, I like dealing with people who play the game, putting their cards on the table. Then you know what you're taking on — much better than a weak, waffling manager. And, at the top, LT's management during my time as Assistant General Secretary was exceptional. I don't think the staff appreciated the sort of management they had. During my period as General Secretary we could have reached agreement with LT for participation in management at the lower level of our negotiating procedures, but the staff could not be persuaded to accept this — it presented too much of a challenge.

Negotiating with LTE at certain levels, instead of facing a BR-type personnel department, you usually met the departmental boss himself, and this meant that you had to know your stuff. Once I was meeting with A. W. Manser, the chief mechanical engineer, about a group of workers called 'pump linesmen' who have a very difficult job and work beneath the tunnels where a lot of the operating equipment runs. Using my British Rail experience I stupidly assumed that he would know nothing about the working conditions. 'Do you know what it's like to work down there?' I asked him rhetorically. 'Oh, yes,' he replied, 'I served my apprenticeship on that job.'

Few of the millions of passengers who use London Transport know of the work performed by this unique grade of railwayman, the pump linesman. The Underground railway system is for a large part below the level of the Thames. It is therefore impossible to prevent water seeping into stations and tunnels — and rain occasionally pours in from above. Not surprisingly there is an extensive system of sumps and pumps to trap and remove this water, and of course a team of men to maintain it. Water always finds the lowest points, and those are where the sumps have to be: under platforms; at the bottom of lift and escalator shafts; under the track in tube tunnels. Often the pumps have been added as afterthoughts, to solve local problems, and access to them can be tricky.

To reach pumps in the old Thames Tunnel on the East London line the pump linesman used to cadge a lift from a train driver, who would let him down at the sump. To return the linesman would point his torch at the approaching train, swinging it backwards and forwards in the hope that the driver noticed and stopped.

Some pump access points seem to have no connection with the railway — like the manhole to be found in the garden of a house in Stratford, below which the Central Line ran, and the entrance to a pump in the middle of a South London recreational ground.

Recently two pump linesmen were arrested in Central London at 2 am. The entrance to Hayes Mews pump, near the London Hilton, is through an iron gate in a side street and our heroes had not been as quiet as they might. A vigilant resident called the police. Not quite so funny is the story from way back of pump staff answering a call at a site next to another well-known West End hotel. They were not able to proceed with their job until hotel staff agreed to keep rats at bay by continually throwing food at them.

Of course, it is not only surface water which finds its way into the tunnels. There are toilets and messrooms at low levels, and waste has to be pumped from these up to the sewers, maybe seventy or a hundred feet above. Many stories have been handed down over the years, and get coloured as they go, but an incident which occurred in 1982 involved a blocked pulsometer (the special pumps required to deal with sewage). Pump staff removed the inspection cover to clear the blockage. Unfortunately they forgot that the system was pressurized and within a split second they, plus everything in the room, were covered with a fine layer of effluent. Nobody can say the pump linesman's job lacks variety.

Robert Dell, the chief signal engineer, was also a top-class man widely sought after as a problem-solver elsewhere. From a management point of view, the disadvantage of departmental chiefs doing their own negotiating was their unawareness of how their agreements might affect other departments. There's nothing more devastating to personnel management to find that one award has an almost exact parallel elsewhere which they have no chance of opposing.

London Transport is closely connected with four main institutional bodies in London's overall transportation planning and policy. These bodies are: the government itself, the Greater London Council, British Rail and the National Bus Company. LT and BR together play a vital role in the capital's economy. The railway they jointly provide carries about 70 per cent of London and South-east commuters in and out of Central London each day. A further 10 per cent of commuters go by bus, leaving only 20 per cent using private cars. This London-South-east sector is a large and important part of the national rail network, from which it cannot be divorced.

Both LT and BR recognize that if they are to provide the service the public needs they must operate in harmony to make the best use of available resources. But obviously under the present institutional arrangements they serve different masters — the Department of Transport and the GLC.

London has the oldest underground system in the world — parts of it were opened over 120 years ago! It has all the consequent problems of numerous long passages, old lifts, badly-designed stations and poor passenger flows, while being expected to cope with enormous volumes during the rush hours. Well before the end of this century the underground will require extensive station modernization, including new lifts and escalators. New rolling-stock, together with new methods of train operation, including new signalling systems, will also become a priority.

This, together with more effective use of manpower, will be essential to bring London's mass-transit system up to the standards now being expected around the world. It implies a much higher level of investment than at present, and much greater annual subsidy.

Clearly, therefore, the GLC is not the body best-suited to run LT (and recent experiences have not exactly shown it to be God's gift to London's transport needs). There is no doubt that some sort of overall transport authority should co-ordinate decision-making in the London area. In my view, the sooner a Metropolitan Transport Authority is created on the lines suggested by the House of Commons Transport Committee Report of July 1982 the better it will be for all concerned.

One year before I became NUR General Secretary local government in England and Wales had been reorganized. A new breed of authority, the metropolitan county council, was established in the big industrial conurbations outside London, among them Tyne and Wear based on Newcastle and Sunderland.

The logic behind setting up the metropolitan counties was that matters like transportation, policing and waste disposal should be a recognized as activities which affect the conurbations as a whole. Previously, responsibility was left to smaller authorities, some of which had 'county borough' status. It was, and remains, a controversial decision. Critics have accused the metropolitan counties of wasteful duplication. They say that the services could be handled adequately by the metropolitan districts, organized into joint committees where necessary. Although legislation for the 1974 reorganization was pushed through by a previous Conservative Government, Mrs Thatcher has declared her intention of demolishing the metropolitan counties, along with the GLC during the present Parliament and has introduced a White Paper to that effect. Is one of her concerns the embarrassment that a strong Labour lobby formed by the metropolitan counties causes?

One undeniable achievement of a metropolitan county which further reorganization will not, it's hoped, harm, is the Tyne and Wear Metro railway system. The origins of Metro go back much further than the reorganization to the Transport Act 1968, which encouraged the creation of passenger transport authorities in the major conurbations, and a land-use/transportation study commissioned by government departments in 1969.

Of the six metropolitan areas — West Midlands, Greater Manchester, Merseyside, South Yorkshire, West Yorkshire, and Tyne and Wear — Merseyside has been the only other authority with the ability to convert this friendly legislation into new transport systems. But where Merseyside's underground is a rationalization of existing lines by a city centre tunnel loop making do with conventional railway equipment, Tyne and Wear's Metro is a complete new system,

149

almost isolated from BR track, with an identity of its own.

In all, forty-two kilometres of former BR suburban lines were taken over for Metro, sanctioned by Act of Parliament in 1973. Parliament had to be satisfied that the costs were justified by greater public transport efficiency, better use of existing track, pressure relieved from the roads network, and likely financial benefits in an area of long-term mass unemployment. Part of Metro's route is indeed along an alignment once reserved for an urban motorway.

Metro's design is a model for other light railway systems. Underground only in Newcastle city centre, it uses 1,500V DC overhead lines to power a frequent service. Passengers operate the door controls at stations, which are completely unmanned. Even ticket sales are fully automatic. Station and rolling-stock design is clean, functional and distinctive. There are forty-one stations on the Metro network compared with twenty-six on the previous BR system. A single control-centre oversees, via closed-circuit television, the whole network, with drivers in charge of their own trains. Metro is integrated with bus routes by interchange points and the unusual creation, in a British city, of transferable tickets.

To adopt the changes implied above meant a revolution in attitudes by the railway unions. Indeed, at first this whole new concept met with strong trade union resistance; the rail unions argued that British Rail should operate the railway and provide the level of service required by the Tyne and Wear Authority to co-ordinate with their bus services; the road unions claimed it was a tramway and should be operated by their membership.

These differences dragged on for many months. The unions reached common agreement only after the intervention of the TUC, who had to use the sledgehammer of their disputes committee procedure. Even after agreement at national level, local disputes on Tyneside caused disruption which continued to threaten the whole project.

Finally, the Minister of Transport, Bill Rodgers, laid down an ultimatum that unless all these difficulties were resolved quickly, and the trade unions guaranteed the whole of the Tyne and Wear Metro scheme a fair wind, he would cancel the lot. This threat concentrated the minds of everyone concerned and after a special meeting held in the House of Commons under the sponsorship of the North Eastern Group of MPs with Gordon Bagier of Sunderland taking the lead, agreement was finally reached between all the parties involved.

With a completely new railway, separate from British Rail, the unions together with Tyne and Wear were able to start from scratch. New conditions of employment were negotiated for a completely new workforce, far in advance of any railway agreement. On reflection, the final outcome was the best possible solution. The alternatives advocated by the trade unions in the early days would never have worked.

The nice thing about Metro is that it is already fulfilling all the predictions made for it. Unlike other big cities in Britain, where public transport revenues and passenger figures are in decline, Metro has started a Tyne and Wear boom. Car parks are having to be enlarged, property near to a Metro station has increased in price, and since Metro began to open up in August 1980 the number of passengers carried throughout the county has increased. Compared with 282 million passenger journeys in 1975 there were 311 million in 1983, with the system still not quite complete.

The final cost of Metro was calculated in autumn 1983 at £274 millions, 11 per cent more in real terms than the original estimate (including four extra stations and facilities for the handicapped). At £5 millions per kilometre all inclusive, it is still a low-cost system. Operational costs, at 8.5 pence per passenger mile, are slightly less than bus and over a penny less than BR.

Quite apart from giving the North-east renewed pride in its railways, Metro has attracted visitors from around the world, has helped the British manufacturers win export orders in Hong Kong and the United States, and has brought consultancy work in Canada and Singapore. This Tyneside success makes the case for investment in public transport in the clearest possible terms.

A JAPANESE EXPERIENCE

I went to Japan in 1972 when, as Assistant General Secretary, I led an NUR delegation. We were specially invited by the Japanese railway union, who were seeking advice about their campaign for the 'Right to Strike'. Their policy was to conduct a week-long spring offensive on the Japanese National Railway.

It was illegal to strike, and in the best trade union traditions they took strike action to win the right to strike. The railway authority's tactics were to sack all the ring-leaders, at which the railway union would take them on to their pay-roll. The union's problem was impending bankruptcy because of the number of activists involved.

The Japanese union wanted to pick our brains over industrial warfare, one British export which appeared acceptable to the Japanese worker. We went there for three weeks and travelled some 3,300 miles by rail, road and air, addressing meetings in various important centres to tell our hosts about the history of the British trade union movement and our railway experiences. Our visit coincided with a general election, which gave added importance to our message. The freedom of public-sector unions to take strike action was an important issue in the 1972 Japanese election.

After the Japanese surrendered to the Allied Forces in 1945 a democratic constitution was established, and three basic rights were guaranteed for all the working people of Japan: the right to associate, the right to bargain collectively, and the right to strike. As a means of encouraging these rights the occupation forces under General McArthur helped to create trade unions. However, in 1949 the Japanese Government introduced a regulation which deprived the workers in public corporations and national enterprises of this right to strike.

Despite our visit, I don't think our message got through, because the Japanese railway unions still operate in the way that they did before our tour. They have yet to win the right to strike. You cannot really compare their union practices with ours for the simple reason that they have so much experience to catch up on.

We were given special facilities to travel long distances, including riding in the motorman's cab on the modern railway — the Tokaido High Speed line — which opened in 1964. This railway runs through the most heavily populated part of Japan and at the time of our visit extended from Tokyo to Okayama — some 420 miles of double-track, standard-gauge electric railway used exclusively by High Speed Passenger trains.

The dead-straight track is tied into existing stations by building a new station alongside the old one, and leaving the old railway to provide slower services (both passenger and freight) beside the new Tokaido Line. It's an automatic railway from beginning to end, controlled entirely from the Tokyo Centre. The line has no signals: it's very much like the London Transport Victoria Line system, operating via impulses from the track. With such hazards as crossings and sharp curves eliminated, the trains run smoothly over long-welded rails at 130 mph.

If the train enters a section where the speed has to be reduced, the signalling aspect in the driving cab changes and automatic braking begins. This is in six stages from 130 mph down to 100, 68, 44 and 18 mph and stop. The motorman only brings the train to a standstill at the various scheduled stops and takes control of the brakes as the train enters the station. Otherwise, his duties are to keep a sharp lookout for any obstacles on the track ahead and to watch all the indications on the driving panel to note how the complex equipment of his train is functioning.

To start the train the motorman simply opens his controller. If the line is clear the electric traction equipment automatically accelerates the train at a rate of 0.56 miles per second per second until the maximum speed of 130 mph is reached. The centralized traffic control office at Tokyo is in complete command. To guard against natural disaster, seismoscopes, anemometers and rain gauges are installed along the entire track. If an earthquake exceeds a certain intensity (Japan is subject to earthquakes) the current to run the trains in the area is cut off. In case of excessive rains and winds, arrangements are made either to restrict the running speed or stop the train instantaneously. Also, for complete safety of the passengers, each train window is made of double-layer glass with a dry air space between so as to guard against flying stones and to minimize noise, wind pressure and condensation of moisture. In fact, every conceivable mechanical device assuring safe operations has been installed on this new railway system. Its record to date: not one accident since the line opened in October 1964.

On the super expresses, two motormen are required; on the

stopping trains, one motorman and one technician. The reason given for these manning arrangements are that in the case of the super express trains with limited stops, the motorman tends to lose concentration and, therefore, two motormen are provided. On the train which stops more frequently, the act of braking the train into the station relieves the monotony and concentration is thereby maintained; so just one motorman and one technician are needed. On the sixteen-coach super express one chief conductor and four conductors are provided and on the stopping trains of twelve coaches, one chief conductor and three conductors. These men combine the duties of guard, ticket-collector and service to the passengers. (The buffet-car staff are non-railway personnel.)

The High Speed Railway is operated by multiple units rather than locomotive-hauled trains (similar to the HST diesel trains in Britain). This makes possible simpler terminal layouts and quicker turn-rounds at terminals. Every coach is driven by means of a motor located at every axle with a continuous rating of 248 hp. A standard twelve-coach train, therefore, has a total of no less than 11,900 hp available for traction.

Each coach measures eighty-two feet overall except the end coaches which, with their streamlined noses, are six inches longer. A complete train of twelve coaches therefore measures 985 feet overall. The coaches are eleven feet one inch wide and have a maximum height of thirteen feet one inch above the rail. By clever design and the use of special materials, the weight of the trains has been kept to the low figure of 325 tons. The Americans named these trains 'Bullet Trains' because of their high speed, silver colour and shape.

The amount the Japanese spend on railways is enormous by our standards. I asked a high-ranking Japanese official how he justified all this expense. He replied that it was vital to the development of a highly industrial society.

'But why do you ask me that question?' he asked.

'Well, we are faced with a different attitude in Britain,' I replied. We were sitting in a restaurant high up in a Tokyo hotel, overlooking the bay.

He pointed to a visiting American aircraft carrier. 'Do you apply the argument of expense to British aircraft carriers?' he asked.

'No,' I said, 'they are vital to the nation.'

'Well,' he said, 'Japan applies the same attitude to its railways that Britain applies to its aircraft carriers.' He added that if Tokyo didn't have its suburban rail network the whole metropolis would seize up.

I discovered on my visit that the possibility of doing without any substantial part of the Japanese railway system was scarcely given a moment's consideration. However, recent discussions with Japanese trade union colleagues and the International Transport Federation Secretariat in London suggest that the situation is changing. The oil crisis caused special problems for the Japanese Government and its national budget. Spending on state-owned enterprises and public welfare was seen as a major problem. The government decided to reshape its state-owned undertakings such as the nationalized railway, postal and telegraphic services, in order to cut back on grants and subsidies. A Special Investigation Committee, appointed to look at the whole administrative problem published its recommendations in 1982. The Committee recommended that a number of state-owned enterprises be denationalized, while others should be split up into small units. Many of the Committee's recommendations had to do specifically with the Japanese National Railway.

The Japanese Government is strongly anti-union, and the greatest concentration of union power is to be found in the railway industry. In order to turn public opinion against the unions and the railway industry, the government claimed they were inefficient and alleged trade union interference in the Japanese National Railways. They also worked up a major anti-union campaign in the popular press, making great play on any aspect of railwaymen's working conditions which are more favourable than those found in private industry and even the private railways which operate in Japan.

The Investigating Committee's findings are now the subject of critical debate and can be summarized as follows:

Since its foundation, the JNR has achieved a major role in the inland transport industry, but it has been running into ever-increasing loss since 1964. The causes of financial deterioration were that the government has placed too many constraints on the railway management and has taken away its power to manage. The railway has anyway become too big to manage centrally.

Furthermore, the management and workforce have lost their competitive urge, because they think that the government will always bail them out. Bad industrial relations have affected productivity adversely, and personnel costs have become too high a proportion of the JNR's income. The JNR has to pay a lot of interest on loans. (Many of these problems are familiar to British Rail.)

The Committee concludes that what JNR needs is:

For management to recover its sense of responsibility, its power to manage and its competitive spirit. Improved productivity, and for excessive demands from local residents and politicians to be ignored. It goes on to say that it is impossible to achieve these things within the present framework of the JNR. The public enterprise system needs to be changed, and the JNR needs to be decentralized.

It will be interesting to see how the Japanese finally resolve their railway problems. We might be able to learn something from them.

THE FRENCH MAKE INVESTMENT PAY

On a recent visit to France I took the opportunity to discuss with French trade union colleagues the latest French railways developments. They described in enthusiastic terms how, in a blaze of publicity, the final section of the Paris to Lyon high speed line had been inaugurated early in 1983. Services involving the Train de Grande Vitesse (TGV) have dramatically cut journey times for many destinations including Geneva, Dijon and Marseilles. Most remarkable of all is the two-hour journey time to Lyon itself, compared with three hours forty-eight minutes only two years ago.

The TGV project is not, however, simply the product of a desire to run high-speed services; it is about railway investment. My colleagues recalled how the original TGV scheme was evolved by French railways (SNCF) in 1969 in the context of government guidelines for the public sector. On this remit the SNCF produced firm proposals for high-speed passenger train services. Paris-Lyon was selected as a corridor with established high demand where about a hundred kilometres of double track was causing capacity problems. In 1970 the French Department of Transport studied the proposal, announcing by the end of the year that it was sound — despite road and air interests lobbying against the TGV project. Final approval was given in 1975; construction started in 1976.

The main feature of the TGV was the decision to build a special high-speed passenger track. There were two principal reasons. First, the TGV's power, needed to produce high maximum speeds, meant that it could tolerate steeper gradients than conventional trains. This allowed a more direct route and fewer civil engineering works. Secondly, by reserving the track for TGV use only maintenance costs were reduced. Axle loads on the TGV are limited to sixteen tonnes, whereas freight wagons are often rated at twenty to twenty-two tonnes. Freight trains are also much slower, rarely achieving 140 kilometres per hour.

The Paris-Lyon route is not the end of the story. Authorization has now been given for TGV Atlantique, a new track from Paris to Brittany and Bordeaux.

There is also a large degree of trust and cooperation between the Ministry of Transport and the SNCF, including exchange of personnel at a high level. The lesson to be learned is that rail can compete in the transport market as a whole and is not confined to certain limited tasks (such as commuting) as some people would have us believe. Like any other business, investment which improves the product will make substantial gains in the market place. It is a lesson which the British government has not yet understood.

According to the SNCF the high-speed venture is already attracting people away from their cars and the airlines in sufficient numbers to show operating profits. Even before it was fully extended to Lyon, TGV made a £50 million profit; by 1984 it is expected to net £150 million for a grateful nation, having required a £1.3 billion investment. These buoyant figures provide the starkest contrast with the miserly British approach to investment.

8 *Railwaymen Talking*

OLD RAILWAYMEN NEVER DIE — they merely reminisce. In the course of my researches for this book I talked to many railwaymen. For this particular chapter I took the opportunity to chat with a number who live and work in North Yorkshire.

First I mustered four working railwaymen — two drivers, a time-keeper and a roster-clerk — all of them based at Harrogate. Between them they have 154 years' service, so what I collected one afternoon was just a small sample of their experience and a taste of their anecdotes...

'WE WERE THE OVALTINIES'

Tommy Cockeran: I started at Starbeck on the first of January 1940. When it closed in 1959 I moved to Darlington, then to York in 1960 and back to Harrogate in 1967. I'm still a driver.

Ronny Broadbent: I started February 1940 at Starbeck. I was a fireman until 1947, was brought off the footplate through rheumatic fever and have been a time-keeper ever since. When Starbeck closed I moved to Harrogate. (Harrogate's a booking on and off point, not a depot.)

Jack Mann: I started in September 1946 out of the armed services. I was in Harrogate in a number of grades up to 1968. Relief shunter and guard, and ticket-collector, having begun as a carriage cleaner. Then in 1968 I went on to the clerical side at York. I returned to Harrogate in 1980 where I deal with rosters and working arrangements of staff.

Roy Brogden: I started on 7 January 1952 at Leeds Holbeck in the locomotive department. I left Holbeck in 1970 to be registered as a driver at Harrogate, where I am still.

Tom: The war was bloody awful at some periods, specially when you were on long hours and nowt to eat, dirty cold and miserable. I worked trains up to Hartlepool and Newcastle, sometimes to Doncaster with the Harrogate Pullman. As for locomotives, we worked Class Rs, G5s, A49s, and all the other classes on the LNER during the war. It was worse if you got with a miserable driver. A few of them were, always reminding you they were your boss. For instance, if you went to carry out Rule 55 for protecting the train at the signal cabin, and you had a fair walk to get there, the engine would start blowing off. By the time you'd walked back your boiler was nearly empty. That was because the driver wouldn't put the water injector on for you. There was another old fellow at Starbeck who issued a stream of instructions — open that damper one notch lad, open it two — and you had to do it. We couldn't object. We were that young we were called the Ovaltinies, after a popular advert. You'd sign on, as today, and look at the sheet for tomorrow, only to find you were with that miserable so-and-so. Then you'd come to sign on tomorrow and the driver would say, 'I'm not taking that bugger — he's a bloody Ovaltinie, he's no experience, I'm not taking him, put him on't pilot.' I was sixteen.

Ronny: I was eighteen, and the seven years I had on the footplate at Starbeck were the happiest years of my life. It was bloody hard work, there were some funny buggers to put up with, but I found that apart from the driver you were your own gaffer. You were out on the track, you hadn't the shed master breathing down you neck.

Tom: It just depended what driver you got with. There were some odd ones. I could tell a few stories about them. One's nickname was the Yellow Peril. I were on Ripon 'pilot' with him. We got our issue of soap in the morning when we signed on. We gets to Ripon and goes behind the warehouse for our breakfast. I starts washing my hands and he says, 'Will you lend us your soap, Tom?' I had it out so I said, 'Aye use it.'
The same night I'm going into the club for a packet of cigs

and as I'm coming out there's the driver. He says, 'Have you any cigs, Tom?' I said 'Aye. There are plenty of cigs on the shelf.'

The following morning I gets to work and it's the same procedure, washing me hands, and he says, 'Can I borrow your soap, Tom?' So I says, 'Use your own bloody soap you got issued with.' 'Oh,' he says, 'I gave it to the wife yesterday to do her washing with, I haven't got it.'

Just as we were finishing our breakfast I pulls my cigs out. He says, 'Give us a cig, Tom.' I said, 'I thought you got some last night.' 'Ah, well,' he said, 'I left them at home for her.'

Ronny: The same fellow left £15,000 when he died. We had a lad at Starbeck, he could crack a joke any time, but he was very inexperienced. They put him on a train to Low Fell (Newcastle) and the driver says, 'You sit there and tell me when them signals are red or green, I'll fire and I'll drive.' So they got to Low Fell and the driver says to the lad, 'How do you like it?' 'By God, my job's all right,' says the lad, 'but tha's is bloody rough.'

Jack: Myself, coming out of the forces and looking for work, all the railway had to offer me was carriage washing. Not having been on the footplate, I think the drivers and firemen (or second men as they call them now) were a different standard to today. That's no slur on people today, but we have lost that comradeship. When I've been in a hole, in the days when Harrogate *was* busy, and things running out of course or perhaps a minor derailment, a fireman would square up for you and move a train set on his own, quite against the rules and regs, but he did it. Even today if someone is ill or sleeps in, as happens now and then, the drivers work the job themselves. The public never suffers any inconvenience.

Sid: Do you all agree that steam engines were hard work, dirty and you earned your money? You weren't sorry to see them go?

Tom: Yes, but there was another point of view. After the war at Starbeck two drivers always shared the same engine. When you came to work in the morning, you knew what to expect.

Jack: Yes, a couple of drivers might have a D49 Hunt class,

The abandoned Wensleydale line amidst the beauty of the Yorkshire Dales.

Class D 20 locomotive passing Northallerton signal box in the early 1940s.

The LNER Shire Class locomotive 'Yorkshire'.

Leaving 10 Downing Street after meeting Harold Wilson in 1975. I was a frequent visitor during my first four years as General Secretary under a Labour Government.

A Gresley Pacific passing Northallerton locomotive shed in the 1940s.

In the cab of an electric locomotive at Euston Station in 1975.

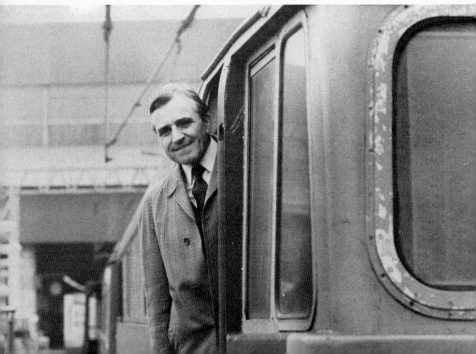

let's say South Durham, and they took a lot of pride in it. Old Baguley, God bless him, got a hell of a rollicking because he wouldn't let his engine go to assist Liverpool once. He wouldn't let his engine go. It was brassed up and like a sewing machine.

Tom: I signed on one afternoon with a driver called Arthur Lord. Our orders were to go to Harrogate from the shed to assist a Darlington-Leeds express in trouble. We arrived in Harrogate to find a G1 Atlantic locomotive on the train. Arthur Lord says, 'I aren't double-heading him.' There was a lovely row on Harrogate station, but he backed us on to the train and says, 'Don't you hang on, Tom.' The station inspector says, 'Get that bloody thing going.' I said, 'My driver says I haven't got to couple up to the train.' So they sent us to the shed. Tanrow was the gaffer, came out and wanted to know the reason why Lord wouldn't help. Lord says, 'I'll tell you the reason. He wants assistance from Harrogate to Leeds, he don't know the bloody road.' Tanrow replied, 'I don't know whether to send you home or not.' 'You can please yourself,' said Lord, 'but I'll get paid for it.' We did our own job eventually. Our gaffer sent a letter off to Darlington, and Lord was right — he hadn't signed the route beyond Harrogate. He wanted someone to guide him.

Sid: Would you accept that in the old days mess-rooms were always full, you would talk about anything and everything? There was a feeling of comradeship. When the steam engine went, that went too?

Roy: Most of the drivers are out on the road all their shift, now, they don't see much of each other.

Jack: There's also been a tightening up of train working diagrams, to use the technical word. We used to have jobs where people had two hours to hang around in Leeds. You don't get that now.

Sid: Would you say the men have changed too?

Tom: Now talk's just about money and sex. Before when you passed out as a driver you'd get one person cracking on about

161

rules and regulations, another about steam engines. There's none of that now.

Roy: Years ago, this involves Charlie Wallis, he were a junior inspector in them days, I'd been on firing about four hours and he says, 'Look, Roy, you'll have to take the express to Sheffield.' I says, 'I won't.' He says, 'You'll have to, there's nobody else to do it.' So me, in bit of a paddy, filled the hole (filled the fire-box with coal) and it didn't burn. Consequently, at West Riding junction we come to an abrupt stop. No steam. We eventually gets steam but lost about twenty-odd minutes before we arrived at Sheffield. Next day I had to go to see this Mr Wallis. He says, 'I'm taking you out to see if it was your fault, to pass you out again for firing.' So I went to Sheffield again and did it all right, as it should have been the day previous. No problems. Coming back through the yard one of my mates, Peter Greenwood, says, 'He won't be taking me for a few months because I'm all right.' Peter Greenwood was with him the very next day.

Sid: Which sort of locomotive did you find the best to work on?

Ronny: I used to like the Class Rs.

Sid: Every Class R I worked on kicked and rolled all over the place.

Ronny: Well, we had a good 'un, 1217, one of the best.

Tom: Aye, but the G5 was the best, the little tank engine used on local passenger trains.

Roy: From Leeds Holbeck (on the LMS) we had the Scots, the 5Xs, the Black Fives.

Sid: Really, you're an old LMS man? Do you remember all that rivalry that used to exist? LMS men always thought the Black Fives were the best.

Roy: We have a driver here *now* whose nickname is Black Five. Black Five Nicholls. Yes, he was a Midland man.

Sid: That stemmed from pride in the company, didn't it? Why did they have that pride? It seems thin on the ground now.

Jack: It isn't there now because we're one nationalized industry.

Roy: I would never admit to an LNER man that the A3 Gresley Pacific was better than the Scot. Eventually, on the latter days of the Leeds-Glasgow run, we got the A3s, and I have to admit they were far superior. But I would never let on to the LNER lot.

Tom: In my father's day, before the war, they didn't pay any national insurance of course. There was no unemployment benefit, but once you were on the railway it was a secure job for life. My great-grandfather, grandfather and father all worked on the railways.

Sid: Do you have any children? Are they working on the railways too?

Tom: One son's still at school but the other doesn't fancy the railways. He's employed as a clerk.

Jack: When I joined from the forces all they could offer me was carriage cleaning. It was summat-or-nothing, but people often said to my mother, 'How did he get on the railways?' as if it were a great thing.

Roy: In my case I would have left school to come on the railways but my old man wouldn't let me. He'd worked shifts all the war, making tanks, so when I said 'I want to go on the railway' he said 'No, thou'll be a tailor. People will always wear clothes.' That were it. He put me into the tailoring trade. But when I'd got a few years on me back I thought well, bugger it, and I went down to Holbeck loco. I were never a train-spotter, don't get me wrong, I just wanted to come on the railway.

Ronny: But today people don't want the shift-work, and that's the great evil of it. The great deterrent.

Roy: Haven't they experienced this to some degree with those lads they got at Leeds Neville Hill — they got a great big batch of them and I think that out of the eighteen they have just two left, and of those one's father is a driver at Stafford. What I glean from that is the lads have seen shift-work and decided against it.

Tom: You see, I was brought up with shift-work, my father being a relief signalman same as yours, Sid. You thought nothing to shift-work. The only thing that deterred me a bit was I couldn't get off on a Saturday afternoon to play football. Unless you could find somebody prepared to swop.

Sid: Isn't it that there are far more attractions these days? You could live with shift-work in my day.

Roy: My eldest lad works on the railways. His problem is that on a Saturday night when he has to go to work for a ballast train job at 11 pm he can't go out with his mates beforehand, because he knows for a fact he won't be fit for duty. On Saturday nights our Scot's got to stop in. He accepts it.

Sid: But are the same calibre of people coming into railways now?

Jack: I don't think so. We've got a hell of a lot of vacancies on the branch on the signalling side. On the level crossing we've two young lads started, came through a Youth Opportunity scheme. Now then. They come along and in wintertime they work overtime every other Sunday, in summertime every Sunday. They've been on a month and they say straightaway — they don't want to work Sundays, and they don't want to work rest days when we're pushed.

Ronny: The wage structure's got a lot to do with it. I'll never forget Smith at Starbeck. He was a labourer. He was sat on the barrow one morning and the gaffer passed him. 'You haven't done much this morning, have you Smithy?' the gaffer says. 'No, not as much as they'll bloody pay me.'

Jack: I came on the railway with reluctance, but the railway has been good to me. And these people who have left have either come back or want to come back. Life's too short to be miserable, so you either get out or you stick it out. The railway is a bloody good firm to work for. No disrespect to you Roy, a lot of people who moan about the railway are the first to want to get their family on it. In my opinion the only thing wrong with the railway is the management and the unions as well...

Tom: In 1947 at Starbeck there were forty-seven cleaners paid off because of shortage of traffic, so they said. Six weeks after, they sent a letter to the same lads asking them to come back. About thirty of them did. They wanted to be on the railway, but it wouldn't happen today.

Sid: I used to work trains round here. I can't help noticing when I go around today that Starbeck locomotive depot has gone, the line from here to Ripon to Northallerton has gone, Ripon station makes your heart bleed. And when you go to Leeds, which used to be a thriving, bustling train centre, you can hardly believe it's the same place... What sort of service are you giving to the travelling public nowadays?

Tom: It's worse, definitely, than before. From Leeds to Harrogate in the old days you had about forty-three minutes with an old steamer, stopping at all stations including Holbeck. Now we've thirty-nine minutes and two fewer stops, driving the diesel units. Once it was thirty-two minutes, but we've gradually fallen back to thirty-nine.

Sid: Yes, I have noticed if you leave the main inter-city routes there's been a serious decline in the quality of service.

Jack: When diesels came to Harrogate all the trains, with the exception of the last one at night, went from here to Leeds Central to Bradford Exchange and through to Manchester Victoria. Some went through to Liverpool, too. It was a bloody good service. Admittedly, it was a long way round to go to Manchester. The train stopped everywhere on the Halifax-Todmorden line. They could have still carried on with that service but now it has gone, and only because of diesel diagramming. A lot of people don't like changing trains, worrying about connections, and they liked being able to get on here in the knowledge they would arrive in Liverpool. It didn't matter how long it took. First the service was restricted to Bradford, then we knocked Bradford to Leeds off and now we've just got Leeds. On Bank Holiday Mondays Harrogate station used to be packed. The changes have all come since diesel diagrams were brought in. We've lost hundreds of thousands of pounds in revenue...

Sid: If we'd electrified instead of wasting money on diesels wouldn't things have been better?

Ronny: Yes, it's got to come, has electrification.

Jack: I understand they're going to bring some new sets (carriages) in with hydraulic doors, like the London tube. Why the hell didn't they do that the first time round?

Ronny: When it was first introduced the West Riding diesel service was Bradford to Leeds, Leeds to Harrogate and Harrogate to Knaresborough. There were thousands of people used it to Harrogate. Thousands.

Sid: Do railwaymen work as hard today as they did in your early days?

Jack: No, definitely not. When I started as a carriage-washer we began at 3 am and finished at ten to twelve, with half an hour meal-break. The other shift was 6 am to 3.20 pm with an hour for dinner booked off. On a Saturday it was 6 am to 11.20 am. You had your own coach to clean, a Pullman, and it had to be clean, no argument. They brought you back if it wasn't right. All hand-cleaned, not long brush, out on the sidings in the dark. If we did well I think we got six shillings and thruppence bonus. The Pullman in particular had to be immaculate. My coach was number sixty-nine, all steel, it was a beauty built in 1926. It had to be hand-polished, then you had to do your brasses, and you were on it from 4 am to 9 am. The Harrogate Pullman had eight coaches. The Yorkshire Pullman, from Leeds, survived until 1974.

Sid: But when did standards of cleanliness really begin to deteriorate?

Jack: As soon as they introduced this so-called work-study bonus scheme. In January 1962. Cleaners went from six shillings and thruppence a week bonus to twenty-five shillings. It was money given away.

Tom: In the old steam days I used to start at 6 am. Left the shed at 6.15 to work the 6.30 stopping train to Leeds. Leeds to Selby via Weatherby. Loose off. Shunt your train. Into the shed. Coal and water, clean your fire, a bloody sandwich in one hand and a shovel in the other. Out. Back on to your train. Shunt it. Back round to Leeds. Get water again. Then back to

166

Harrogate. You got down to the shed about twenty minutes before your day was up and the shed master would say, 'Just time to clean the smoke-box, laddie.' You'd done fifty-two stops and they wouldn't give you twenty minutes.

Sid: One thing I noticed in the early years of the war was the number of Form Ones for petty discipline problems flying around.

Jack: Even in my time if you came five minutes late in the morning you were stopped the time, and you lost your bloody bonus as well. There are very few Form Ones these days. I can only remember two cases recently at Harrogate, issued to guards for leaving ticket money in a case in the mess-room.

Sid: It's a cleaner job, a better job, but what about the shift-work? In recent years have efforts been made to make it easier?

Roy: Well, they're trying to minimize it, aren't they, the flexible rostering helps cut out the early-hour starts, the worst part of shift-work.

Jack: It also means more long weekends and more time off in clumps. And more social hours. Take the twenty-week roster for guards (drivers are very similar). Out of those twenty weeks there's four weeks of late turns — the earliest late turn finishing at 10 pm and the latest late turn at midnight. It's a bloody doddle. It's office hours.

Tom: In the old days at York out of thirty-six turns in the link we had nineteen turns straight off the belt end, going to work between 7 pm to 2 am. The other turns started between 7 am and 2 pm. You hardly got a rest day. You finished at 7 am Sundays and out again at 1 am Monday morning. That's all gone now.

Roy: As a passed cleaner I spent many years at Holbeck. Then I got registered as a fireman and my first links were with the Carlisle lodging. The next week you might be on the Birmingham lodging link. Coupled with these two lodging links the only turns you had were afternoons. There were twelve of us in this link as firemen. I said to my mates, 'I wonder why we can't have a week of days?' So I went to the

LDC and said, 'Look, can't you stick us a week of days in?' He replies: 'The Carlisle and Brummagem link has always been like that, and will always remain like that.' When they knocked the lodging off that improved my life no end. One of the Birmingham lodging houses was Saltley, right agin the gasworks. If you weren't tired when you got in the gas soon used to put you to sleep.

Tom: On those York turns all the drivers on that link signed a petition to put to the LDC to split them up with the other seventeen turns. We were politely told to mind our own bloody business.

Sid: You enjoy better all-round conditions today, so why is it there's a staff shortage?

Jack: Sometimes you can get more on social security. We had a character recently, well-liked, a nice lad, with six children. He got a shunting job after only three years, very lucky too, but as soon as he lost his regular overtime he gave his notice in. Said the world was upside down, because what with all the social security benefits he was better off on the dole. He was forty-four. He'll never work again, never. His self-respect will have gone when his family has grown up.

Roy: At the finish he didn't want work, having found out that he could get sufficient to keep him and his family on the dole.

Jack: On another tack, since nationalization I've seen a huge number of bosses' jobs created. At one time there were five assistant general-managers based at York, all living at Harrogate and catching the 8.15. The whole management system is top-heavy.

Tom: Sometimes these managers come up and you don't know who you're talking to. In the old days you knew who all the inspectors were.

Roy: There are a lot of young lads coming into this job now with university degrees. This has been my university for thirty-two years. If they're going to argue with me I'm not saying I'm brilliant but I can hold my own.

Tom: I had an experience on a train from York. All the

managers were on it when I overshot Knaresborough station and finished on the viaduct. The guard waved us back. The following night when I'm stood in York station they all come up, 'We don't want any extra mileage tonight, young man.'

Sid: You must have worked with some characters during your time on railways?

Roy: In my early days firing the Ossett Lane shunting pilot, there was an old shunter who spent his time talking to the wagons — 'Where were you last week? You went to Leicester last week, didn't you? You should have been here yesterday. I don't know where *you've* been but come on, off you go' — as he shunted them into a different siding. He knew them all. The men used to call him Tootles. I can't remember his real name for the life of me.

Tom: Like old Frank Braithwaite, working a train from Leeds with a Class R loco, he would always stand in the corner up against the boiler end talking to the engine — 'Come on lass, you can bloody do it. Come on lass, get your bloody toes stuck in,' all the way to Harrogate. You wouldn't say that to a diesel. If anything went wrong with a steamer you could find what it was in five minutes but it took twenty-four hours to put right. If anything goes wrong with a diesel it takes twenty-four hours to find what's wrong and five minutes to put it right.

Sid: Didn't most of the funny railway incidents happen on rural branch lines?

Tom: Yes we got some of the early diesels, Class 350s, at Starbeck to run up the Masham branch line. George Harris was the driver; he knew the 350 but he didn't know the road, so they sent me as a second man to conduct him. It was a single line to Masham and the farmers as usual were in their heaven during the summer waiting for you to set their corn fields alight with your sparks so they could claim compensation. George said, 'If anybody wants to know owt about engines send them to me; but if anybody wants to know about t'rules I'll send them to thee. I know bugger all about rules and regulations.'

So we gets up to Tanfield, the first station after Melmerby

and we does our shunting, goes into platform. Eventually the porter comes out and says, 'The station gaffer wants driver in't office.' 'Tha's better go, Tom, it's no good to me, I can only talk about engines.' So when I goes the police are in there. The station gaffer says to me, 'Isn't the driver coming?' 'No,' I says, 'he sent me instead. I'm the man concerned anyway, because I was the conductor. What's the trouble?' 'There's Mr Green sitting here complaining about his field of corn being set on fire.' 'His corn? My God,' I says, 'that's quick, isn't it?' (We'd only been at the station about fifteen or twenty minutes.) 'But I think he's barking up the wrong tree. He wants to get his glasses on.' This police sergeant warns me, 'Be careful.' 'Well,' I says, 'we haven't set it on fire.' He says, 'Are you sure?' 'Perfectly sure,' I replies. 'Couldn't a spark have done it?' I says, 'Will you come out on the platform, please?' So out we goes. I says, 'Look, how can we set the bloody thing on fire? — we've got a diesel.' 'Bloody hell,' says the sergeant, 'this bugger's trying to work a quick'un. Right, I've finished with you.' What happened after that I don't know. But I went back and told George. 'Ho, ho, ho, that's capped the bugger.'

Sid: I didn't know farmers were up to that.

Tom: I'll tell you another thing they used to do. You know the route you used to work up to Leyburn and Garsdale on the Wensleydale line. They used to put bottles on fences and walls so you could have a throw at them with bits of coal, and when you'd gone by they would come to pick coal up.

Sid: I don't know. If they ever wanted coal we used to stop and give them it — for a couple of rabbits.

Jack: I remember an incident with a bear. It was 1968 and I'd been at York only about a fortnight in the trains office, charting trains, but I'd already got to know one or two people in the divisional office at Leeds.

One day Leeds rang me up and said, 'Jack, I'm sorry about this, but you're the only bloke I can contact. I'll tell you what it is, I don't know if you can help me or not. I've got a bear...'

I says, 'A what?'

'A bear, in the passenger train guard's brake van coming from Poole in Dorset tonight. It will have been tranquillized but not crated. It's due to arrive in York at 1800 and it's to go forward at 2320 to Dundee. Can you arrange for it to be examined, to see if it needs another tranquillizer via a local vet?'

'Well,' I says, 'I'm a stranger at York.'

'Don't worry, you'll find the consignee's name and address on the collar to send the vet's bill to.'

So with that I rang the station-master, Thompson, and said, 'I've just had a notification from Leeds that they're sending a bear...'

'A what...?'

'A *bear.*'

'Oh.'

'What I'm after,' I says, 'is do you know any vets locally?'

'There's one on Blossom Street, Mr So-and-so, I'll get you the number.'

So I then rang the vet. The receptionist answered the phone.

'Good afternoon,' I said, 'this is British Railways at York, what it is, I've got a bear coming...'

'A what?'

'A *bear*' — I were getting pig-sick of this — 'what I'm after is do you think your boss could possibly...'

'Just a minute,' she says, 'I don't want to get too involved, I'll put you through to Mr So-and-so.'

He picks up the phone and says, 'Good afternoon, can I help you?'

'I've just had a word with your receptionist and what it is, it's British Railways at York here and I've got a bear coming...'

'A what?'

'A bear.'

'Oh.'

'It may want tranquillizing...' I told him the story so far.

'What time will you want me?' he asks, without more ado.

'If you come to the ticket barrier at 1800, when the train's due I'll get the assistant station-master to meet you in.'

'Yes, that'll be all right,' he says.

So with that I rang the ASM at York and says, 'Oh, Jack [Jack Craggs he was, dead and gone God bless him] short and sharp. I've just been advised that there's a bear coming from Poole.'

'A what?'

'A *bear*. This bloody bear's coming' — and I gave him the story too.

'Yes, I'll meet the vet, all right,' says Jack.

'Well,' I says 'I shan't see you until tomorrow so will you put in your ASM's log if everything was all right?'

'Right-oh, Jack,' he says and that were it.

So the next day I looked at the log. 'Bear arrived. No tranquillizer required. All in order.'

That were it again... until 1400 when Jack Craggs arrived on duty.

'What a bloody going on,' he says. 'For a start, you told me that bear were crated.'

'It *was* crated, wasn't it?' I knew it weren't but I daren't say owt.

'Oh no it wasn't,' says Jack.

'It must have been a small 'un,' I add.

'You what? It were nearly as big as me,' says Jack. 'He were all shackled to the rings in the brake, staring at us from the corner. He looked to be lively. I'd taken Maurice Harland with me into the van with the vet.' This Maurice Harland stuttered.

'Now Maurice,' I says, 'get the name and address off the collar for this gentleman here.' M-M-Mr C-C-Craggs,' says Maurice, 'Y-y-you're the boss, b-but I'm refusing to do it.'

'Go on, it won't hurt you.'

'N-n-*no*. Not b-loody likely.'

Bear's there, still shackled in corner.

With that the vet says, 'Oh, I'll do it.' Then he looked at the bear and reports, 'Oh, I think it's all right, doesn't need tranquillizing...'

'Oh, lovely.'

With that they got it out of the van and shackled it to a pillar on platform fifteen. That was it for the York staff, but I wasn't any too popular for weeks.

EPITAPH FOR A RAILWAYMAN

Jack: Anyone who has to do with staffing on the railway like me is a miserable bugger. Staff clerks and roster-clerks have all the worries in the world. Anyways, this staff clerk died. Some guards, a couple of drivers and porters got together and said, 'Look, we'll try to save his widow a bob or two, we'll act as pall bearers.' So the six who volunteered were shouldering the coffin. As they walked into church they heard a knock on the sides. 'Hello...' a voice said, 'How many's carrying this coffin?' 'Six of us,' one driver replied. 'Well, I'm only paying for four.' He must have been a Yorkshireman.

TALES OF A TRACK-WALKER

Then I visited Harry Hartley, recently retired NUR branch secretary at Northallerton. Harry, a magistrate in my father's tradition, had worked on the permanent-way from 1946, including a long spell as track-walker on the Wensleydale branch line.

Harry Hartley: I left the Army in 1946, after several years as a prisoner of war. I went on a building site hoping to become a bricklayer but this proved unacceptable to the unions at the time because I wasn't fully trained. So I started looking around.

I belong to a long line of railwaymen — my father, my uncles and grandfather all worked on the railway — all in North Yorkshire. My dad was at Leyburn. We went to Leyburn when I was thirteen, so I finished schooling there. I've always classed Leyburn as my home town; my brothers and sisters are still there. My father worked there from 1930 until he died. Both my parents are buried there. I've lived near Northallerton for twenty-three years now, myself.

Anyway, in 1946 I went to see the railway engineers' department at Darlington where I was living, having got married while in the Army. I was still in my Royal Engineers uniform. I didn't know, but there was a big connection between the railway engineers and the Royal Engineers. Apparently, in the days of the Territorial Army in the 1930s a lot of TA engineers' regiments came from railways, just as the Signal and Telegraphs people always went to the Royal Signal Corps. Anyway, going there in uniform wearing RE flashes I were made. I was given a job in a matter of days.

This vacancy proved to be at Oaktree, between Eaglescliffe and Darlington just near Dinsdale Station on the Stockton line. I started there on the permanent-way. The first morning I reported, the ganger introduced me to the other fellows. Then, for a couple of hours, we two just sat in the hut talking. He was pointing out to me what they did on the railways, for safety and everything else.

It just so happened that day that somebody reported a pair of fish plates broken (fish plates joined lengths of track together). I was sent with Jack to change them. Off we went with a fish plate apiece and a spanner to do the job.

In the afternoon I joined the gang as one of the gangmen. We were lifting and packing joints with ballast under the sleepers. The ganger who was looking on, says to me, 'Come here. Get down on your knees and tell me where that track wants repairing.' This was my first day, don't forget. He did well for me did that fellow. From then on I just joined the gang.

Sid: In those days permanent-way gangs were small, with just a few miles of track to look after ...

Harry: We covered from Dinsdale station down to Eaglescliff station, about five miles of double track. We also had a few sidings at Urlay Nook to look after. Nowadays, apart from station areas, gangs are bigger, mobile, transported around a much bigger area in vans to work with permanent-way machinery on site.

Sid: Is that better, though?

Harry: No. If you've got ten or twelve men in one of these vans working, let's say, only ten miles away, they are travelling one and a half hours a day — so that's fifteen hours a day dead time.

Sid: Haven't they different equipment?

Harry: In the old days we used to jack the track up with a Simplex jack with teeth and steps. But in later years we used these flat hydraulic things which fit completely under the rail. If you are caught by a train with one of these under the track the train doesn't hit it, it just squashes it down; the old jacks which stood proud above the rail, could do damage to equipment under the train.

Sid: How did you check the track for safety?

Harry: It was inspected every day by a patrol man, sometimes called a track-walker. He was required to put a report in each day on maybe ten to twelve miles which he walked, covering at least two gangs' lines. If the defects he noticed were serious they were corrected immediately. Otherwise they were done when the gang next went into that area.

On Saturday mornings the ganger would walk our length of track himself. He would then plan his workload for the next week. At the same time there was a standing card, like a yearly calendar, for the seasonal jobs. In the summer you didn't lift off the track unless it was really necessary because of the heat, which might buckle the track if it were disturbed. In winter you wouldn't bother to cut grass — you might burn the dead grass off on a dry day. In November, when the weather was expected to be bad and foggy your calendar said fences and guttering, things like that. Round about March was always the time of year for oiling fish plates. You would take them off, oil the back and inspect the rail ends ready for expansion and contraction during the warm summer months. It was interesting work but always put on one side if more urgent jobs came up.

Sid: You had no protecting clothing then?

Harry: Not even overalls were issued to permanent-way gangs. We had to supply our own.

Sid: That was why you went in as soon as it rained?

Harry: We used to have one old boy who prayed — 'Oh Lord, if it lies in thy power send it down till half-past fower.' (We started at 7.12 am and finished at 5 pm.) Saturday mornings we worked four hours to make forty-eight altogether. Sundays were not part of our normal working week then, but there was always a lot of Sunday work available. All the heavy work like re-laying was done on Sundays.

Sid: Sunday's work had to be completed on that day, didn't it?

Harry: Yes, the engineers were given a possession time, say midnight Saturday to midnight Sunday, and they had to plan the work they could get through in that time while trains were cancelled or diverted.

Sid: That's why permanent-way workers always got double time on Sundays, because of the pressure on them.

Sid: Was it dangerous?

Harry: I've seen some dangerous things done. We had to load sixty-foot flat-bottomed rails by hand, for instance. They would probably allocate twenty men for the job but if, as often, two didn't turn up on a Sunday morning it was hard work. And you weren't lifting off a level floor — you had to pick them up from a ballast shoulder. Your feet could start slipping. It was really dangerous work. I'm pleased to say this side of it has now been replaced by machines. I wouldn't like to be holding rails with some of the blokes we have these days.

Sid: Were permanent-way men more experienced then?

Harry: Well, they grew up with it then. They knew nothing else. Machinery has taken a lot of the hard work out — and the navvies who built the railways worked a lot harder than we did — but the sad thing about machinery is that it has done away with a lot of men.

Sid: In those huts where you sheltered I believe you had no washing facilities. How did you wash?

Harry: In 1946 soap was still rationed. We used to get a small amount issued. It was hard stuff anyway, you couldn't get a lather out of it. To get hot water we used to heat up a fish plate in the stove until it was red-hot then plunge it into a bucket of water!

Sid: You had hard winters to face too...

Harry: Yes — 1947/8 was the winter of the big snow storms. I was on snow duty for about twelve weeks. I was one of two delegated to Urlay Nook, near Darlington. We worked fourteen-hour shifts, one week of days another of nights. When the snow was really bad it was impossible to keep the points free of snow and ice. So we started one at each end of the points; when the person from the facing end had got his gap clear we pushed the rail over and gave the signalman the tip; then we used to clamp them. The train would push the trailing end over as it went through.

Sid: I was on the footplate at that time. I remember they had to call the Army in up Barnard Castle way to help clear the line.

Harry: Yes. They tried jet engines mounted on wagons to blow the snowdrifts away. The problem was they buckled the rails and set fire to the sleepers. Or they melted the snow, which quickly froze and you could not get at the other snow for ice.

Sid: Did you have any protective clothing issued for snow work?

Harry: Just a heavy top-coat. I think they were mainly for fogging duties — standing out at fog posts with flags and a coal brazier. You could be called out any time in the night for that duty. After a certain time on the permanent-way you were trained by a signalman on flagging and fogging rules. You obviously had to know how to read signals. If you were on a 'distance' signal you had a detonator on the track, which you only removed when the signal was at green. If it was yellow (caution) you left the detonator on and showed a red flag. Sometimes if the train got too near to you you didn't bother to take the detonator off anyway — you let them have it. That could be dangerous because bits would fly from these detonators. I once saw a bloke get his eye cut underneath. Working on the permanent-way always has been the most dangerous of railway jobs. Every year permanent-way men are killed, mainly by rolling-stock.

I left Eaglescliffe and eventually went to Aysgarth on the Wensleydale branch as a track-walker. I was there for ten years. In between I went to the Charity length at Darlington, nearer to home, on the Bishop Auckland branch past Darlington North Road station. I went there as a sub-ganger, even though I'd been on the railway only two years. The old ganger there was getting on in years but thought he had six months to do until one day the permanent-way inspector called him aside. When he returned he had tears in his eyes. He didn't, it seemed, know his own birthday. He was six months over his time, and the permanent-way inspector had given him three weeks to finish. He was one of those blokes who used to say, 'By God, I wish my time was up. I'm sick of this.' But when it came to leaving it really broke his heart.

I was at Darlington for about two years, then went up to

Aysgarth. My job was to walk eleven and a half miles of the Wensleydale branch line from Redmire station to Hawes station every day, rain or shine. In really bad weather the ganger was supposed to walk with me. But the fellow said, 'Ah'm not going, thou's not going' — so we didn't. I took the good with the bad when I was up there. I started in February 1950. For that first week it just poured the whole time. I was soaking wet every day. The old boys up there told me it was the worst flood they had had in thirty years. I thought, 'My God, this is a right baptism.' So I stuck the job.

Sid: What did you do? — you didn't just look at the track?

Harry: You had to key up the sides of the track, keep an eye on the fencing. Then you had to watch the farmers. When I first went I was warned by the local permanent-way inspector to watch out for dead sheep being left on the line, getting run over and the farmers claiming compensation. I thought I would play these blokes at their own game. More than once I found sheep that *had* been killed by the train dead by the track. Then I would get a spade and bury them, saying nowt. I could go to places even now where there's a sheep buried that nobody knows about.

Some farmers were in the habit of kicking fence rails off and letting their sheep in to graze on the banks. One time there had been a special train on a Sunday — to bring racehorses from Scotland to Garsdale, then on to Leyburn for Middleham where the famous stables are. The train ran into a flock of eighty-three sheep. It didn't kill many, but when the footplate crew stopped and looked up the fence rails had been kicked off by the farmer. Of course, that farmer never claimed anything, he daren't. He was stuck with it.

Another farmer, a bit further up the line, had a one-horse grass-cutter. He was standing there by some crossing gates. I said, 'Come on, if you want to cross you're safe.' He said, 'No, I'm not going across. I'm waiting till you get out of the bloody road then I'm going to cut some lineside grass for myself.'

After scheduled passenger services stopped on the branch in 1954 I was still walking the line, but only two days a week up to Hawes. The other three days I came down the other way towards Spennithorne, on the Northallerton side of Leyburn.

They cut out the middle track-walker on the line, which of course carried on stone train services from the Redmire quarry.

Over the years I got to know the windiest and the wettest places on the branch. We did have line-side cabins, but if you knew you were in for bad weather you just got suitably prepared. By then we were issued with proper protective clothing — waterproofs and leggings.

Sid: Did you measure your walk exactly with the sleeper ends?

Harry: Yes. I got used to it.

In 1958 the bonus scheme came in for permanent-way men. That did away with a lot of jobs. I never liked it. Men were thrown out of a job, it were blood for money in a lot of cases.

At about that time a vacancy occurred at Danby Wiske on the main line between Northallerton and Darlington. Nobody seemed to be interested in it. So one day the area supervisor said to me, 'Look you're on a dead-end job up here, why not come down to Northallerton?' 'Well', I says, 'I realize it's a dead-end job but I'm not keen to move.' We had five kids by then, and we lived in a cottage at Aysgarth. But Jean, the eldest one, was about six months off leaving school and there was no possibility of a job for her up there. So I said we would consider it.

This was a ganger's job at Danby Wiske, a grade higher than I was at the time. I met the supervisor a couple of days later and told him I would take the job on condition that nobody else wanted it. I was never one to chase promotion, preferring to make my own life around a little job. Nobody did want it. So I took it in 1960 and stayed on that length with two good mates (sad to say, they're both dead now) until 1966, about the time that the machines came in and working practices changed.

In the six years I was at Danby Wiske on the main line I won the prize three times for the best-kept length of track. I got it twice, then missed it once, then got it again. The year I missed it Peter Chalmers, our boss, the engineer at Darlington, came to see us one day. I respected him greatly, he knew exactly what was going on and you could always talk to him. So I said to him, 'How come we haven't got the prize this year?' He said, 'I don't know, it's just the way the points were added up I suppose.' I said, 'I'll tell you why we didn't get it — to stop us winning it three years in a row!'

Sid: Did winning the track award give you a sense of pride in the job?

Harry: It certainly did. One of the sad things about the new way of working was that all that went out of the window.

Sid: Did the water troughs on your length create any problems?

Harry: Well, there was spillage on the north-bound trains. I always said the spillage of water was taking the life out of the steel. Of course, the track has now been changed and the water troughs used by the old steam loco have gone.

Sid: But because trains move faster today, the standard of track maintenance and permanent-way has to be better than in your early days.

Harry: It's long-welded, which means no joints. Joints were always your trouble on the permanent-way. That and drainage. Now they've put huge amounts of ballast under the track — they've maybe lifted it up two feet in places — so you have better drainage. We always used to joke and say, 'Keep a bad joint outside the plate-layer's cabin so that when the engine tender strikes the joint coal is dropped. That was your main coal supply!

Sid: In your early days there was the pick, the shovel, the barrow and the jack. That was about your lot. Now today, what do you use?

Harry: The basic tools are much the same. Except that the jacks are hydraulic now. And, of course, the work that we used to do packing under the rails is now performed by special tamping machines. I used to operate one of them. We also have ballast-regulating machines, so if a permanent-way train goes through tipping ballast and it doesn't come off even, or you tip too much or too little, these machines can pick up and re-distribute the ballast. Some machines have a little brush on the back sweeping all the surplus ballast off the sleepers making a tidy job of it.

Sid: So it's highly mechanized, the old type of permanent-way man is gone — and the job's much better paid?

Harry: Yes, it has been regraded, certainly, but we have a lot of responsibility. At certain times we can move our machines up to fifteen miles without a conductor. I was this kind of 'driver' — I passed out over certain lines. We went through the rules and regulations with the loco men. We've had loco men come to us and discovering one of these machines for the first time — 'How the hell do you sort that out?' they ask. They drive trains at 120 mph but they don't like these complicated permanent-way machines. They're not small, either, they're as big as a loco sometimes. So why shouldn't we have their rate of pay? All they've got to do is stop and start...

Sid: Is there the same comradeship around today?

Harry: There's a certain amount, but I wouldn't say there's the same. You get a different kind of fellow coming on. I've said many a time to my friends that railwaymen are dying fast. These blokes who come on today — very few of them are honest railwaymen. Railwaymen were, in my opinion, the same as miners, really dedicated to the job. Our fathers, grandfathers, uncles, spent their whole lives on the railways. They were really dedicated and interested in the job. Some of them today couldn't care less.

Sid: Everyone I talk to seems to think the same.

Harry: I've said for years that if anyone showed any interest in the railways the management's there to knock it out of them. They don't want you to be interested in the job.

Sid: Is that because the industry's having a rough ride, or is it because different kinds of people are coming on?

Harry: No. I blame middle management. The BR Board have good intentions, but they delegate too much power to regions and areas. It's these people in the middle who just couldn't care less. If you have a complaint, you ring someone up, they say, 'I know nothing about it.' You send a letter in — it gets lost. They always pass the buck. Over the years I have always advised anyone who has run foul of middle management: 'Sit still. We'll go to the top, to the Divisional Engineer.' I guarantee you'll hear no more about it.

Then there's unwritten rules. You can go to areas where the

bloke in charge says, 'Oh, we have a rule here — we do this, that or the other.' I say to them, 'Look, if that rule isn't in the book I don't want to know about it.' Any unwritten rule will backfire on you. You only have to sit and wait and it will come back to you. You used to get a lot of this. You would say something to the supervisor — 'See about my holidays or my lieu days,' or whatever. He'd come back: 'They say at Newcastle, they say at Darlington...' I used to turn round and ask, 'Who's *they*? Put a name to it. If you're not putting your own to the decision put somebody's. I want to know who *they* are.' I used to advise the lads if they sent a letter which seemed to have got lost to pin the next one to their timesheets.

No, incompetence is due to middle management. A lot of young blokes these days with engineering degrees haven't a clue about practical work. The wiser ones will go on a job, tell you what they want doing, and get out of the way. The other type comes knowing everything in the book. You say to him, 'Right. From now on *you* do it', and he hasn't a clue.

Sid: Do you take more precautions these days now that trains are going 120 mph — do you have double safeguards?

Harry: Where it's necessary, yes; in general, no. If there are curves we do get extra men. There are also curve warning systems — the nearest one to here is on the main curve at Thirsk. If a gang is working there, or even the patrolman is going through, he switches on the system at the beginning of the curve. Then any train coming into that curve, from either end, sets an alarm off. It works from the track. So when the permanent-way men hear the alarm they know a train is coming, though they may not know from where. When the patrolman gets to the other end, if he's on his own he switches the alarm off again. If a gang's working there all day the alarm will be kept on all day. There will also be a lookout man to see the direction of trains.

Sid: Weren't you personally a guinea pig for high-visibility clothing?

Harry: Yes — that was in about 1966 when we came off the lengths and I went back to track-walking. I was walking from

Northallerton to Croft (near Darlington) at the time, for about a year. I was on LDC, the local rep for permanent-way men. The chief accident prevention officer came out one day for a meeting. This chap said he wanted someone to try out a high-visibility jacket they were experimenting with. Being a track-walker, I volunteered. I wore it for quite a while. It was obvious that drivers could see me better. They were blowing their whistles a lot further back. Funnily enough, they also got gangers to travel in the cab of the loco from Northallerton to Darlington to observe me wearing this thing, to see what the driver saw, trying to educate the permanent-way men into accepting the new clothing. A lot of them didn't want to know, so the idea was to pass the message down through the gangers. Now, you have to wear high-visibility clothing. It's in the rule book.

Sid: But it's amazing how men try to get round safety measures.

Harry: There was a case recently of someone sacked for not wearing his high-visibility jacket, after three warnings. He claimed unfair dismissal, but he got no sympathy.

Sid: In the old days I remember officers' specials, with permanent-way engineers, inspecting the track. Do these still run?

Harry: Yes. They have a special Diesel Multiple Unit now. The last one I rode on was an old coach pushed by a steam engine. You would set off from Darlington with all the gangers on board from Darlington to Northallerton or maybe York. As you approached your own length you had to sit next to the engineer right at the front. You were on the spot — he would ask, 'what about this, what about that?' You could throw questions at him too, especially if you wanted materials.

Permanent-way men were jacks-of-all-trades. If anything happened it was always the permanent-way men who got called out. The signalmen would stand there watching out of the window, from their warm cabin, while you were wet and cold outside. Permanent-way men were always on call. I've been at football matches at Darlington when they used to come round with a board with your name on it. When I first started you had to leave your name at the cabin if you were going off to the pictures — in emergencies your name would be flashed up on the screen.

You got nothing extra for stand-by — only if you were called out. You could refuse to come out — but you were expected to do it. There were those who abused the system. I can remember one cabin, it's gone now, where they had the signal lights out in the best of weather. If a signal light went out you could be called out to go and light it.

Sid: On the railway you often have to take your own initiative. How adequate is the rule book?

Harry: I've always believed that if you work to the railway rule book you'll never get anything done. One thing ties another up. But if you make a mistake and it goes to an inquiry they sit there with the rule book and say, 'Didn't you carry out that rule?' If you didn't you are in the cart. It doesn't matter how many times you've got away with it and broken the rule.

Sid: What was your area then, on this tamping machine you operated?

Harry: Mainly Yorkshire, main lines and branch lines.

Sid: Are standards higher on the main line?

Harry: Well, we did each job as well as we could. But where you might go on to the main line twice a year tamping you could visit others only once every two years.

Sid: You didn't have responsibility for tunnels and bridges?

Harry: The track in them, but not the tunnels themselves.

Sid: I remember the men who worked in Bramhope Tunnel between Leeds and Harrogate, used to wear moleskins because they were constantly in the wet.

Harry: There was a full gang in there, you know. That was their life, inside, working in that tunnel. I could never have done that. They got a tunnel allowance, but not much. Each large tunnel had its own gang.

Sid: So in many ways life is much better, now?

Harry: Oh, yes, there are big improvements on the railways but it's sad that they have cost a lot of fellows their jobs. The machines have inevitably put other fellows out of work.

Sid: New technologies and closures. A lot of the lines that you worked on have gone. Are you glad you've recently reached retirement age?

Harry: I am in a way. I've had a fair crack, thirty-seven years, and when you finish on the railways at sixty-five you know you're getting on. But to find a better job or a more interesting one, I don't know who I would have worked for, or, among the older workmen, better mates to work with. Going back to the earlier days — you could hang your jacket up with all your possessions in it, including your wage packet, and nothing would be touched. Today you can't put a cigarette down without somebody nicking it. In the old days you never thought of having lockers; nowadays you have lockers which get broken into.

Sid: In the old days you knew your job, you did your job and that was it.

Harry: I never went home at night fearing that something might happen on the job I'd worked at during the day. As far as I know I always left the job satisfactory.

Sid: And most railwaymen were like that...

Harry: That's it, they were a race on their own. Two more things. I can't prove anything, but I suspect I went a long way towards changes coming into being. Nowadays, if a driver blows his whistle at you on the track you are supposed to acknowledge his signal. I believe I was the instigator of that years and years ago when I was track-walking up the Wensleydale single line. All the old drivers like Dick Pashby and George Raine always used to blow, they were good. When they blew at me I would acknowledge it. I like to think that I started something there, which they passed on by talking to their mates and superiors, or the LDC representatives and gradually worked through the system until it became a rule.

One time I was caught by a Signals and Telegraph inspector track walking — I had two crocodile clips and a bit of wire, so that in an emergency all I had to do was put them across the two bond wires to cut off the track and put the signals at danger. Now the rule book says you go back a mile, put three detonators on the rail, wave a red flag and all the rest of it. But it takes you twenty minutes just to walk back. This S&T inspector, when he caught me, said, 'Don't use that contraption any more — carry out the proper rules.' Fair enough. But years later the track circuit clips came out. Just the same thing. I wonder who passed on the idea?

STOPPED BY A SWARM OF BEES

My last interesting discussion, also in Northallerton, was at the house of Ernie Alvin, a relaxed, alert eighty-five-year-old of my father's generation. Ernie joined the railway near York, where his own father was a signalman, as long ago as 1914. A signalman all his life, Ernie was auditor of the Northallerton branch and still enjoys using his railwayman's pass to travel abroad with his wife.

Ernie: I started on the railway just before the First World War broke out. I began as a lad porter at a small station called Hutton's Ambo, near Malton. My home was at Pocklington, near York. My dad took me up there — I'd be about sixteen.

Sid: That was only about a couple of years after my father, who started in 1911 then.

Ernie: Aye, I went to fight in the war and when I returned my dad, who was a signalman, saw me back into the service. I finally passed my signalling grade exams and arrived at Northallerton in 1920. I was allotted a job at Hutton's Wood signal box, south of the town; your dad once relieved me there...

Sid: That was in the days when there were fifteen signal boxes in and around Northallerton.

Ernie: Yes, and I have worked most of them, apart from the station box and the south box. I ended up at Low Gates, where your dad again relieved me, in between the wars.

Sid: Were you issued with uniforms in those days?

Ernie: Oh yes. We were the favoured grade, particularly compared with permanent-way men. When I first got a job on the railway, living at Pocklington, my school friends were very envious. 'By, you're lucky, you've got a job for life.'

Sid: Were all railwaymen proud of being on the London and North Eastern Railway?

Ernie: They were at that time.

Sid: And there must have been great volumes of traffic by rail.

Ernie: Yes, the York-Hull line was very busy in those days. And at Northallerton, too.

Sid: So you earned your money as a signalman?

Ernie: Yes, you did.

Sid: In those days Low Gates, a gate cabin, must have been catering for horses and carts over the crossing as much as motors.

Ernie: Aye. Gradually the motors took over. Inside the box things began to change, too. We began to get slightly better conditions. When I first started we had just three days' holiday a year. You hadn't any money spare to go on holiday, either. We used to put twelve hours in on a Sunday. Six am to six pm. Do you know what we got for that Sunday? A straight five pounds. You got a weekend off in every three. The normal week was six days, forty-eight hours. So in effect you got one day off every three weeks.

Sid: But did you enjoy working on the railways?

Ernie: Yes, I did. What I always thought about my father as a signalman himself was that it must be great to stop a train. That was real power.

Sid: You've stopped hundreds since yourself...

Ernie: When I was still at Hutton's Wood do you know what stopped the train? A swarm of bees. The old semaphore signals needed oil lamps, of course, and we watched them very closely with it being the main line. One light went out, so I had to stop the trains and investigate. They sent someone down from the station, a lamp-lighter. He went up the signal post, but came down quicker than he went up. Those signal lamps normally burnt seven days without attention. It was the Scots express I had to stop for the swarm of bees.

Sid: Were you always in the old manual-frame boxes, never in the more modern power boxes?

Ernie: Low Gates became half and half in later years.

Sid: Did you notice a falling off of traffic before you retired in the mid-Sixties?

Ernie: The closure of the Hawes branch made a lot of difference, especially to freight, losing all those milk trains and cattle trains and much less freight went down Teesside.

Sid: Were you one of those signalmen who wouldn't let other railwaymen into his box?

Ernie: No. We weren't supposed to allow anyone in, for good reasons. And we'd ask other grades to make sure their boots were clean. After all, we had to clean the boxes ourselves, taking it in turns.

Sid: What about cooking?

Ernie: We did a little bit. The box at Low Gates had a small oven which we sometimes used. Toilet arrangements were primitive too. But we did let the permanent-way men into the box to warm their hands on fogging duties, when they had to stand by the signals with lamps and detonators. Some of my colleagues didn't, but I wasn't as bad as that.

Sid: But the signalman did exercise some authority, didn't he?

Ernie: Oh, aye. You're the boss in that box. There were no controllers before the war, you regulated traffic as you saw fit. You and nobody else decided to give a certain train priority. The station-master was your superior, but you took the decisions yourself. If there was any resulting delay you took the responsibility.

Sid: You must remember the days of those slow Teesside freight trains. Once they set out from the Newport marshalling-yards on Teesside for York they didn't care a damn when they got back.

Ernie: Aye, those loose-coupled freight trains were only allowed to go twenty-five mph. The drivers didn't care because the longer they took the more money they made. So if you had an express coming up behind you you couldn't let them go from Northallerton because they would hold everything up. The next place you could put them inside so the express could pass would be South Otterington. If they had a twenty-minute margin they might get away with it, but if the express was held up York would be wanting an explanation.

Sid: During the war years life must have been pretty hectic for you?

Ernie: Well, you had to work in the dark all night. You could hear bombs dropping on Middlesbrough and we just sat there hoping they wouldn't get any closer, feeling our way about. I remember once we had an angry air raid warden in the box saying, 'You're showing a light.' It was the glimmering of the fire in the hearth. You got used to the dark, but I always had a heavy heart sending trains into the bombing raids on Teesside. When you got a red warning you just had to carry on.

Sid: I worked on those trains. On the footplate we carried blackout sheets to stop the glare from the fire-box. All the bombers had to do was align on the track. Sometimes you could see the flare from the fire-box for miles.

You'll remember Northallerton when it was brimming with railway traffic. It's changed a bit now, hasn't it?

Ernie: All gone. There were fifteen signal boxes at Northallerton and now there are just two — the station and Low Gates. All the crossings are now automatic barriers. When I was first at Low Gates we used to average about sixty trains, mainly freight, a shift. Nowadays there's next to nothing, and Northallerton station itself is more like a cattlepen. I went by train the other day and I couldn't believe the state of the station.

Sid: For anyone coming into Northallerton on the A167 along Boroughbridge Road, the station used to dominate the skyline in the old days. There's nothing left now...

Ernie: No, it's terrible. You can't understand it.

Sid: Was your grandfather a railwayman too?

Ernie: No. He was a farmer.

Sid: Like my great-grandfather — the same generation. Can you recall my grandfather?

Ernie: Yes, mainly as a passenger guard going up the Wensleydale branch. He was a nice fellow. I knew your grandmother as well.

Sid: You were the NUR Northallerton branch auditor?

Ernie: Yes. Oliver Ellis was the first branch secretary I remember, with your dad as his assistant. Oliver was a signalman, too, and a magistrate. My father was a signalman at Pocklington, about fifteen miles outside York. He'd been there all his life. He was secretary of the Market Weighton NUR branch. He joined me. He paid my first subscription. 'You're in the union now, you've got a card, keep it up.' I did.

Sid: Signalmen tended to be branch secretaries because they were good with the pen. Take the Northallerton branch. Every secretary that I remember — George Playforth, Oliver Ellis, my own father, were all signalmen.

Ernie: My father could do branch work in his signal box because the line was relatively quiet.

Sid: Yes, what he had was a little office provided by the railway company. Busier boxes were different, but I can remember father taking his typewriter to the box on a Sunday.

Ernie: I was a member of the NUR for fifty years and proud to be a member.

Sid: So the NUR in Northallerton, whether the town agreed with them or not politically, was of some standing, with a tradition of public service. And yet this Tory town was not favourably disposed towards trade unions and what we stood for.

190

But if you had your time over again would you start on the railways?

Ernie: Not as things are now. In the old days we were all one happy company. There's nothing like that now.

Sid: Did you ever think you'd live to see the day when Northallerton was stripped of its railway heritage?

Ernie: Oh, no, I didn't. My wife and I were on the train to York the other day when a woman doing a passenger survey came along asking if we had any complaints. 'Aye,' I said, 'I've got hundreds of them.' She left us. It's different altogether, now. I never expected that things would deteriorate as they have done. We've known the railway in its good days.

Sid: Are you enjoying your retirement?

Ernie: Yes. The nicest thing they ever did was form the railwaymen's touring club. We've been with that several times, all over Europe, and that was a lovely thing. We have even been to Canada, travelling right across the continent by train on a free pass.

I can certainly agree with Ernie and his wife that to travel across Canada by train is the trip of a lifetime.

I can well remember on one visit to Canada with my wife Joan, taking the two-day train journey over the Rockies from Banff to Vancouver. This was during the Canadian Fall (Autumn) and the views and the colours were breathtaking.

9 Reflections on Life at the Top

Coming back to the North has meant a complete readjustment for me. After living in the South-east and commuting to London for over twenty-five years I've had to reorientate myself to new-found space and the time to stop and talk. Out of the big cities, anyway, there's a completely different attitude to life. People who recognize or remember me actually want to talk about themselves and their own railway connections.

I don't particularly enjoy being spotted, but I have learnt to live with it. When I was General Secretary, some travellers were hostile during disputes, but generally speaking I was treated reasonably.

I remember on one occasion being at Liverpool Street about 8 pm one night, sitting alone in a compartment waiting for the Bishop's Stortford train to leave. One irate commuter started banging on the window waving his fist. Then he entered the compartment. So I said to him, 'Before you open your mouth I know all about your railways problems. I travel like you. There's my ticket. I pay for that, too.' That cooled him down. So then we talked in a more rational way about the service and its problems. Before he left he even asked me for my autograph.

By the time I got home at night I had my bellyful and I just wanted to put my feet up. My wife Joan doesn't talk politics as a rule and that suits me. But towards the end, as my role of NUR General Secretary seemed more and more controversial, she became distressed at the job coming in through the front door.

A locomotive picks up water at troughs just north of Northallerton.

I visited China in 1978. Here I am with Union President, Dave Bowman, making a presentation to Chairman Mao's engine driver.

With a group of Chinese engine drivers in front of a French-designed main line diesel locomotive.

A girl operator at work in the control tower of Nankin marshalling yard.

At Monkwearmouth Station Museum with the nameplate from a Class B 17
locomotive no. 61654 'Sunderland'.

The sad sight of the once-proud station at Ripon.

Addressing a rally at Central Hall, Westminster during the 'No rail cuts' campaign of 1981.

At times we had the press camped outside, waiting for me to emerge. They were obviously under instructions, just sitting there in cars for hours. They usually wanted a picture of me at home, or leaving home for what ever reason.

Once, I was in the garden at the weekend, digging, when all of a sudden two press photographers appeared in the garden. They had just walked round, without even a knock. I told them to get the hell out, but if they had simply approached me and said, 'Look, my editor wants a picture of you gardening,' I would have obliged. My attitude was that I gave the press ample opportunity at work or at conferences to contact me, and that they should leave me in peace at home.

Sometimes I was picked up from home by the office car. At crisis moments this was a natural for the press, who snapped me getting into the car and added a caption like, 'He's all right...but what about the poor commuter?'

But by and large I didn't get a bad deal from the press because I made myself available to the media whenever possible. Not like some trade union leaders who insult them yet clamour for their attentions. Call them capitalist lackeys then bask in their attentions.

My job as NUR General Secretary meant operating in a tough world. During my last three years, especially, I was constantly watching my back. There was continual conflict with government, with BR management and with extreme elements within the union. Everything was a battle for survival. I spent my time advocating a shorter working week for members while putting in over seventy hours myself.

Unless I exercised the strictest discipline over my diary I was never at home. This is partly because the Labour and trade union movements do lots of their business at the weekend — it's the only time when most members are free to engage in conferences, etc. A crisis would always keep me at work but I had to learn to say, 'This weekend, come what may, I'm going to spend at home.'

I had two diaries. My own one and the desk diary kept by my private secretary. There was a nasty tendency for my desk diary to fill up with engagements if I didn't watch it. I found that the pace and pressure of work was such that I hardly had time to think, let alone read all the documents which landed on my desk. All my senior colleagues were under the same type of pressure and I wonder how we ever succeeded in taking the right decisions. Often we didn't.

In the early days, my predecessors would be involved in working out agreements which could last years. Indeed, Charlie Cramp, General Secretary from 1920 to 1933, never negotiated a pay increase during the whole of that period. In fact, the union was forced to accept pay cuts of 5 per cent in March 1931 which was not finally removed until August 1937. Through these years railway staff had sacrificed over £28 millions from their wage packet to help arrest the fall in railway dividends. These days, you've no sooner concluded one national pay deal than you're starting on next year's. And the agreements themselves are far more complex. With clauses on productivity, new technology, etc. they become great memoranda, whereas before they might have been just three paragraphs.

Right up to my last moment as General Secretary I didn't fossilize, I was always trying to find ways of improving the union, making it more effective. The higher up in the union you go the bigger the problems get, and the more important are the consequences of your decisions.

During that time I also learnt to deal with different elements in the union. In the Fifties and early Sixties the main political 'opposition' in the union were Communist Party members. I have no quarrel with a CP member being active in the union. He believes a particular philosophy, and most have the courage to stand at union elections under that ticket. Communists were tough and disciplined, and I could work with them because, at the end of the day, the communists of that time were loyal to the union. Not so today.

I'm not a right-winger. I have always been on the left of the movement. By that I mean the intelligent left. These labels put on by newspapers are totally misleading. I would just brush them aside. Like the militant label they put on some trade unionists. What do they mean? They're often the one who's shouting like hell, but when you get to the barricades they're the first to run for cover. I know. I've seen them.

I'm not the one who carries bags on behalf of somebody else — that's not my idea of being a leader. I preferred to lead in the direction I believed was right for the lad on the job — and so the battles got rough. The problem is that many people in Britain are oblivious to the battles which are taking place within the democratic institutions. If they don't get off their backsides one of these days they'll find out that they have no democratic organizations remaining.

To ease the pressures this sort of life creates, my son Anthony and I would go fly fishing together just as often as we could. We've fished in many parts of Britain, depending on where he has been based — first as a university student at both Keele and Aberystwyth, when we fished trout rivers in Derbyshire and North Wales, then later when, as a geologist for Britoil in Glasgow, we found streams in plenty in Scotland.

When I was General Secretary I found that fishing was the only way I could escape from the pressures of London, where crisis followed crisis. At home in Bishop's Stortford, even though I was ex-directory, the phone rang continually. Once on the river the peace and quiet of the countryside were just as enjoyable as catching fish. I'm only interested in trout or grayling, fishing which entails anything but sitting. You can walk miles working a stream and return tired. I once fished the River Swale one hot summer when the water level was low. It's a rocky river, and many heavy boulders were visible. I spent the whole week scrambling over those rocks like a commando course and returned home feeling terrible. The doctor told me I was suffering from exhaustion and was amazed to hear I had spent the week fishing.

EXPORT OPPORTUNITIES MISSED

In my grandfather's and father's day British locomotive manufacturers capitalized on their know-how by building specifically for export markets and selling traction and rolling-stock around the world. They had the advantage of Britain's show-piece railways at that time.

Britain's position as number one locomotive builder declined quickly after the Second World War when Western European countries were modernizing their systems and we were just hanging on. Even after our own modernization programme, very little attention was given to the export market, which could have been an obvious support for jobs at British Rail Engineering's workshops.

As soon as I became NUR General Secretary in 1975 I made it my business to ask government ministers about export credit facilities. I pointed out that, for instance, whenever the French President visited a foreign country to make an arms-supply deal a clause stipulating railway supplies was invariably slipped in. British governments were doing nothing to promote their rail products abroad.

Under my pushing we finally obtained better treatment, including proper export credit guarantees, and as a consequence British Rail Engineering Limited's export trade has become worth about £50 millions annually. I firmly believe that BR can take a leading role in developing the export of railway equipment and know-how. There is a growing worldwide market for rail products; what is now needed is a firmer government commitment for a national venture which provides business and jobs both to BREL and supporting industries. BR should not be hanging on to the hem of a consortium for major contracts, but should take a lead. Victories in the export field could do a lot for BR's reputation here.

But British exporters have obviously suffered from under-investment at home. Most prospective buyers need to study what they are being offered in conditions of hard daily use. There has been some success selling a slightly-remodelled version of the HST to Australia and the early experience of the Tyne and Wear Metro promises well, as I mentioned in Chapter Seven. The Railway Industries Association, representing the interests of rail manufacturers, numbers more than fifty members, including big names like GEC, Hawker Siddeley, Plessey, Vickers and Westinghouse. British manufacturers are of course selling traction and rolling-stock, electrification equipment, signalling and telecommunications, plus track and permanent-way materials around the world. But they could do much better. What we require in Britain is a totally modernized railway system to show off our products to foreign buyers. The potential remains enormous.

During the late Fifties and early Sixties there was a realization among railwaymen that business was slipping away from us. It was the period of the first motorway building and the arrival of the attractive small car like the Mini which was nippy, reliable and economic to run. Meanwhile, many lines struggled on with increasingly outdated steam locomotives, old rolling-stock and unreliable diesels.

We were beginning to realize the power of the road lobby in Britain: the motor manufacturers, the road builders, the Road Haulage Association, the National Farmers Union. The size and power of the lobby is reflected within the Ministry of Transport, where only a limited number of staff deal with railways and all the rest with roads. Even when the railway case is overwhelming — like the East Coast electrification — the pro-roads Transport Ministry will haggle and nit-pick to prevent any progress. To be bottom of the railway electrification league, as described in Chapter Seven, is a graphic example of the stupidity of transport planning in this country. A nation the size of Britain just can't afford to squander land and pollute the environment the way it has done by covering itself with motorways and permitting huge trucks on the road.

Society will look back on this time and realize that we have been totally senseless. While we went ahead covering Britain with concrete, the railways were already there, under-utilized. All that was needed was an intelligent level of investment.

When people hear me saying things like that they claim I have a vested interest — which I had. So that was why I set about creating an environmental group, Transport 2000, in the early 1970s. This proved to be a useful umbrella group for various environmental interests, and we put NUR money into backing it.

In this venture I was ably supported by George Curry of the Railway Industries Association, who appreciated the value of this organization in making the railway case. From his position as director of the RIA for over thirty years, he knew at first hand of the enormous possibilites in promoting good railway products, and that the best in Britain was equal to any in the world.

George Curry's organization was of tremendous help in those early formative years, they provided a great deal of experience in the presentation of a number of policy statements, including 'British Rail 1975—2000', 'An Electrifying Case', 'Scotland's Transport Tomorrow', which enhanced the reputation of Transport 2000.

I realize that, in a modern society, you have to balance the environmental arguments. I'm not a rabid conservationist — things do have to change. What's lacking in Britain is the commonsense, rational discussion between two sides who forget their vested interests and ask what the nation really needs. There has to be a sensible, middle road between those wanting to go back to nature and those advocating a concrete jungle. With Transport 2000 we, the NUR, became the counterbalance to the more extreme conservationists and the combination worked. I even persuaded Sir Peter Parker to put money from the Railway Board into it. We brought an expertise and a credibility which protest groups don't often command. From my own point of view, it became a lobby in the national interest, not a narrow railway union cause. The beauty of the rail case is that the network is already there.

Transport 2000 is still a vigorous organization. As a pressure group it can only claim moderate success so far because it has not yet altered the attitude of government or industry to the case for railways and other energy-efficient methods of transport. But as a body with many regional limbs it continues to provide impetus in the struggle to win over minds to the need for an integrated transport policy.

Britain has no energy policy, but it is at present rich in oil, gas and coal. Britain has no transport policy and its transport lines are a shambles. With the vast majority of heavy goods now going by road, what happens when the road system falls apart? Goods, theoretically travelling at an average sixty miles per hour on the motorway network are, as often as not, caught up in horrific jams while motorways, worn away by the pounding of heavy traffic, are feverishly (and expensively) rebuilt.

Meanwhile the government brings in new legislation to

permit bigger trucks, which will do even more damage to the road network. And by-passes which ought to have been built are stopped in the spending cuts so that these even-heavier trucks are causing environmental misery in villages and built-up areas. At the same time, the railway lines which pass nearby — where the environmental nuisance is easily contained — are desperately under-used.

Transport 2000 is among the groups campaigning for a more realistic analysis of the relative costs involved in sending freight by rail as opposed to road. It also campaigns for giving more priority to public transport, including buses, both in town and countryside, and for an end to the silly price war which sets bus against rail. It wants better industrial use of Britain's waterways, more understanding of the needs and potential of cyclists, and a new deal for pedestrians.

All its arguments return to energy use and environmental impact. It makes no attempt to deny the attractiveness of personal motoring or of road-based freight. They would play a big part in an integrated transport system which employed to its full the splendid rail network history has left Britain. If the competition were fair — comparable investment, comparable subsidy criteria — railways could compete very favourably with road in many freight areas, just as Inter-City can take on and beat the private car.

I argued constantly that some 50 million tonnes of long-distance freight which currently goes by road each year could be economically put on rail. This would make the total carried just 220 million tonnes annually, compared with 1,500 million tonnes by road.

We accepted that much shorter-distance freight would always go by road, it's the heavier, long-distance stuff we should be after. The only way rail can compete over short lengths is through the specialist, merry-go-round trains. But road transport would be less attractive than it appears today if the government made road hauliers pay the true costs the lorry imposes on the community. I believe the present 'competition' is unfair. British Rail has to cover the cost of maintaining track, signals, rolling stock, and so on. It provides a highly-skilled workforce which operates under controlled conditions. All the cost of this is a burden which road users don't have to carry, even though they pretend that the road fund licence meets the cost of roads.

We need a change of government policy which recognizes the environmental and social costs of road haulage and provides a formula allowing rail to compete commercially. This makes sense because the more heavily rail-track is used the better the cost ratios.

HOW I MET MAO'S ENGINE DRIVER

The job of General Secretary was not all blood, sweat and tears. I travelled extensively around the world, sometimes accompanied by my wife Joan. I think the most memorable of these visits was to China in 1978, and in a roundabout way I invited myself to this strange land.

We had sent a delegation to China several years earlier and it occurred to me as General Secretary that we had been remiss in not inviting them back. So I wrote to the Chinese Embassy extending the invitation. Back came the reply that the national centre for the trade unions was no longer in existence (as a result of the Cultural Revolution), but they suggested that we ourselves visit China — indeed, why not come for three months? Well, that wasn't on but I went to the Embassy to discuss the proposal. I wanted to know who we would be the guests of, who do I write to? They told me that the People's Friendship's Society would be responsible.

We went for three weeks rather than three months, and happened to arrive at Peking at the same time as Tony Crosland, the newly-appointed Foreign Secretary. He had just left Environment (with responsibility for Transport) and I had been trying to arrange a meeting with him for some time. He invited me to meet him and his wife at their apartment, where we spent a very enjoyable evening. I pulled his leg saying I'd been trying to get hold of him for months and had had to follow him half way round the world. The only problem was that my concerns were no longer his.

Every time I go to communist countries the first thing I try to reach agreement about is the programme. I like to know where I'm going and what I'm expected to do. It's not that you can dictate your programme — you are always in the hands of your hosts. What concerns me is the intensity of the

200

programme laid on. You find you are expected to be on the go from six in the morning until late at night. I also wanted to try to ensure that the programme was balanced, so that we saw not only the railway system in China but gained some insight into Chinese society and had time to relax and recuperate between stops.

At the end of our first meeting I asked our hosts whether it would be possible to meet Chairman Mao. I said that I understood President Nixon was over a couple of months before, so shouldn't Mao now meet a representative of British workers? Mao's health had of course been the centre of much speculation. Several days later I was told it wasn't possible to fit in a meeting with Mao because of his medical problems, but at his special request he wanted me taken to see his personal locomotive and meet his engine driver.

Both I and the NUR President, David Bowman, being old footplatemen, weren't exactly thrilled with the substitute offered. In our Western way we thought it was a brush-off. Anyway, we accepted it philosophically. We went to see Mao's locomotive. It was huge, immaculate, with a stainless-steel head-and-shoulders carving of Mao on the smoke-box door. The engine stood perpetually in steam in case of need. We found it in a normal motive power depot in Peking, possibly a bit cleaner than the old English sheds were, but with all the usual dust and ash.

Mao's locomotive was the most gleaming, highly polished machine I had ever seen. His engine driver stood on the footplate waiting for us. I indicated that I wished to drive the locomotive, was allowed to move it twenty or thirty yards, then brought it back. It proved well worth seeing, even its coal had been washed. The significance of Mao's engine only dawned on me a few months later, when the great man died. Of the three people who read funeral orations at the great gathering in Peking's Square, one was Mao's engine driver.

So being taken to see the engine and meet his driver certainly wasn't a brush-off. Railways were a crucial part of Mao's long rule, and his engine a symbol of his power and authority. It was one more lesson I gained in learning not to apply English standards to experiences in the Far East.

In Peking I was shown the railway station, not unlike our

201

largest railway termini, except that it had none of the commercial trappings of Western society. This was in the years before any sort of consumerism arrived in China. Everyone wore plain denims — it was difficult to tell women from men. Shops carried the bare necessities without any glitter and with limited choice.

At the station we were shown the booking-office. I couldn't understand why one queue was longer than the other. I asked why — was it first-class and second-class? No, my interpreter replied. So what was it? Soft-seat and hard-seat, he replied. So what's the difference? I wasn't quite clear, thinking maybe the soft-seat ticket holders got a cushion to sit on. A couple of days later we set off on our travels by train. It proved to be the sort of railway you might have found in Britain in the mid-thirties. But the train was very full because, as we could easily deduce, railways were the main means of transport between towns and cities in China. We had reserved seats in what looked like a dining-car, with a certain amount of luxury and ornament. So this was a soft-seat carriage? Yes. Could I then see a hard-seat one? Yes. I walked down and sure enough the next carriage had hard wooden seats and tables. Oh, I said, that's first-class and second-class. No, not in China, said my guide, that's soft-seat and hard-seat. Is the price different? Yes, the price is different. Well, I said, that's first-class and second-class. No, he replied, there are no classes in China, just soft-seat and hard-seat.

A good illustration of how China uses every inch of arable land to feed its huge population is seen from the railway, where crops extend to the trackside without any protective fences to keep people or animals off. In marshalling-yards, I found that if there was any space at all big enough to plant anything it was planted.

As we travelled about by train we couldn't help noticing the sheer numbers of people employed on the railway. Overmanned is hardly the word for it. I got on one footplate of a steam locomotive only to find four staff; on a diesel I found three in the cab. We passed a relaying gang of at least 1,000 people, who dived to both sides when they heard our whistle. The gang — women as well as men — lived, we were told, beside the line, moving camp as one job finished and another began.

202

On the train itself we found staff in each coach who would serve China tea. When you stopped at a station the steward stepped down from each coach to ensure people got on and off safely. Some of the engine drivers proved to be women. At one station where we stopped three women jumped out of the cab to polish the diesel locomotive. When I asked about the numbers employed on specific tasks the short answer was that they had a lot of people in China, and they might as well have them doing something as doing nothing. There was no pressure of wages on the economy, but the manning level to our eyes looked somewhat ridiculous. It was the opposite approach from our society's, where the pressures are to reduce the labour force. When I asked how many people were employed on the railways they were unable to tell me. Trains and bicycles are still the main transport methods in China.

We were taken during our trip into all sorts of places, including hospitals, where, embarrassingly, we were treated as if we were members of the medical profession. They made us wear long white coats. The hospitals were clean but rudimentary. We were introduced to the wonders of acupuncture and without any hesitation patients would be asked to show us their scars from an appendix operation or whatever. There wasn't the same sort of concern for personal privacy which we have in Britain. They even took us to wards where acupuncture was being practised; one man had needles sticking out of his eyebrows. I also had a taste of the herbal medicines which they use extensively. I had a throat infection and, being desperately anxious not to end up in a Chinese hospital, asked to see a doctor. A proper doctor, not the 'barefoot' doctors I had been told about, volunteers who tramped the land administering first-aid in the early days of the Revolution. The proper doctor arrived in his Mao hat and tunic, looked at my throat, and prescribed a variety of herbs. I had to take twenty of those, twenty-five of these and thirty of the other. It cured it, but I had to eat a colossal number of tablets.

While we were staying at the Peking Hotel we were treated to a number of banquets. One menu I remember well included delicacies like consommé of white fungus — it tasted all right — sauté of sea cucumber and fish maw, sauté of quail eggs with vegetables, boiled fish with hot oil, pastries and mixed fruit. I was sitting next to a high-ranking fellow from the Chinese Friendship Association who liked ducks' feet. Following the Chinese custom of extending your favourite dishes to your guests he kept helping me to them, but I found them impossible to get down. Black sea slugs were another delicacy I tried to avoid.

Everywhere we went, to schools, hospitals, factories or wherever, we were greeted formally and introduced. Then our hosts would read out a prepared text. This would always include denouncing the former leader Deng Xiaoping, the running dog capitalist roader (this was during the Cultural Revolution). You got to expect this, and I couldn't help feeling that the text was read mechanically. In the schools and everywhere else we went they would then turn to explain to us what they were doing, and you could see the change of expression: their faces would light up. They were always proud of what they could show. We dropped in on a class of eight- or nine-year-olds sitting round the teacher. The interpreter told us that this was a political education course. One after another the children stood up with fierce expressions on their faces and they too denounced Deng Xiaoping and all the deviationists. Outside I remarked that they were a bit young to understand that sort of thing. The interpreter replied that they had to start young. 'All right,' I said, 'what if they go home and the parents don't agree with this capitalist running dog stuff?' 'Well,' he said, 'the parents have to be educated too.' They almost seemed to be encouraging the kids to spy on their parents.

That was the bit of 1978 China that I found hardest to accept. Not long after, of course, Mao died, Deng Xiaoping returned along with his running dogs and is now in a position of great authority. The masses have just had to accept the opposite scenario as the new truth.

As we went round China I wanted to see to what extent the state controlled people's lives, so I kept a look out for any hint of private enterprise. I was disappointed. When I saw rickshaw-drivers I would ask, 'Is that private enterprise?' 'No, state,' replied the guide. They must have needed a tremendous bureaucratic machine to administer that one. Another fellow was selling something resembling ice cream. Wasn't that, surely, small business? No, state control. I saw a cobbler in a corner of a little street we walked down. 'What about him, there. Isn't he working for himself?' 'No, state employee.'

As I toured around I was aware of the sharp contrasts which existed side by side — modern workshop next to a medieval-looking scene with an old lady pushing a handcart or a bullock pulling a plough. But on what basis did they reward the workers? The priorities, I was told, were attitude to the party, attitude to work, rather than skill at work. There were very small differentials anyway between one worker and another. At one factory we visited, the works manager, who happened to be away, had been given the job, we were told, because he had been on Mao's long March. Workers were so integrated, men and women, that women appeared in every job you could name. Women seemed to be equal in every sense so far as industrial jobs were concerned.

In China women are to be found everywhere, chairing trade union committees, driving engines, or whatever. The only times when women appeared any different were the occasions we were taken by railwaymen for entertainment at their clubs. These working people's clubs served the local community, and were so popular (partly because places of entertainment were scarce) that locals could only attend by rota. There they drank tea and watched other railway workers entertain them in music, dancing or conjuring tricks. On the stage they were a blaze of colour, with the women brilliantly dressed and made up. But in the streets they were back to the same drab denim.

Once, in a works council, I asked the women why they didn't wear wedding rings. Because they are the badge of the slave, they replied. I only ever heard one Chinese woman say that she would like something better. She said that she objected to using a communal kitchen in her block of flats. She ventured to suggest she would like something better. Everyone else you spoke to always referred you back to the old days before Mao — things were far worse then, they said. Now they had food, a reasonable roof over their heads and education — they weren't going to argue about freedom of expression.

The railway workers had a union but quite unlike ours, being part of the state machine. They never went into wage negotiations. The national plan was fixed and the workforce had to tie in with it. If something was bad it was shrugged off with a philosophical excuse that the priorities would change some time.

As we went round the country, sometimes by plane as well as rail and road, we stayed in guest houses which had apparently been built under the Japanese occupation and lived in by the Japanese officers.

I found a tremendous resentment against the Russians. There was one graphic example we saw of Sino-Russian non-cooperation. The Russians were building a combined rail and road bridge over the Yangtze which, when relations deteriorated, the Russians just abandoned and returned home. The Chinese, however, carried on the job with great difficulty, and completed it. The bridge is very similar to the one over the Tyne at Newcastle. The Newcastle high-lever bridge must have been built in the 1850s; the Yangtze bridge in the 1970s, but both are on very similar lines. The main difference is that Newcastle's bridge has rail on top rather than under the road, and the Chinese bridge is much longer.

On reflection, the best way to describe my visit to China is that it was like stepping on to another planet. I was told repeatedly that by the year 2000 China would attain the same level of industrial development as Western societies. I found this difficult to accept. I don't think the Chinese appreciated the size of the task facing them.

10 Sir Peter and the Union 'Crack Up'

~~~~~~

SIR PETER PARKER'S spell as Chairman of British Rail coincided broadly with mine as NUR General Secretary. We often found ourselves, by the nature of our jobs, arguing the toss, but always with mutual respect.

Parker, appointed by a Labour government, and re-appointed by the Thatcher government, was personally committed to the mixed economy and to public enterprise. Together we developed an approach which, even though upset by the disastrous rail strike of 1982, still looks like fashioning a new era of railway investment and productivity.

Sid: When you took on the chairmanship of BR in 1976 did you realize what a difficult mission it was?

Peter: Well, I had already served for ten years in the public sector part-time, one way and another, before I accepted the chairmanship of the Railways Board so I was not innocent of public enterprise problems. I was first approached to take the railways on in 1967, remember, and had studied the scene then.

In 1968 I joined the British Tourist Authority. In 1969 I was asked to take on the job of the Chairman-Designate of the National Ports Authority. In 1971 the Conservative Government appointed me to the British Airways Board. So by the time I arrived at British Rail in 1976, I was perhaps the least innocent of 'outside' chairmen appointed to a national industry.

Now, when the late Tony Crosland appointed me there was no special financial remit for me. He handed me a consultative document — a green paper with an orange cover — called

'Integrated Public Transport'. He had become very interested in transport during the last stage of his time as Secretary of State for the Environment — Transport was part of that Department; his hand showed, not only in references to Proust — in the tilt of the paper against railways. I admired Tony in many ways but not in that argument.

Anyway, Tony had left for the Foreign Office by the time I actually took office. In fact, Peter Shore had come and gone between my appointment and full-time arrival. Ministers of Transport prove most mobile. The day I walked into my office Bill Rogers became Minister. We met at once. And I could see he wanted to distance himself from that consultative document.

Back to the point — I came full-time to public enterprise knowing that the frontiers were troubled — I'd seen that in many different ways. Specifically, I knew there were great tensions between the Railways Board and government — a reorganization of the Board and its objectives was something that I decided on from the start — and one thing to establish was our objectives, at least as we understood it. That's where the idea of a Contract came in. I said: 'We'll take the Public Service Obligation* deal as a contract. We are "obliged" to run economic services, all right, but let's make it clear we have a payment for that: government wants to be a customer, so there's a contract, we get a payment.' Politicians don't like that, nor does the Treasury of course: they prefer the language of subsidy — but actually the subsidy goes to the passenger. Railways should have a contract, clear and definite. The contract idea has got to be continually refined but I'm sure it's on the right lines.

Within two months of taking over I was made aware by my colleagues that the changes, the modernization of the railways, would always face the risk as they developed of a major conflict with ASLEF. We made a great deal of progress but the real problem was always going to be ASLEF. First because of the old tangle between the craft union and the industrial union — and in the internal strife between you, NUR was

*This is explained on p. 226.

awkward, too, you know. Second — I faced hard but constructive debate and battle with NUR — though you were slow too — but ASLEF did not seem to have a leadership capable of coming along at the pace of change we needed. We all knew change was afoot, had to happen, including many members of ASLEF, but when the crunch came in 1981, the leadership seemed to crack.

Sid: All right, you came in and then about 1979 you proposed to us the creation of the Rail Council as a management-union consultation forum...

Peter: Earlier than '79. It happened in '78, at the Great Western. But we'd been preparing for it some good time before that. It was a necessary move to break out of the negotiating rituals. We had to communicate policy, clearly, regularly. In the preparatory stages, you stayed up very late one night, paid me the courtesy of meeting me and Cliff Rose, in a vast empty lounge at the Charing Cross Hotel. You listened to me for a while and said, 'It's worth a chance, let's try it.'

Sid: What did you anticipate would develop from that?

Peter: Well, like creating Parliament, you know, when they started it they weren't quite sure what they were doing, or where it was leading to. But something like that had to happen. My thesis was that industrial democracy as being defined by the Labour Party — and I wrote a long letter to the Secretary of State, Bill Rogers, about it — was up the wrong alley with worker-directors. I remember meeting you once, before I took over, when you told me that you didn't have any confidence in the idea of being on the Board.

Sid: I told you that I couldn't do two jobs...

Peter: Right. I felt it was an absurdity: a trade unionist on the Board, a trade unionist from the industry, would get entirely confused about his commitments and loyalties. Both you and I said — if we've got a problem, it will be hammered out between us. Many nationalized industries have a trade unionist on their Board — it is often a symbolic gesture, perhaps, but the trade union experience and perspective can be valuable. But it doesn't make sense to have a trade unionist from inside the industry. Management has its job to do, to manage; that means consulting, of course, listening carefully, but then deciding — that's its responsibility, no messing about on that.

But if we weren't going to have trade union representation on the Board we still had the problem of communicating and keeping you in touch with Board thinking and strategy. How could we do it? We couldn't hope to use the British Rail Joint Consultative Council because that was a very limited operation, where all the talk amounted to progress-chasing. How should we convey the total problem, the economic facts of life and death in the industry? The only way to do it was to create a forum which would not be progress-chasing or negotiating, and where the unions would have the same commercial information that the Board had. The central point was to develop an understanding of the policy of the industry — not to negotiate.

Sid: I know I was strongly in favour. But did it work, in your opinion?

Peter: The strikes disrupted it; but in my view it worked until then — and it has started up again. It's never easy to measure success and failure in human relations in industry. The sheer fact that the Board was ready to be plain and open in its dealings could not prevent a strike if some elements were determined to block progress ultimately — but I'm sure the final result, the inevitable result of general support for the Board's firm line to get ahead with modernizing working practices — that certainly had something to do with the fact that the Board was plain and open — ready to talk and listen — and decide.

And the Council worked well from the start — one instance, the first meeting in Paddington. ASLEF attended even though, I believe, it had not constitutionally agreed to take part: they lived with schizophrenia, wanting to be part of progress but not participating. Although they never accepted the Council, they came — and would complain about the lack of papers.

I remember at the first meeting we were slipping into the old business of progress-chasing when you said 'What are we doing wasting our time like this? I thought the Council were going to be different, Peter. I thought we were going to discuss strategy, problems of the industry, problems between ourselves, and the problem with government...'

I said, 'Fine, that's what we're here for.'

You turned round and said to me 'Peter, I know your problems. You know my problems. How close can we bring them?'

'All right then,' I said, 'let's face the long problems of the industry.'

That moment gave the basic chance which has stood the industry in good stead. And the Council has survived the strikes. At the last meeting I attended, all the unions were there, and there were a lot of tough items on the agenda: the British Rail Engineering problems — and the Corporate Plan to 1988 (my last) were also coming through: a lot of tension and, beforehand, reports that the ASLEF members were going to walk out after ten minutes — actually they didn't. They didn't stay for lunch, which was a most useful and for me a memorable occasion. Now that sort of Council strikes me as one of the best industrial democratic mechansims to take the strain of change in any dynamic corporation. The Council survives. There will be moments of confrontation, even break down, but it can survive. And you helped create it.

Sid: I thought that it was the nearest thing to participating in management. We did not take the final decisions, but the influence trade union representatives had was profound. That vehicle is the one we used in November 1980 at the crisis conference held at Watford when you told us we could be in a plughole situation by 1983 and put the Balance Sheet of Change idea up for consideration. You stated that you weren't going to government with a begging bowl. On reflection do you still think that's the best way forward, for the unions and management to get together, agree a strategy, then go and present it to government on the understanding that government has to come in as a partner, too?

Peter: Yes; in the sense that government is the banker and shareholder and needs to be confident that the Board and management can deliver their plans. If the industry is tearing itself apart, then bang goes that confidence. The approach of

211

the Council, united for change, impressed Norman Fowler: he met it twice in his time as Transport Minister. Then when he was switched to Health, David Howell came in, and he met Council once. But by that time, ASLEF was showing signs of going back on the specific commitments. NUR was fulfilling them, ASLEF backing off. How could Howell argue in Cabinet for railways if that historic 1981 package was not being delivered? The moment we couldn't deliver, the Balance Sheet of Change began to go wonky. That was autumn 1981.

Sid: But we still had a rhythm going, with both sides expecting to deliver, until the flexible rostering dispute hit the industry in December 1981.

Peter: By Christmas, we had to call ASLEF to account on its commitments. Then, there was no way I would — or could — press government to electrification until the Board had won through. Only the industry in unity, committed to efficiency, could be worth the millions of the East Coast electrification — that was the Board's position.

Of course, electrification is simply a renewal of the railways — it's in the logic of the future railways — as the government itself agreed in its ten-year approach. It's not a sudden switch-on, it will be a step-by-step business. But it became inevitably the talisman of confidence in our industry. Howell said once, 'Peter I've got the bat, if you can only throw the ball.' It was not a question of the government denying something to railways by that time. There was no question of the Board throwing the ball until we'd sorted out the crisis of commitment to change. The ASLEF strikes cost us nine months, and our image got a bloody nose before we'd won.

Sid: Shortly before you left BR in August 1983 you published the corporate plan 1983-8. It was written to meet a very tough remit. In it you accepted that BR would only have five years to assimilate a subsidy cut of £200 millions. In October 1982 Nicholas Ridley, the new Transport Minister, cut the five years to three. Doesn't this present the industry with very serious problems?

Peter: Of course, it'll be tough. But — and I cannot speak for them now — they will know how to deal with the tough remit in the timetable. Your question raises the whole complicated question of corporate plans and government departments. I've not been in this latest discussion, and so I'm not privy to the details. Generally speaking (and I'm not just talking railways) there are a couple of things to remember. One is that in any big corporation, when you're controlling budgets and plans, you realize that their only certainty is they're uncertain. Sometimes I think big corporations take corporate plans like sedatives. And in any planning process, there have to be contingencies at every level. The other thing is that no minister is going to Cabinet with whatever he's given by the industry he's responsible for — he can't say to the Cabinet 'that's it'. He's going to say that he's screwed the industry down — or up (though I doubt he'd ever say the latter). You of all people know that as a negotiator you keep trying to slice the salami — you're not justifying your job unless you do better or is that possible? I think so.

Sid: You travelled extensively round the network, and in preparing this book I've been talking to many ordinary rank-and-file railwaymen. I couldn't find one man, in any grade, who wasn't demoralized. I've found third-generation railwaymen who tell me, 'I'll be bloody glad when my retirement comes — I'd go tomorrow if I could.'

Peter: I wouldn't accept that whole-sale, down-beat view. But, off the rails on a general point, public enterprise has been depressed, I believe, by what I've called the climate of insult that has been generated in recent years. This government has made criticism of public enterprise a form of conventional wisdom — and it has massive support from the media. And traditionally, the unions have been strongest in public enterprise — that increased the intensity of the politics around public enterprises and their efficiency.

Now, I'm a believer that there will always be some public enterprises in the British economy — and that, therefore, we should make the most of them, make the best of them not the worst. Shake out inefficiencies, but acknowledge their achievement when praise is due.

That said, I don't expect any mercy working in the railway industry — it's always been an exposed, highly-visible business. And there's been a love-hate relationship going cheerfully back into the last century — I've got a *Punch* railway joke-book, given to me when in 1976 I left a merchant bank I chaired in the City to join the railway: it's full of jokes from the 1880s, just the same jokes we have today — you can live with that. We're deep in the folk-lore of the country.

But in the past four or five years it has become a shibboleth that public enterprise is a mistake. Some ministers speak this gospel with theological arrogance. Now, the Thatcher Government genuinely believes that the only way to get vitality and realism in an industry is to push it close to the market. I too believe that where you can apply the test of the market, fine. But it's not always possible, it it? And if you are up against a propaganda machine of a successful government saying that all public enterprise is a bad thing, that is demoralizing. Under those conditions railway workers live in a very cold climate indeed.

On top of that, the industry has lost over 400,000 workers since the war; in continuous retreat over numbers, people are dropping off the sledge the whole time. So unless you can counter that by generating an atmosphere of positive confidence, of light at the end of the tunnel of change, a feeling that an excellent new service will be forged, morale is dead.

That's why we started our own propaganda for railways in 1976, and for four years, it is widely accepted, this was entirely successful. There was a railways debate in 1978 in the House of Commons, a wholly bipartisan debate that is the best focus I can think of, showing railways can be taken out of party politics, with timescales far longer than any single government. That Commons debate of 1978 had both sides of the House agreeing that railways were doing well. We took a transcript of the debate to show to the US Congress to help win the contract as consultants to the Federal Rail Administration. The Committee Chairman opened proceedings by asking me: 'Are you here to peddle nationalization?' I said: 'Absolutely not. That's not how Britain regards railways.' I circulated copies of the debate with all parties saying railways are an essential component in the public transport of any advanced industrial society.

That was a high mark of understanding of the railways' role.

Then with the change of government, there was a deal more controversy about that role. Not so much at ministerial level but within Cabinet and its powerful economic advisers. And then in 1982 the railways community had a crack-up. In the throes of that, it is simply not possible for you, the railwaymen and women, to feel proud.

But that necessary battle is over — 1983 results show that. Bob Reid, the new Chairman of British Rail, has got the confidence of all sides, I hope. The corporate plan is clear. The objectives are clear.

You'll find that electrification will budge forward; it'll come, all right; we will get the East Coast main line up to York, bit by bit. Even the Channel Tunnel is a 'goer' again, perhaps. It's not all sackcloth and ashes. But the Thatcher Government thesis is still to privatize as much of the railways as possible.

Sid: But how will this corporate plan be put into action — it means again shedding men, changing work practices...

Peter: If you looked at the engineering industry as a whole, it has been slammed up against the wall by recession and by competition, having a horrific time. There's almost been a wipe-out of British engineering going on in the Midlands, the North and Scotland. Relatively the BREL redundancies are far fewer — though the sad circumstances of one-company towns, Shildon for instance, are very, very hard.

Sid: Yes, but there are some very thorny issues to tackle — like taking guards off trains.

Peter: That'll happen. They will come off, I promise you that. We're set on that course and there is no going back.

Sid: But isn't it a sullen acceptance by railway workers?

Peter: Not if we can point to the prize of a strong, modern railway. You know, people often come up to me when I travel by rail nowadays and we talk, railway people: I don't find they're against what we are fighting for. And if this government can begin to take some pride in the railways — my conviction is that in a couple of years' time Nicholas Ridley, the new Minister 'in', will be able to turn round and say, 'This industry's doing extremely well.'

Sid: In the meantime, the shipping division will be privatized...

Peter: Yes, this is an elected government: it will privatize what it can in public enterprise. In BR, we are committed to privatizing Sealink. Gatwick-Victoria is certainly a candidate for private operation. I put that proposition up four years ago, saying if we couldn't get the money to improve vastly that prestige piece of the service from the normal investment programme, somehow we'd get it another way. Same thing, remember, with hotels, with the Gleneagles deal. We kept a stake, did it carefully, bringing other investors with us. That has proved a good business deal altogether. But then the rest of the hotels were put on the chopping-block later — not in as business-like a style, in my view.

Sid: We sweated blood on the Gleneagles transaction.

Peter: But it was the right pilot scheme.

Sid: I produced £600,000 of NUR money to secure an interest in the new company. I also secured a closed-shop for NUR staff.

Peter: You called me up asking how much you should put in. We discussed, and you asked, 'Does that mean we get a member on the board?' Answer — no. I am sure BR wouldn't be frightened of private capital if it really works, and if it really sets a pace as to how things can be done. But if it's simply used to destroy public enterprise, I'm not for it.

The French SNCF for instance go to the market to raise capital. Incidentally, I was recently in Japan where there's a huge sector of private railways operating alongside the Japanese National Railway. In Japan they're becoming very interested in the way we are organized. They're beginning to admire the sector organization we've now achieved over recent years: dividing BR into businesses. The Japanese are, of course, worried now because of a huge public expenditure deficit on railways. There has been an Act of the Diet to privatize the whole thing.

Sid: Are you saying the Japanese did it wrong with their massive investment in railways?

Peter: Not that simple really. First of all they have a total transport policy. We haven't achieved that in Britain, post-war, it's been *per ardua ad hoc* for us. Secondly, the Japanese use the railways as an instrument of social policy. As a startling instance, at the end of the war, they demobilized their troops into the railways. Something like a million men. And they are still highly overmanned. They're roughly the same sized system as British Rail but they employ over 400,000 people. Naturally they are asking themselves — how on earth can we carry on like this? JNRail is 20 per cent of their public expenditure deficit — in five years it could be 50 per cent. That's why they are saying that it has got to change, even that the railways as presently managed are unmanageable.

Thirdly, there's the private sector of railways there which makes comparative comments pretty confused. Private railways around Tokyo, fourteen of them, make a great deal of their money mostly from residential developments, leisure parks, department stores; in fact property developments, the sort of money-spinners which we have to sell off, though BR's a very successful property company . . .

Sid: All right, but is there any model in Europe you see as an example for BR?

Peter: I believe we could be the best, once we get government committed long-term, because it's arguable we're the best organized, now, internally. If you look at the international scene of railways in the last few years you'll find volcanic upheavals. The whole of the Russian railways board — sacked; the Japanese board — in turmoil; the French board — changed and pushed around; the West German board — nearly all out; same with the Spanish and the US boards. Ours is a scene of consistency by comparison. Nobody, in my view, has thought it through as well as the British have, with all our problems. What we haven't yet got is the governmental confidence — but that's coming more and more, I reckon. We've been starved of all sorts of resources just when we know what to do. The people who get ahead best, in terms of clear government back-up, are the French.

Sid: Why have *they* got it right?

Peter: Geography is a bit on their side; their scale suits the logic of what railways do well, but they are much more logical about overall transport policies. For example, they saw that their great megalopolis, Paris, needed high-speed transit systems to survive. De Gaulle saw he couldn't hope to develop the Paris region unless he got public transport sorted out. So, in the late Sixties the French Government put the money down and Paris's Metro has become a formidable instrument. Another example: their Train de Grande Vitesse (TGV) — they put down new track as far as Lyon, just as a first step. They have proved themselves capable, in France, of the big decisions for the infrastructure of their industry.

Sid: But they also manage a bipartisan government. They don't have this left-right split which thwarts us.

Peter: That's the heart of the matter. They see their railway in a long-term perspective. The French have had a series of about nine railway development plans — we haven't had one — no matter what government is in power they've been able to think for the future. Recently, they've stumbled. But their post-war record has been formidable. They were in fact planning a modern railway before the last war. They've proved capable of taking big decisions. This country sometimes seems to have lost the knack of taking big decisions.

Sid: We took one on Concorde...

Peter: I remember the jumble of varied vested interests round Concorde, because I was on the Airways Board at the time. Heseltine, when he got up in Parliament to announce the BA decision to buy Concorde, said that there 168 MPs who would be interested, because they, from all over the House, represented constituencies with employment related to Concorde. Concorde, Maplin and the Channel Tunnel had all been running at the same time. Britain couldn't really afford to do any of the three schemes properly. Two were knocked out — and magnificent as the Concorde is as a flying machine, as far as the country's infrastructure matters, they held on to the wrong one. They should have got on with the Tunnel.

Sid: I remember presenting to you the Railwayman's

Charter... setting out the objective of a new pay structure, thirty-five-hour week and better holidays.

Peter: Yes, a remarkable thing...

Sid: But there was a clause in it which said you (the management) could have any change you wanted — I had a terrible job getting that one through. But then we didn't make much progress. I couldn't sell change when we were standing still.

Peter: Synchronization was critical, synchronization of change and sensible investment. I went to the Department of Transport in the summer of 1981 arguing to get part of the East Anglia electrification under way — self-evident proof of the future of the system. If it was to be done, 't'were well it were done quickly — in my judgment. In negotiating change, over time, you are climbing the mountain, you pull hard on the rope, ease a bit, pull again. But in the public sector, the relationships within Whitehall, between Departments and the Treasury and No. 10 are all part of the bigger scene — and the negotiators themselves turn out not to be the only ones on the climbing rope. Some day, it will become clearer what those other Whitehall factors were, and their effect.

My line was plain enough. We needed to be strong in negotiation but positive about the future, too — it was vital to keep the balance. Actually, the 1981 negotiations — the toughest you could remember, I once heard you say — these were concluded in the late summer, and there were celebrations over the package. The industry was on the move: there was an agenda for action. Not that, eventually, the later switch of direction at ASLEF executive, led by Mr Fullick, the new President, could be dealt with in any other way than it was finally in 1982.

By the time David Howell arrived it was obvious that ASLEF meant to reopen the 1981 package. We couldn't deliver it without a fight. That was the point.

Sid: I remember going to see Howell in February 1982. I met him in his private room at the House of Commons. I asked him, 'Why have you abandoned the industry? You're battling with one isolated group, the train drivers.' He brushed me aside and said, 'Until you lot get your own house in order don't come back to see me.'

Peter: And that made sense to me too. We'd spent a long time bringing our plans to modernize the industry into focus, a long time talking through the importance of moving into modern practice to match a modern railway — then at that moment ASLEF foxed it all. We straightened things out but it took months and cost millions —

Sid: But do you see a future for railways? Think, fourteen million private cars. Inter-city buses developing rapidly. In that world, will we still have 10,500 route miles five years on?

Peter: Nothing is guaranteed — but I wouldn't be surprised. Railways are doing rather well again at the moment. If the industry can keep stable, act in a confident, reliable way — if it can keep cutting its costs to be competitive, it's role remains. It's not all doom and gloom. One of the last visits I made was to Glasgow — have you seen it recently? Go to Glasgow Central: see the new travel centre, see how smart it looks — there's confidence.

Sid: You want to try Hartlepool...

Peter: I know — there are plenty of contrasts on the rail. But it's a great thing for us to clean up the scruffy stations; and it's been happening. You can't look as if you're winning in a commercial service if you're scruffy.

Sid: But what about all that lack of investment?

Peter: We've got to have a new product for inter-city travel ready in 1988. The High Speed Train has been marvellous, but there'll be a new product by the end of the Eighties. It may well be the adapted APT. The machine should be exciting — maybe not quite as exciting as the original idea the aeronautical engineers were dreaming up in the late Sixties — but still remarkable.

BR has to maintain smart inter-city service, otherwise the planes or the buses will have us. Have you been on these smart new buses? The hostess greets you, offers you a drink, the bus driver is trained to smile, handles your luggage for you.

Everything about that service is thought out to compete.

Sid: Price is the key, though.

Peter: And fair terms of competition.

Sid: I accept that.

Peter: The bus operators will get caught eventually, probably find things getting tougher — with petrol prices and perhaps higher road costs. But we've got to meet the challenge now.

Sid: In the meantime we've got to live.

Peter: Yes, and we've got to live by looking competitive and commercial. We could not live when people were convinced that the railways were run by the unions. That's why we had to have the crack-up. We had to have it.

Sid: Don't you think the Board should have faced the problem of the train drivers much sooner? Their conduct was a certain recipe for conflict and would have had serious consequences for the future of the industry.

Peter: You didn't think so at the time.

Sid: I agree I didn't accept your ultimatum in 1982 — Go back to work or be sacked. But I did put it to you over the pay-train guard issue which dragged on from 1977 to 1979 that the ASLEF attitude was totally irresponsible and that the Board let them get away with murder.

Peter: You wouldn't expect me to accept that. But the main point is — if you are going to have to fight be sure you're in condition. When I came into the industry, there wasn't much confidence around, was there? In government, in unions. We decided that we had a job to do to champion the industry. We took every opportunity to proclaim some pride in BR performance — advertising, on TV, through a new emphasis on marketing — we appointed a Marketing Member of the Board, it was Bob Reid, in fact. We were determined to have public enterprise with a smile on its face. Our first objective had to be to show we were performing successfully in the market, and, of course, fulfilling our financial commitments with government. Once confidence had built up, other challenges of change could be tackled.

You know, it's easy to find something to fight about in railways: with over 200,000 people on the job in BR it's a combustible scene. I remember, for instance, the Class 56 loco row — when the Labour Government was not keen to see the chips down. But we've managed change without brawls most of the time, without wrecking our customers' lives. When it came to 1981-2 we'd achieved our breakthrough, but ASLEF went and tried to ruin it. In fact, the line is now cleared for progress.

Sid: At the end of the flexible rosters dispute, the TUC Finance and General Purposes Committee decided after ninety minutes that ASLEF didn't have a case at all.

Peter: At last. But the damage done by the TUC's backing at the start of the ASLEF nonsense was incalculable. That muddled things most dangerously, you know; months of muddle while silly questions were let loose to confuse public opinions. Had the negotiation of 1981 been vague in the first place? Was the Board ignoring safety? Rubbish — as you know. NUR and TSSA were lining up to the specific commitments.

Anyway, the moment came when David Basnett and Moss Evans as senior TUC figures came to see me: they took the initiative in reversing the TUC position, and we stayed up all night, and ASLEF had to toe the line. But it all took too long — and what wounds this inflicted on BR's reputation.

Sid: I remember going to the House of Commons to a meeting of the Shadow Cabinet when Michael Foot had declared his support for ASLEF and demanded an explanation from him. I asked him point blank, 'Do you know the facts?'

Peter: He came round to see me, too — I think after you'd had a go at him. I found myself asking him, too, 'Michael what are you doing?' I had come to the point at which I was to make a statement about closing the railways down. He wanted that postponed — one hour, two hours — for more talk. Obviously by that time, the Labour Party had no grip on the reality, no measure of the hollowness of the ASLEF position, no recognition that the Board and management of BR were utterly determined. Michael Foot had been given 'a bum steer' — very sad.

11   *What Future for Railways?*

~~~~~~

RAILWAYMEN'S LIVES, AND livelihoods, are directly affected by the industry that employs them. In Britain, as in the rest of Western Europe, with few exceptions, that industry is controlled by the state. But here in Britain the railways are expected to run on a commercial remit, with the gap between revenue and costs met by the so-called Public Service Obligation grant, subject to continual trimming.

I argue in this final chapter that the basis on which this grant is supplied has proved fallacious and quite unsatisfactory; that the rural line services are a glaring example of how the system is bleeding to death; and that British Rail will not stand a chance until Parliament decides to take it out of the political arena and guarantee long-term investment. The question is, will that decision come before it is just too late?

BR'S BURDENS ARE KILLING IT

My submissions in July 1982 on behalf of the NUR to the Serpell Inquiry into the finances of the railways, left no doubt about my concern over the crippling financial burdens the industry was being forced to carry. I explained how the financial state of the railway industry was regularly discussed at the BR Council (the railways' top consultative body, see p. 209) and the unions were kept well informed of the problems that confront the industry. During 1981 the BR Council went jointly to the government to discuss these problems and to offer constructive proposals to help overcome them.

The present crisis facing railways is not one that has suddenly appeared overnight.

In 1976, in response to the Labour Government's consultative document on transport policy, the NUR argued that the existing (1976) level of investment would lead to a serious decline in the railways and in the level of service provided to the public.

The British Railways Board (BRB) had warned successive governments of the difficulties that were being created by unrealistic financial policies towards the railways. Peter Parker in his first report (1977) as Chairman of BR stated:

> our success (in 1976) is short term, is being bought at a calculated cost in terms of our future ... The present level of investment in railways during the economic crisis is too low to sustain essential renewals to the existing system and service patterns.

This was the consistent theme of the Chairman's comments over the whole period of his office.

I argued constantly that the reason for the industry's present financial problems was indecision by government — their total failure to agree on a long-term national transport strategy. Despite fine-sounding phrases on the need for transport policy to be built on fair competition, the government had failed to produce the necessary framework.

Additional problems have been caused by the government's unwillingness to recognize the now-critical need to replace assets and infrastructure brought about by the modernization programme in the late Fifties and early Sixties. Individual ministers have often offered sympathetic words, but they have been unable to translate these into the action necessary to create the modern railway system this country so obviously needs.

The result is a dispirited workforce who now find themselves under attack for 'low productivity' as another excuse for government to delay essential investment decisions; yet real improvements in productivity can only be achieved through greater investment. As the BRB argued in its document 'Opportunity for Change' in 1976:

> the overmanning of which many British industries are fre-

quently accused is largely traceable to inadequate investment. Significantly, most of the European railways with whose productivity that of BR is adversely compared have in recent years benefited from levels of investment per employee, per traffic unit produced, or per kilometre of track, substantially higher than those available to BR.

During my years as NUR General Secretary, the NUR demonstrated its willingness to look realistically at structural changes in the industry and to accept changes in working practices. I argued that continued co-operation was entirely dependent on the government creating a climate in which change is acceptable. The government must lay down a proper financial framework in which the industry can function efficiently. It requires approval of a rolling programme of investment including electrification and other key projects.

For years, railway workers have been faced with an ever-present threat of cuts, closures and redundancy. This is not the best climate to persuade workers to consider radical changes in working practices. A real improvement in productivity and efficiency requires a commitment by the government to the long-term future of the industry; a commitment in deeds as well as words.

My constant complaints about the financial arrangements were based on the fact that government financing of British Railways conspires against both a constructive policy towards fares, and, more importantly, long-term financing. By that I mean the External Finance Limits (EFL) and the Public Service Obligation grant (PSO), the principal elements of BR's financial relationship with central (and local) government, depend on yearly, hand-to-mouth financing.

Short-term financing in the way necessitated by the current PSO has had inevitable costs. These are now all too apparent on BR's services. The diet of near-starvation investment rations and short-term expediency are responsible for the fact that today much of the industry's equipment and infrastructure is all but worn out. The problem is acute now, because a sizeable part of the rolling-stock is the same age. It was introduced as part of a huge investment programme — the modernization plan in 1956 — and is beginning to show widespread signs of permanent deterioration. Further, the system is struggling, and losing, in a battle to cope with a massive backlog of renewals in track and signalling.

Indeed, this was the principle conclusion to come out of the 1981 Monoplies and Mergers Commission's Inquiry into the commuter network, which gave an official seal of recognition to the fact that under present financial arrangements neither the government nor British Rail, nor indeed the passenger, is clear as to what level of service should be provided. And on top of this the Commission recognized that successive governments had not confronted the question of who exactly pays for this service — taxpayers, local authorities, commuters or employers? In its conclusion, therefore, the Commission urged the government to give clear objectives to the Board. In other words, the Commission concluded as we in the industry had concluded long since that a more meaningful 'contract' between the industry and the government should replace the outdated and insubstantial PSO.

It went on to say that the government was getting as good a service as it could expect from the money it was providing. I believe that this applies not just to the commuter services, but to the whole of the passenger network.

This Treasury jargon requres some explanation: There are four central aspects of the financial conditions under which the railways now operate: the Public Service Obligation; The External Finance Limit; an Investment Limit; a commercial remit.

PUBLIC SERVICE OBLIGATION (PSO)

The government pays a PSO grant to the Board annually — currently running around £900 millions a year — to compensate the railways for activities (basically passenger services) which the Board would not undertake, or undertake to the same degree, if it considered only its commercial interests. It is not £3 millions a day of taxpayers' money poured down the throat of British Rail, it is a form of contract with a difference.

Its level is entirely arbitrary. It is imposed by virtue of government policy towards public spending generally rather

226

than on the particular circumstances of the railways at a given moment. The level of the PSO grant is not assessed according to the real needs of the railways. The cash limit for the PSO has been set yearly at its 1975 rate up-dated for inflation by the GDP (Gross Domestic Product) Deflator. Consequently, the real value of the PSO is being eroded yearly. The GDP index by which the cash limit is annually up-dated underestimates the real increase in the costs of running the railways, because real costs are running well ahead of the costs assessed in the GDP index.

In spite of this, the Board has been proud to announce that it claimed a lower PSO than that of the limit in each year between 1975 and 1980. Such an achievement is manifestly a Pyrrhic victory when one looks at the standard of service now being offered by rural passenger operations, or the major part of the commuter network. Railways staff have also made considerable sacrifices which has had a part to play, a situation I repeatedly complained about at the Rail Council, until finally the Minister of Transport of that time, Bill Rodgers, agreed with me and some restitution was made.

The PSO reflects the traditional dislike of subsidy of any kind in this country. The PSO as a method of subsidy stands out compared to governmental support amongst other European railways. Subsidy in most European countries is seen as an essential part of running a railway: it is not something to be paid in the last instance only if commercial profit-making fails.

EXTERNAL FINANCING LIMIT (EFL)

Put simply, the principles of control of external finance for British Rail, as for all nationalized industries, were established in the White Paper, 'Cash Limits on Public Expenditure, April 1976'. The EFL represents an absolute constraint on the funds the Board can raise externally and is as such the overriding financial control on the business. In fact, strict cash limits on the industry have become a permanent development of what was originally a temporary measure. On its introduction in the mid-Seventies, the government of the day well recognized that a punitive cash restriction could only be imposed on the railway, with its mounting investment needs, as a short-term policy. It included in its White Paper, 1977, a special status for the railways.

> The Government hopes that the developing prospects (for the railways) will justify the case for some increase in railway investment as the plans for public investment are rolled forward.

Quoting this, the former Transport Minister, Bill Rodgers, said in the House on 21 June 1982 *that it was the clear intention of the Government of the day that 'the door should be kept open for railways'*. But the door has been kept firmly shut. And while investment needs to recoup the backlog of renewals in track, signalling and rolling-stock mount, the EFL is so tight that even government-authorized investment schemes cannot be taken up.

The EFL is thus working in contradiction to the PSO. It is now operating in a way far removed from that of a legitimate means of control on public spending. Perhaps the most illuminating illustration of the operation of the immutable EFL came in 1981 when the Board put forward its plan for what is called the introduction of private capital into the industry. The Board's original plans were thwarted when they discovered that even private investment would count against its EFL. The EFL thus proved counter-productive to even the Board's plans for the privatization of the system — something that is clearly consistent with current government thinking.

The price of compliance with the EFL is annually revealed to the trade unions. Consider, as an example, the list of projects that had to be sacrificed in 1980 to stay within the 1979-80 EFL: non-purchase of an additional ship for the Channel Islands Ferry routes (£5 millions); reduction of revenue investment by the deferment of track relaying (£6 millions); a reduction on British Rail Engineering's working capital (£5 millions); a reduction in staff costs before the end of the fiscal year (£3 millions).

In recent years the EFL has become more and more of a constraint. The short-term measures like those I have listed, necessary year after year to stay within its ever-tightening limits, are taking a heavy toll of the future viability of the industry. Furthermore, its operation, as a yearly limit, makes longer-term or even medium-term investment planning impossible.

I suspect that this government has been content with this arrangement because it is adequate for short-term finances — the long-term financial needs of the railways could easily be left for the future. As long as the cracks in the system did net get too large, investment could be put off. Time has now run out and the backlog is threatening to overwhelm the industry.

INVESTMENT LIMITS

The Investment Limit is, like the EFL, an aspect of government's concern wherever possible to limit the freedom of its nationalized industries. As if the Investment Limit and the EFL were not enough, the Board is required to put any investment proposal above £5 millions to the Minister for approval. In a multi-million-pound business this condition is absurd. Many good investment schemes have been put to the Minister and have subsequently been dropped because they have been overtaken by cash limits or opportunities have been missed because of long delays in approval. Others have become more costly when eventually put into effect because of changed circumstances (electrification is sadly becoming an example) for the same reason.

COMMERCIAL REMIT

There are two directives to the Board laid down in legislation: (a) to operate a network roughly the same size as that in 1975 with the aid of the PSO; and (b) to break even.

The first of these gives implicit recognition to the railways as a public service; the second is in effect saying that the railway is a business. The foundation of what we have called the Board's commercial remit is its policy to set fares (clearly the main source of revenue) to cover costs as far as possible. I seriously question this approach to the running of the railways because it cannot guarantee the maximum use of the railways' assets, or the provision of the railways the country needs. I firmly believe that the railways should not be run as a commercial exercise, on the same lines as a grocer's shop. The whole of the passenger railway is a public service and should be utilized as a part of a coherent strategy towards transport as a whole.

I believe the railway's cardinal commercial remit adversely affects its fares policy and its investment plans. In the case of the rural network, fares should be low enough to attract as many passengers to the system as possible. For inter-city services, however, the working of the Board's commercial remit is particularly brutal. Inter-city services normally (in other than the present dire conditions) are expected to be the most important source of internal income for the whole of the passenger network. Fares are pushed up to their limit to provide the bread and butter for the whole of the passenger network. Hence, as the 1982 BR-Leeds University study of European railways reveals, we have the highest mean fares in Europe. They are, overall, much too high.

In order to make money, the Inter-City services have to be fast and frequent. Investment chases Inter-City needs because this makes sense under the logic of a commercial remit. The price of this is that short investment funds cannot be spread evenly throughout the network, so the rural passenger networks and some commuter services have become the rump of the system. There is a pressing need for investment on passenger lines besides the Inter-City lines, for instance on interchange facilities, light trains for rural lines, and so on. This investment could transform the railways.

The solution lies in government recognizing that its present financial contract with British Rail has serious flaws and that its present attitude to the railways is making this contract impossible.

BRANCHES ON THE BRINK

Rural branches perform an important service to the community. In many areas the train is the only public transport available. But services are expensive to run and revenue fails to cover even the direct costs of operating, let alone provide for maintenance and renewals.

There are about one hundred of these rural heavy loss-makers on British Rail. The services are financed partly from fares, in some cases partly from local authority contributions, and also from the Public Service Obligation grant, which is the contract the government makes with British Rail each year (see p. 226), but like other nationalized industries, British Rail has had to operate within increasingly tight cash limits. The PSO grant which was first established in 1975 has been reduced in real terms every year since it was introduced, and the most recent government directive is to get it down to £635 millions by 1986. What's more, and here's the contradiction, while cutting their global support the government has insisted that the railways go on supporting the loss-makers.

So far British Rail has, in the main, managed to better these severe financial targets, but this has only been achieved against a background of strict economies. On rural lines it has made significant savings by paring operating costs to the bone. It has reduced buildings and facilities to cut costs, unstaffed stations on a massive scale, and widely introduced a pay-train system where the guard issues the tickets.

Even so, the gap between revenue and direct costs on the one hundred rural lines has widened relentlessly. The time has come when major decisions affecting their future have to be made.

Both track and rolling-stock are wearing out fast. Track renewal is essential if services are to continue; already speed restrictions have had to be imposed to maintain safety standards, and most diesel railcars are at least twenty years old, increasingly unreliable and expensive to maintain.

If we take a closer look at rural lines, no two are quite the same. They serve town and country, upland and seaside, carrying shoppers and holidaymakers, schoolchildren and commuters. All of them benefit the community, but at a price. Underlying the decline are three decades of road expansion and increasing car ownership, with growth in private cars particularly marked in the areas served by our rural lines.

While the government and local authorities fund, maintain and police the roads, British Rail is faced with the total costs of maintenance and renewal of all its assets to a safety standard that makes it seventy times less likely that you will suffer serious injury on a train than in a car. On top of this, the costly capacity for peak times, like moving thousands of summer

231

holidaymakers to the coast, has to be paid for in winter too, when there are far fewer passengers.

In exchange for an £90 tax disc, the government gives the motorist the freedom of the road. To give you a local service it costs the railway industry more than £5,200 per year to maintain every mile of track; £18,000 per year to man and maintain a level crossing; £25,000 per year to man and maintain a signal box; £60,000 per year to maintain and run a two-car train. Even lineside fencing, which BR must provide by law, costs hundreds of thousands of pounds every year.

The railways have struggled desperately to live within tough financial limits. They have simplified track and cut costs by switching to mobile maintenance gangs. Signalling is down to the minimum, with many signal boxes eliminated. Pay-trains, with the guard selling tickets, are a familiar part of daily life for the regular passenger. Stations are back to basics — no staff means no buildings to keep up, just simple facilities to keep people dry. It's an impressive list, and railways are carrying more people with fewer resources — that's real productivity.

But the industry still cannot bridge the gap between revenue and costs. Up to now they have managed to keep going to make do and mend, saving money by doing only essential work to maintain safety standards, but it's a vicious circle. Old track costs more to maintain, and speed restrictions make trains slower than they need be. Refurbished railcars brightened things up for the passenger and allowed the industry to soldier on a little longer with obsolete trains, but this enforced policy of deferred renewals can only lead to closures if we can't replace tracks and trains. So branch lines will go, not because British Rail wants to close lines, but because there won't be enough money to make them safe to use.

In the short term the Board appears to have decided that there are still economies to be made, like converting double track to single and restricting the time of day during which trains run. These will mean a reduction in service standards at busy times, but the industry is really at the limit of what it can do at low cost and within the confines of traditional railway operating methods.

What the industry must do is look at new ideas like radio control, which would save money by reducing the number of signal boxes as well as replacing open communication lines and obsolete semaphore signals. The easing of regulations on level-crossing operation could save staff and money by automation or conversion to open crossings. Local authorities could help by allowing railways to close little-used crossings, particularly where several are close together. Others could be automated, easing the problem of recruiting crossing-keepers and cutting delays to road users. It costs over £60,000 to equip an automated crossing and local authorities could help to cover some of this cost.

New trains have been developed with rural lines in mind, and the introduction of the new Class 141 railbus is proving to be a real innovation, using low-cost bus body components on a new lightweight four-wheel chassis. Capital, maintenance and running costs would all seem to be lower than for a conventional diesel railcar. Again, there is a price tag on this; even this economy train costs nearly a quarter of a million pounds to put on the rails.

Lightweight trains could allow British Rail to save on track and maintenance costs without prejudicing their high standards of safety. In Britain, we could give rural lines a new lease of life if only the investment cash were available.

I would like to see a real appreciation by both national and local government of the social benefits our railways bring to rural areas and their potential in attracting tourist travel, in the form of practical help and more financial support. The authorities should not just think in terms of keeping lines open, either. I believe that a case can be made for reopening railways in attractive rural areas like Wensleydale, whose past I described in Chapter Four.

Wensleydale is a particularly interesting example of what could be done: for commercial reasons — ferrying limestone from the Dales to Teesside — the bottom half of the line remains open and in good repair. The track has gone from the upper half but the bridges and embankments survive. Some stations have been converted into private houses. The one at Hawes is a visitor centre and folk museum created by the Yorkshire Dales National Park Authority.

Visiting Hawes was a strange experience for me. The old station buildings have been restored and look fine — much better than most working stations, in fact. Photographs inside depict the locomotives that used to run the line, similar to the ones I drove. But Hawes station is 'marooned' in fields. I couldn't help looking for those tracks which should be connecting it to Redmire and Garsdale.

Nobody is suggesting that Wensleydale could again be viable on an ordinary service basis. But I wouldn't be at all surprised if estimates showed that reinstating the track and running trains as a joint enterprise between, let's say, the local authorities, the Dales Park, the tourist boards and a group of rail enthusiasts would be far less of a commercial risk than businesses people speculate on every day of the week. BR could also stand to gain in laying on specials as far as Redmire.

A timetabled service up Wensleydale, obviously much more frequent during the summer months when holidaymakers pour in, would also provide local residents with an assured method of transport during the long winter months when roads can become impassable. Any extension of the line beyond Hawes would, of course, depend on whether objectors manage to prevent BR's scheduled closure of the dramatic Settle-Carlisle mainline route, which the Hawes branch used to meet at Garsdale Junction.

Railways do get limited assistance from the community — but much more is needed. Local authorities have in some areas helped to fund improvements. This, together with the provision of interchanges to improve coordination with local bus services and strong local promotion to win more people back to rail travel, could bring real changes. Financial support to the railways in Britain is the lowest in Europe. Unless this alters we won't be able to maintain the rail network for a larger role in a future clouded by energy shortages.

Rural railways are part of this strategy. A vital lifeline for many today, tomorrow they could be the key to mobility for millions.

THE WAY OUT OF THE WILDERNESS

The plea for a positive plan for the railways is a plea I have been making over and over again for as long as I can remember. But has there been any evidence of a real commitment to a thriving railway at any time since the Labour government took over a somewhat struggling, sorry system from the railway barons in post-war Britain?

Twenty years ago the French government began a long-term programme of investment in its declining public transport, and in particular its railways — a policy that still continues today. (The Paris Metro receives more financial support than the whole of British Rail; and there is the impressive £1-billion high-speed TGV — Train de Grande Vitesse — as further evidence.) A massive programme of revitalization was begun. A plan which involved thousands of millions of pounds and spanned years. The point is not the amount of money involved, although this is important, but the fact that underlying such a programme was a clear commitment by government to the continuing and indeed developing role of the railway.

I have constantly argued that this sort of commitment is not a luxury, or a railwayman's pipe-dream, it is *vital* to the running of a railway. Yet it is a degree of commitment that is sadly lacking in the history of British Rail.

In addition, looking around at the railways of Europe, far from France standing out as unusual it is Britain that is the odd one out. British Rail has the distinction among its European counterparts of having the meanest government sponsorship.

Looking back over the past twenty years or so of transport policy in this country, one can trace many of the root causes of today's problems. And in looking at the policy of Westminster towards the railways I cannot help but notice the other side of the fence — how in contrast the country's roads policy has fared: a contrast not just in terms of track or tarmac but of public versus private ownership as well.

The never-had-it-so-good 1950s, with their rapid rise in standards of living and car ownership, saw a dramatic decline in railways throughout Europe. But whereas France, and many other European countries, began to take determined steps to reverse this decline in the 1960s, in Britain the assumption that supplies of cheap oil would continue to be available for the foreseeable future remained unshaken. In the Britain of the 1960s — the future of a continuing plentiful supply of oil was questioned only by cranks (this was even more true in the USA). The motor car and the lorry were set to replace the train. Now, after, the oil crisis in the early 1970s, this assumption looks strikingly naive.

Why was Britain slower than its European neighbours in picking up the pieces of its public transport? One important point is the difference between the prevalent opinion in Britain and in the countries of Continental Europe to their state industries. The other European countries had a much longer and more firmly established tradition of public ownership of transport undertakings, as well as of other important sectors of their economies. State ownership of transport was unquestioned because it was regarded as providing the essential infrastructure for prosperous economic development. And in this attitude there was — and still is — no disagreement between the various political parties.

Contrast this with the dominant attitude to state ownership of transport (and indeed even basic industries) in this country. So strong is the tradition of 'free enterprise' in Britain, that even the most radical Labour administration was forced to make some concessions to it.

It is no exaggeration to say that British transport policy, especially towards the railways, has been something of a political battlefield. The bloodiest battles have been fought over the principle of public or private ownership. Labour administrations in 1945-51, 1964-70 and 1974-9 of course favoured public ownership, although they couldn't decide on whether public transport should make profits or offer a public service.

In between, Conservative Governments have generally sought to reduce the role of public transport and to encourage the growth of privately-owned road transport of all kinds. Their traditional dislike of publicly-owned industries of any kind made the railways a prime target.

The Transport Act of 1947 was perhaps the closest we have got to the Labour Movement's ideal; but even this had enormous problems. The Attlee administration clearly felt at the time that mere ownership of transport was enough to guarantee its transport policy objectives. Little or no provision was made for active management and control of transport — to enable the co-ordination and integration so vital to the objectives of Labour transport policy.

236

This fundamental, and peculiarly British, disagreement over the principle of public and private ownership of the nation's transport resources is largely responsible for the dramatic reversals of policy. Sir Stanley Raymond declared when he retired as BRB Chairman in 1968: in his twenty years' service in public transport at least half his time had been devoted to 'organization, reorganization, acquisition, denationalization, centralization and decentralization'.

In spite of the policy inconsistencies, however, there has been one all-too-consistent and enduring fact: the railways have throughout been a shrinking and declining service, while road haulage and the motor car have climbed from strength to strength. This decline is something that I fought to reverse, because I believe we have all the arguments on our side. Let no one get away with the idea that railways are the transport of the nineteenth century. Railways have a vital role to play in the transport of the future.

How does the history of the last decade or so affect today's industry and today's problems? To the railwaymen who have to make the system work, the obvious lack of real commitment from successive governments to their industry has led to a build-up of feelings of insecurity and at times frustration. There is no fulfilment in working for an industry that appears to be slipping down the drain with governments' blessings.

As Sir Peter Parker has argued on many occasions, the railways' legacy of short-term policies and under-investment has led to a crisis point. The vital investment projects which have been piled up before us for years cannot be neglected any longer.

And yet, with the writing clearly on the wall, what has this government got to offer? Has this government learnt from the mistakes of the last thirty years?

Apparently not. The Minister of Transport, Nicholas Ridley, confirmed shortly after his appointment in October 1983 the BRB's tough remit by accepting its corporate plan for 1983-8, which cuts the PSO grant by some £200 millions and which will mean a further deterioration in the standards of service, line closures, even more exorbitant fares for passengers, plus, of course, a further threat to jobs in the industry.

During my time as NUR General Secretary, I made it clear the railway industry can only be operated successfully if its three partners — management, the unions, and the government — all play their full parts: if all three recognize their responsibilities.

During that period I showed that we, the unions, were willing to take up the challenge of the future, and adapt to the changing face of the industry. In spite of its pious statements of support for the industry's future, what part in the partnership has the government played?

Let no one be mistaken. Their apparent quest for more 'productivity' from the industry is a sham. It means no more than a cut in railwaymen's jobs and conditions. Most importantly, it has nothing to do with efficient and successful railways — the sort of railways I and most people would like to see.

What hope has 'productivity' when the unreliability of clapped-out stock and track, is daily turning passengers away from the system?

What hope has 'productivity' against a background of disinvestment in the railways? When old track and stock becomes increasingly difficult to maintain or clean?

What hope has 'productivity' when lack of government revenue support makes railway travel a luxury fewer and fewer people are able to afford?

No — 'productivity' has nothing whatsoever to do with a more cost-effective railway.

If the government succeeds in bleeding railway workers dry, will this contribute to better railways, and a better transport policy for the nation? Of course not.

If the government were truly serious about its commitment to more productive, cost-effective railways it would start now on a programme of essential renewal and investment in the industry before it's too late. For one of the strongest arguments for a commitment to greater investment in the railways is that it will *save* money. Pound-for-pound the money now being spent on patching up the system is money badly spent. Money spent on basic investment will relatively quickly pay for itself in reduced costs, etc.

There is little sign of such foresight on government's part now. Not only are they apparently intent on following the

238

drip-feed method of financing that has dogged the industry for so long; but they are intent on rehearsing the bankrupt and crude argument or private versus public ownership, which has likewise frustrated long-term transport planning.

I have said that these issues are not a subject of serious debate on the Continent of Europe. Public ownership and investment in its railways is taken for granted as the best way of managing a country's transport resources. We need the same 'taken-for-granted' stability of policy in this country. We need a bipartisan approach joining both Conservative and Labour parties. There are some fundamental principles that should not be subject to party political bickering. This is a fact increasingly recognized by many people in Britain. The railways are just too valuable to remain a party-political shuttlecock.

Glossary of railway terms

Assist   Provide a second locomotive for special loads or journeys
Backshift   Work shift starting after midday
Bait   Sustenance carried on shifts
Black Five   LMR locomotive
Blowing off   Steam issuing from safety valves
Brassed-up and like a sewing machine   Highly polished
Classification   Pay grades linked to skill and responsibility
Conduct   Accompanying drivers to show them the route
Control   Centralized train operation introduced in World War Two
Dead man   Safety handle to halt train with driver indisposed
Diagramming   Organisation of train services
Dispose of engine   Cleaning and preparing steam loco at end of shift
Distant signal   First warning signal under semaphore system
DMU   Diesel multiple unit (small passenger train)
Double-header   Two locomotives together pulling special loads
Filling the hole   Filling the firebox with coal
Fire-dropping   Emptying a steam loco's firebox and ashpan
Fishplates   Track joints which permit expansion
Fogging duties   Standing beside signals in fog to warn drivers
Form One   Standard disciplinary form for railway offences
Gauge glass   Visual indication of boiler water level
Hang on   Couple loco to train
Lighter-up   Steam engine fire lighter
LDC   Local departmental committee, grassroots forum for railway problems
Link   Set of shifts worked by each grade of railwaymen
Lodging link   Shifts entailing overnight stay
Loose-coupled   Old system of wagon coupling without braking system
Multi-aspect signal   Modern, colour-light signal
Pilot   Shunting locomotive
PNB   Physical needs break for one-man cab operations
Possession time   Track closures for permanent way repair
Power box   Modern automatic signal box
Route card   Card a driver has signed showing he knows a route
Rule 55   Rule to protect a stationary train by informing the nearest signal box and putting detonators on track
Running pilot   Shunting locomotive traversing operational lines between yards
Semaphore signal   Old-type arm signals moved by lever
Shed master   Man in charge of locomotive shed
Steamer   Common term for steam locomotive
Tablet   Safety token used in single-track working
Track-circuiting   Signalbox display of train positions in lighted panel
Track-walking   Regular permanent-way inspection on foot
Turn   Daily or weekly shifts
Wiring   Telegraphing train movements between signalboxes